LEGENDS

Charles Bronson

with

Stephen Richards

Mirage Publishing

A Mirage Publishing Book

Publishers of Investigative authors
New authors welcome to submit manuscripts

New Hardback

Published in Great Britain
By Mirage Publishing 2000

A CIP catalogue record for this book is available from the
British Library.

ISBN 1 902578 1 1 2

Mirage Publishing
PO Box 161
Gateshead
NE 8 4WW
Great Britain

Printed and bound in Great Britain by
C.P. Print Ltd., Swalwell, Newcastle upon Tyne , NE16 3DJ.

©Cover designed by Artistic Director: Sharon Anderson

This book is dedicated to my old pot and pan

Joe Peterson

A Real Legend
A born fighter to the end

Winner of the Charles Bronson Open Arts Competition for 2000
Inside Time (Prisoners Newspaper) bottled out and refused to run one so
apologies to all the prisoners in the UK who were denied this chance.

Fight, fight, fight

Refuse to accept it
Don't take it as the norm
Death was not an option
You ticked on the form

So fight, fight, fight
But not to the death
And fight, fight, fight
But not to the point
That you have nothing left

Do not lay down easy
Do not let your soul go
Turn him away
Just say no

Just because you've seen the reaper
You don't have to leave
Just stay alive
All you gotta do is believe

So fight, fight, fight
It's a battle you can win
Your life is sacred
Refuse to let death in

© Nigel Roberts - A winner

Foreword

Charles Bronson, where in hell does one begin to tell of and to describe this Legend of legends? Charlie has my utmost respect, those who hide behind a cloak of decency have labbelled him a 'monster', but they needed someone like Charlie, a man full of pride and heart, to fit this tag.

What they didn't realise though was Charlie would be too much for them because he couldn't be beaten so the role's reversed, they've become the monsters in taking every ounce of dignity and trying to suck the life out of Charlie, but NO, they can't beat this man.

'Nonces' or in legal terms child molesters, they don't get treated like Charlie because the men in white coats with warped minds treat them as patients, but Charlie they treat like a wild dog for they fear him and his principles.

I've purposely held back this foreword until after Charlie's latest trial and I can't believe what the bastards have done to this man, a alife sentence, and do you know his crime, let me tell you. It's because he exposes the brutality and degradation that goes on in Her Majesty's prisons. In this book Charlie tells it all and I shall be behind him whatever avenue he takes.

Respect,

Joe Pyle

INTRODUCTION

What makes a legend, well you might ask. Is it being hard as nails, being able to take mental pressure or being able to dish it out? I'll tell you what makes a legend, it's someone whose life has had a memorable impression on you and that might be for good or bad reasons. You've probably heard of people talking about so and so, "He's legendary for his apple pies..." etc, etc. So you see he or she don't have to be an Einstein or an Attila the Hun to get in here but they've got to have had the ability to have an affect on my life – and that means good or bad.

My ideas of a legendary character will differ greatly to your idea but I hope by time you've finished this book that you'll have an opinion as to what it's all about. My life's been enriched by some of these characters and because of that I have to take my hat off to some of them, characters that've become legends within the penal system and some from outside of it as well as people who've influenced my life because of what I've heard about them.

'Charles Bronson the serial hostage taker', 'Charles Bronson the notorious killer', 'Drawings of a killer', 'Most dangerous prisoner in the penal system' and 'Killer on a roof' have been ways of describing me in newspaper reports over the years – all lies! I've got a heart and a soul and for any of you that've read *Silent Scream* you'll know of my past and how I've been treat by the penal system in this country. I'm not an angel but I'm not a paedophile either.

I've had nothing but lies told to me from the people in high place over the years and that's what done my canister in – lies and more lies. My family visiting prisons after travelling miles and miles only to be told, "Sorry, Charlie's been moved last night." My poor old mum travelled all the way to Broadmoor, she'd booked the visit and had to book bed & breakfast for an overnight stay. She gets to the

Legends

gates of Broadmoor and they tell her she can't see me! Why, I'll tell you why cos I was beaten up fucking black and blue that's why. So my dear old mum argues that she's got a right to see me and stands her ground. Eventually she gets to see a guy and he says, "Who was the one making all the fuss at the gate?" My mum replies, "It was me, I've got a right to see my son and this visit's been booked for some while now and I'm not going until I've seen my son." The guy replied to her, "You're the one he gets it from, you're the one that's mad!" The guy's name, Dr Lucas, I'll not forget in a hurry, not because I'd want to hurt him but cos I'm gonna see him in hell – anyone for toast!

I've had my ups and downs in prison just like you've had yours out there and it ain't no different for me except you can walk away from the pressures, in prison you don't get the chance to walk away from trouble, you are the trouble – I am the trouble. I'm coming up to 27 years total time served, look at paedophiles, they rape and kill and walk out after serving an eight stretch or maybe a 10?? I've done enough time for more than three stinking evil paedophiles and yet I've not killed anyone.

I was lied to big style at Hull Prison Special Unit by John Golds, boss of the CSC units. He told me I'd be staying on there for a number of years and yet weeks later I was being moved cos the place was closing down. Okay, fair enough it wasn't his decision he says in court when I was up for false imprisonment of civilian education worker, Phil Danielson. So who's fault was it then – a bunch of clowns sitting on a committee at HQ!

Anyway we'll have to wait for my appeal coming up to see what's what, as I'm confident even more truths will come out and you'll have all the reports coming out that I've said this and I've said that. Well unless it comes from the mouth of Steve Richards then it's a load of bollocks. Robin Ackroyd told a load of lies about me when he did a Sunday newspaper piece on me. He wrote that I'd spoken to him from prison after being sentenced – bollocks! He wrote that I'd said I had nothing to lose now – bollocks! Wrote a load of bollocks and he admitted later on to my lawyer, T, it was because of sensationalism that he did it – bollocks!

It was for money that he did it. People out there think I make money out of this – bollocks! I can tell you that I haven't been paid one red cent or one brown penny for any of my work. Other's have benefited from it and ridden on my back. Robin Ackroyd even set

Legends

up a website in my name and it was as if though it was me saying things on there and he used photos he still hasn't returned. Photographs given to him in good faith on loan, which he's hung on to regardless of many, many verbal and written requests to secure them. Some photos he got from my mum and he promised faithfully to return them to her – he's broken that promise and that makes him a clown. He's mugged me off but it wasn't that when his website was closed down because it was illegal. When he first visited me and made out he was a man of his word – he lied. Now you see where I'm coming from about all the lies spun to me over the time.

Joyce Connor mugged me off good style too; she was serving 5 years for drug smuggling. Smuggling drugs strapped to her body through an airport. We've never met but have been pen pals for nearly four years and she was released without parole. She swore down she'd not let me down, that she'd stand by me, blah, blah. Well when she got out it was Dave Courtney who picked her up from Northampton train station in a white Roller. She gave some sort of excuse about not being allowed to be picked up from outside of the prison – bollocks. What prison do you know that doesn't allow anyone to be picked up from outside, anyway Dave humoured her, he's not daft. On the way to the party that Joe Pyle had laid on Joyce said to Dave, "We have to call to Milton Keynes to pick my friend up." Dave obliged and because of that they turned up at the party some three hours late cos he's a gentleman and picked her friend up.

We've got people like Joe Pyle, James Nicholson (Le Prince), Andy Jones of Crime Through Time Museum, my lawyer; Mr T, Roy 'Pretty Boy' Shaw, Tony Lambrianou and a good civilian friend of mine, Reece Huxford, standing about waiting for her to turn up. Even my old mate, Ray Williams, turned up and even the lead singer from 'The Swellbellys', Needles, turned up in a suit! I mean anyone who's ever seen Needles will take my point but he blew them away on the night – he travelled all the way from Scotland for the do.

Dave put Joyce up at a hotel for the night and the following day Joyce was supposed to be waiting by a telephone she'd prearranged with me to phone her on. I called from prison on the Sunday afternoon…'brrrr brrrr, brrrr brrrr,' nothing, it just kept ringing. "Fucking hell, something must've happened to my

Legends

princess," I thought to myself. But nothing had happened to her at all, as I later found out.

That same Sunday a piece appeared in the Sunday Observer where Joyce was saying she was going to be my wife, blah, blah. She couldn't even get to be by the phone so how was she gonna be my wife? It was nearly two weeks later when I received a letter from her but only after I asked Steve Richards to call her on the number I had. He bollocked her and she went running telling every Tom, Dick and Harry that he'd been giving her what for over the telephone – they didn't listen to her, as they all knew what she was. I've since blown her out and I'd like to apologise to all who went to that party for wasting their time, I mean no one knew her, it was only out of respect to me that they all went. So there I was let down once again and you know what, I didn't cry a tear or even think about it cos I've been getting in plenty of practice these last 27 years from the let downs and lies I've been told by the system.

My new lawyer, known simply as 'T', is the dog's bollocks of legal representatives alright! He's a legend to the end and it's people like him what turn it around and make me think that maybe there's some sort of good out there after all. You've gotta take a butchers at his write up in here cos it shows what a legend's made of. I'm not gonna prattle on, as I know you don't want to hear any more about me, do you? I mean you wouldn't want to read about my life would you; okay then you've forced my hand. I've already written the manuscript for Insanity and that comes out later in 2001. Now I wouldn't want to spoil a good read so I'm off. Keep up to date with any news on me by logging on to my 'OFFICIAL' website: www.bronsonmania.com.
see ya there.

Your old china,

1

A-Z

Angry Angus

I met this legend in Parkhurst Prison in the early 70s. What a nasty bastard! He had to have at least three good arguments a day. One of these arguments was in my cell...with me!! He came steaming in shouting about somebody's radio being on too loud. "Hold the hell up Angus...I've got no radio." But even if I had, so what?? I stuck the nut on him and broke his nose. I had no choice, as he was still getting angry. We remained pals but people like Angus have gotta be in small doses with me. He's a legend best kept at a good pace away.

Ape Man

This con's the nearest thing I've seen to anybody to play the part of 'Planet of the Apes' and I mean without make up. I first met him in Ashworth asylum in the 80s and again in Belmarsh Prison in the 90s. He hadn't changed a bit; just to see his face makes my day, it's so funny. He got out of the asylum and killed, so now he serves a life sentence.

    Ape Man was having another trial over the murder of 'Cat-Weasel'; Cat-Weasel was a member of a paedophile group who killed kids. He got strangled in his cell at Whitemoor jail. Cat-Weasel got what he deserved, I think the Ape Man should be sent a crate of bananas; he's a blinder – a legend amongst Ape men. These characters have influenced my life and now they can influence yours, a real madhouse on your bookshelf. This is the real thing you couldn't make it up.

Bible Man

I met this dude in Broadmoor in the 80s: he was a big black guy

LEGENDS

with big pearly white teeth. I don't know why he was sent to Broadmoor, I don't think he knew himself. I was there for 4.5 years and I can honestly say there wasn't a day he was seen without his bible, he read it in the shit house, in the TV room, in the kitchen, down the football field, in the garden and in the bath but it got a bit much when he would break out with 'Onward Christian Soldiers' at 5am!! The Bible Man was a legend I often wonder if God helped him get out?

Big H

H got five life sentences in the 80s and he's still fighting his innocence. The only evidence on him was that of a super grass named John Childs. I met big H in Parkhurst.

He's a legend in the system for his electronic wizardry. He can fix a broken radio in no time and he's even made a computerised chess set.

I'll never forget the time H let me take one of his budgies on a visit, his budgies were his world and he loved them. This day I'd taken one called Harry on a visit to show my visitor. I was told afterwards that H was all concerned about Harry, "Was he alright?" "Was he being looked after?" "Was he hungry?" And so on. This budgie had never been out of H's cell for 10 years. We laughed about it later.

H helped me over a bad period in my sentence. For a man that stood 6 foot 7 inches and had supposed to have killed five people, I've never met such a good-hearted man. Nothing was ever too much for him

Bill the Bomb

Billy's saved my life twice – once inside prison and once on the outside. Inside the prison I got stabbed in my back four times while at Parkhurst Prison and it was Billy who plugged up my holes. It kept me alive while I got whipped away in an ambulance to St Mary's Hospital on the Isle of Wight. Outside Billy pulled off half a dozen men who were having a go at me and were planning on shooting me at a later stage.

He always helps a fellow fighter who's in trouble. He was a promising heavyweight boxer who went to America and done some serious sparring with top contenders. He had it all style, strength, speed and a punch. I believe Bill the Bomb could've been a world champion. He turned to crime like so many of our great fighters end up doing.

Billy Boy – R.I.P.

In the early 70s a cop got shot in the nut seven times, Billy got natural life for it. He once told me the gun had a faulty trigger – that's the sense of humour Billy had. I say 'had' cos he died in Full Sutton jail in the late 80s. He was a nice guy to have about and he always used to say things that stuck in my head, way out things like, "Life on other planets" or "Life under the ocean." I used to go back to my cell thinking about all he used to say. He was a very deep man, maybe too deep.

The one thing I'll always remember Billy for was his sense of humour. He got nicked in Full Sutton Prison on the cookery class for nicking a tin of beans. Billy came down the block where I was at the time. He shouted to me, "Here, Chas, the slags have fitted me up over a poxy tin of beans. I hope they don't throw the key away on me." You've gotta smile, a tin of beans, as if Billy Boy was to give a monkey. I miss you mate and I hope you made it to one of those other worlds you always went on about.

Birdman of Broadmoor

This guy just had to have a page in my book. Lots and lots of convicts have budgies and canaries - part of their lives. This man went one better! He had a bloody big magpie!

To my knowledge the Birdman had been locked up in Broadmoor for 20 years. He was a cheerful chap, always polite and respectful to everybody, which made me wonder what was such a nice bloke doing in the most notorious asylum in Britain?

He found a young magpie, which had fallen out of a tree. Since Broadmoor has been around for 150 years it has some massive trees in its grounds. The magpie was tamed and eventually grew into the most beautiful bird, roosting on the Birdman's shoulder.

LEGENDS

Sometimes it would fly up into the trees but it always returned to the Birdman's shoulder.

That magpie was his happiness; it was a great sight to see, as a fully-grown magpie is a splendid bird with its distinguished black and white markings. I often wonder what happened to them both after I moved on? If the Birdman moved on then what would've become of him or the magpie – both dependent on each other's company. Thanks for the memory.

'B' is for Blagger

That's what I was, a pavement artist, a robber, a highwayman, a gun totting blagger. Blaggers are a special breed of person, I say person cos there have been women blaggers. Ned Kelly, Dick Turpin and Charles Bronson - all blaggers. I've never shot anyone, never killed anyone, never really got away with much in my robberies and here I am doing life! Makes me wonder why I took the profession up. I mean I could've been a brain surgeon but I doubt you'd want me opening up your crust , would you? S o now maybe you can see my point as to why I became a blagger? I wouldn't advise anyone to follow in my footsteps, it's a mugs game, don't get me wrong, years ago it was a good business to be in - now, though, it's bad news.

Born fighter

Sammy won the flyweight championship of Great Britain in the early 60s. A true fast fighter and a true gentleman. His boxing talent made him a celebrity and a highly respected man. It even got him on This is your life. A true legend in every sense of the word.

He later ended up in prison with a 15 year sentence for armed robbery and he practically served it all in Albany prison on the Isle of Wight. For most of those years he worked in the prison gymnasium and was without a shadow of a doubt the most likeable guy in prison. Not only liked by the convicts but also by the jailers, everyone loved Sammy.

There's not a more polite man in the world than Sammy. Sometimes his politeness was so much of a shock to the younger convicts that they mistook it for a joke and a couple felt that right hook over this attitude. But even after they come round Sammy was still polite. A dear friend and now free.

Broadmoor Bob

This guy I met in Long Larten Prison, he's a classic we all love Bob he can play the guitar like a pro, he can sing and do impersonations. You should see him take off UK comedian Ken Dodd. Bob's serving life and spent time in Broadmoor. He cheered Ronnie Kray up and cheered us all up. Without guys like Bob we'd all be depressed.

Bruno

Big Bruno smashed a screw's nut in Long Larten jail a few years back, ever since then he's been kept in solitary, he's a big black guy, 6 foot 6 inches tall and 17 stone. Recently he was moved to Broadmoor asylum, Bruno is basically a nice guy but he gets mad moods and when he's mad he's on Mars. You can't get through to him; he's unapproachable like he's a Martian. He believes he's got a computer chip in his head and that he's on a mission.

Captain Bob

I met this guy in Frankland Prison in the 80s; he'd copped 14 years for a couple of ton of cannabis on a boat. Bob's always good for a laugh and he took everyday as it came. They ended up putting the Captain on the top secure unit in Parkhurst as word was flying about that a helicopter was coming to take him out. It was all a load of bollocks but as usual they panicked and took it serious so the Captain spent a few years in total secure conditions. He's out now so happy sailing Bob.

Chester Charlie

I met this guy in Wakefield block in the 70s. He killed a guy in a pub fight and ended up doing life. He was forever setting fire to things a right pyromaniac. He went too far one night and almost died from the fumes. Now most of the stuff in prison cells is fire retardant, like my concrete bed and my compressed cardboard

LEGENDS

furniture – not that I'm looking to get toasted but this guy was nearly laughing all the way to the crematorium – anyone for toast?

Chilly

This guy comes from my hometown – Luton and he's a real character. Some would call him a pill head, as there's no pill he hasn't taken in his lifetime.

We first met in Parkhurst Prison unit in the early 70s. At that time he was serving a five-year sentence. With the amount of pills he's taken over the years he becomes confused and easily forgets things! I've been locked into a conversation with him and suddenly he'll burst into laughter or cry or even jump up and down. He doesn't even know why he does it himself!

To an outsider he would put the fear of God into them, but to me it's part of life. I've seen him be ironing a shirt and just run off and leave the hot iron on his shirt. He's run the bath and forgot and as a result flooded the unit. He's burnt all of the pots and pans. He's even set fire to his own bed - whilst still in it!

But I love him, as he's unique and always good company - never violent to his own breed. I've not seen him for years now, but I've heard he's still knocking about!

Coke

I met this guy in Leicester Prison; he was serving 10 years. At that time I was on remand for armed robbery and I first came across him in the prison gym. He's a big Pakistani guy, always smiling; they say he's a millionaire – no wonder he was always smiling. He marked my card one day over a sex case, so one day in the shower I grabbed this nonce's bollocks and told him if he ever came to the gym again I'd tear them off and make him eat them. We never saw him again. I later met Coke again in Gartree Prison in the 80s and he was still smiling, that's how he is. I know he's a big face around the Midlands but for me he stands tall and has my respect.

I hate them nonces and the screws know I do, so to antagonise me they often put them in the same area as me. It was at Woodhil Prison in 2000 when they put a sex case, Miller, a few cells away from me. Miller raped and killed a 12-year-old boy. The screws know what they're doing and it winds me up to see these sex cases around me and at Woodhill I cracked up and set about his cell door. The 8 screws escorting me were wearing MUFTI gear but they just ran off. But they soon returned with 16 more and I held the 24 of them off for five hours whilst still trying to kick my way into Miller's cell. More screws came and there were about 60 of them. When I was captured I was slung in a van and shifted to Whitemoor. I mean, how many people say, "Let me in a cell with them sex cases and I'd soon sort them out," fucking millions of people but when it comes to me doing the business then the whole world shits on me, can't make people out.

Cool Hand Cliff

Cliff was passed a life sentence for shooting a bloke. He was only a boy when it happened at the age of 18. He's now served the same amount of years in prison, half his life.

I first came across him in Full Sutton Prison in the 80s and several times since. I took to him straight away simply because he's a character and great company to be with. 'Unpredictable' is the only word I can use to describe Cliff. He's had it rough in the time he's been inside.

It's difficult to pick a story, as there are so many. But I guess I have to choose the one where he started laughing in Lincoln block and never stopped for a solid hour. The screws put us on the exercise yard together for an hour a day. I'd told Cliff a funny story

and he began laughing. I don't remember the story, as Cliff laughing was far funnier. The laughter started when we entered the yard and he was into a fit of laughter when we left. I could even hear him still laughing when we were in our cells - talk about mad? Madness and sanity's the same thing and for me that's what makes the world go around. I'm the poet from hell reaching for a rainbow and wanting to kiss the stars. All my fellow cons give me support and we chase dreams and laughter to keep us sane.

LEGENDS

Crazy Horse

This convict has to be the ugliest man I've ever met in prison. No disrespect to him, but he makes the elephant man look good looking.

Crazy Horse had a head like a donkey and a brain like a peanut. I first met him on F-wing in Parkhurst Prison some years ago. He was always up to crazy things and fighting with other cons but he always lost.

I've never known him win a fight in all the time I've known him. I recall one fight he had where he kept getting knocked down, but he kept jumping straight back up.

He has to go in this book of legends for being so ugly, for being so crazy and for trying.

Cry Baby

This guy's only getting a mention because his face is inside my head and will be until the day I die.

It happened in Rampton secure hospital and it was my first ever time in an asylum. This guy was a big plump chap and a little bit simple. He'd one of those rosy red chubby faces with big rubbery lips and tiny piggy eyes along with massive shoulders and large hands.

I guessed he could be dangerous so I trod carefully. I was sitting at a table in the association room and he came over and sat opposite me. "Play you at chess," he said. I asked, "Can you play?" "Yes I am a Grand Master," he said. There was no way this pea brain was a Grand Master, I just knew it. So he had a big smile as we set the pieces up. I'm no great player myself but I did know where the pieces go but he was just putting them anywhere he fancied. This loony never had a clue how to play let alone be a Grand Master. I beat him so easy that it was unreal. He started crying and I mean real crying with tears rolling down his face, I couldn't believe it. It really opened my eyes up, as I never knew crybabies like that ever existed. Since then I've progressed on the chessboard of life and become a decent chess player. I even challenged Carlos the Jackal to a game by post, I'm still waiting to hear from him - maybe he's bottled out; old one ball Carlos. Oh yeah, didn't you know that, same as Hitler, he's only got one.

A-Z

Dangerous Dougie

I first met Dougie in the block in H M Prison Armley, in Leeds back in the 70s. Since then our paths have crossed many times. There isn't much Dougie hasn't tried on his life sentence, he's even killed a fellow con and got an extra life sentence added but I guess the one incident that would give him legendary status was the time he took a jailer hostage and demanded a cat. For me that's the making of a true legend and Dougie made it, he's still locked away coming up to 30 years. I hope one day you make it Dougie and that they take your danger label away.

Dave Mc

I met this guy in Parkhurst in the 80s he was a good pal of Reg Kray. Dave's a game sort he'll attempt anything but he became a legend the day he escaped from Hull Prison Special Unit. It was one of the most dramatic escapes of all time he just walked off with one of the civilian education teachers. It was really amazing how he accomplished it, as Hull unit was a top secure unit before it closed down in February 1999. Sadly he was caught a week later and he's now serving 28 years. Dave will survive it though. If you wanna see inside of Hull special unit take a butchers at the video documentary on me – Sincerely Yours.

Del

I met him in Walton Prison in the 70s, he's a scouser and a living legend, he's survived it all, dungeons, beatings, bullets and knives you name it and he's experienced it. I respect the man for how he conducted himself.

Once in the prison workshop we all had a sit down, I grabbed a pair of shears in case of trouble. Delroy was the man to cool things down; he knows how to control a situation without acts of violence. That's why he's a successful businessman and drives about in a Roller. Del for me is a winner and it's men like Delroy I look up to.

LEGENDS

Digger

This guy I have so much respect for, as I know how much he's suffered over the years. 1988 he was in Brixton prison awaiting trail for armed robberies and shootings. One day he stripped off in his cell and covered himself in baby oil. Then when his cell door was unlocked he came running out wielding a table leg. He steamed into the jailers but as much as they tried they couldn't restrain him as he kept slipping out of their grip.

After this incident they banned inmates from purchasing baby oil. Digger later received a 22-year prison sentence.

Eric the Russian – R.I.P.

I met Eric Rubin in Parkhurst Prison; he got 12 years for his part in the Knightsbridge safe deposit box robbery with Valerio Viecci. Eric was the last member of the gang to be captured, he's a sick man that's why he only got 12 years – even £60m can't buy health. I loved to listen to his stories and he had a one for every day I seen him on the exercise yard. He'd lived a fast life and survived some hard years and he's even spent some time in the Russian salt mines in chains. Parkhurst was a bloody holiday camp to Eric compared to what he'd experienced in other parts of the world but as I used to watch this legend cough and see emptiness in his eyes I often wondered what judge could be so cruel to send him away for 12 years.

Fred the Clock

I met Fred at Parkhurst Prison in the eighties. He'd shot a cop dead in Blackpool in the 70s. Fred's already served over 20 years.

Fred must be the best clock maker in the system as he's spent years in Maidstone Prison making beautiful clocks. Big ones grandfather sized ones, small ones and mantle clocks. All beautifully varnished. People used to make jokes saying, "you got the time Fred" and "Time will never run out for Fred" and so on.

The best clock I ever seen him make was one he gave to fat Bob, it was 6 foot high. Bob used to store his food inside it on shelves. Fred used to make clocks to keep his mind active. Prison draws out a man's skills and a lot of guys have discovered their true vocation in life once they've been inside and I say to anybody that you've never experienced life till you've seen the inside of the belly of the beast. (Prison.)

Fred the Head

Prison legends are created by the system. Fred's a typical case of what the system can do to a man. Fred's a man's man. He lives his life by a code of honour – but to an outsider he could be described as a ruthless character, a heavy, a bruiser, and a born fighter.

Fred's fiery temper got him into all kinds of scrapes until he was labelled incurable and untreatable. The system could not control him so eventually he was certified insane and sent to an asylum.

So there was Fred in the asylum with all the madmen and it became a new battle for him. He had to fight for his sanity 'the hardest fight of his life'. Fred was always handy with his head. In a fight he always got his head in first. I've seen him bust up a man's face with one crack of his nut – lethal.

But his head became infamous throughout the asylum. Fred became known as Fred the Head. He butted the cell doors off – incredible but true. Obviously it became a total embarrassment to the asylum until in the end, they invented a double door cell. Sadly it did the job. Poor Fred's door smashing days became a myth. But it still lives on throughout the asylum. Fred the head remains a legend.

For me he lives on in my heart, as I know Fred's other side. He's really a good, honest and loyal man. He has a heart of gold. To his friends he's a diamond – but to the system he's a major problem. I chose Fred to be in this book of prison characters as he's a worthy man who's suffered terribly all his incarcerated years and I'm privileged to have spent some time with the man through both good and bad times.

I just hope I never have to witness doors buckling under Fred's mighty head butts and see his head bleeding from the smashing of his skull on steel doors – not a pretty sight. Fred's a real character

LEGENDS

and a true friend. Good luck and stay strong.

General Hoffman

This guy was in the cell directly opposite mine at Long Larten Prison, he's Spanish, a small guy but with so much bottle. I only spent a month with him but it was plenty long enough to see where he was coming from. He was what is known in the game as an International Hood, he knew how to conduct himself in any situation he had to face. He'd survived bullets and was a fast mover, obviously prison clips the wings but one day our wings are free.

Gentle Giant

He was as black as coal and one of the biggest guys I ever set my eyes on inside prison. He was 6 foot 10 inches tall with giant hands that resembled shovels and fingers like bananas.

I met him in the asylum some years back. When he arrived there was nothing to fit him! His shoes were a size 16, his chest was a 56-inch and his neck was 21-inch. So he had to settle for a pair of pyjamas until clothes could be arranged.

I'll always remember that first day I saw him towering above the attendants with great big shinny eyes and a big smile of pearl white teeth. He truly looked a sight, but the thing I'll never forget is the words he shouted out! "I want my mum". This was a man in his 30s, 6 foot 10 inches, 20 stone and a giant of a man and all he wanted was his mummy, as frightening a character he looked.

He was just a real nice guy who had the mentality of a young boy. I don't know what he'd done to end up in a top security asylum. Obviously he must've been a problem and no doubt could still be a problem! But this gentle giant really planted himself in my brain. As I still can picture that giant of a man arriving and asking for his mum.

Grizzly Adams

I met Billy in Gartree Prison in the 80s; he's a Londoner who was serving 18 years for armed robbery. A big man of 18 stone, a man with amazing strength who's well known for his cooking skills but he was a bit handy in smashing his frying pan over the occasional head. Some cons don't know when to stop, they keep on and on so a tap on the crust is sometimes necessary. Rumour has it there are more dents in Bill's frying pan than in a stock car.

Hate 'em all Harry – R.I.P.

Strange enough I first met Harry in jail some 20+ years ago. He was a short stocky man very powerful and always fighting. A hell of a punch.

He was named 'Hate 'em all Harry' by the Kray twins whilst in Parkhurst in the early 70's. Quite simply because he hated everybody, he would even argue with himself. But Harry was a character. He was always up to something and he was forever on the move from jail to jail.

He became infamous after he cut George Ince in Long Lartin prison. As Ince had been knocking off Dolly Kray outside whilst Charlie Kray was inside. But I've chosen a classic story that I'll always remember at Gartree prison.

Harry was up to his usual tricks. He was cooking a stew and I saw him look inside another convict's pan. Suddenly, as quick as lighting Harry grabbed a piece of meat out of the other convict's pan and dropped it into his own stew.

Obviously a massive argument broke out later when the piece of meat was found to have gone. But Harry had scarpered off to his cell and eaten it. Later the convict pulled Harry and all what the convict got was a bust jaw. Harry was saying what a bloody liberty blaming me, he winked at me and smiled that crazy smile of his.

I chose to put Harry in this book of legends simply as I liked him – the same as the Kray's liked him. He was a character. He livened up the jail with his wit and wicked ways. Plus he was always loyal to his mates. Sadly he passed away but he lives on and always shall – legends don't die. God bless Harry.

House Brick

Tommy received his nickname well over 30 years ago when in a gang fight. He got smashed in the face with a house brick. The name stuck with him ever since.

LEGENDS

I first met him in Risley Prison in the late 60s. He was on remand for a tie up in a warehouse and I was on remand for nicking a removal van – a full removal van! Tommy received a four-year sentence and I received three months detention.

Strange enough we only lived about half a mile away from each other, but until we met up in Risley Prison we were unaware of this fact. We'd heard of each other through the criminal fraternity but that was it. We became good friends and bumped into each other many times over the years due to our crimes.

We'd made six gallons of hooch and it was a good brew. We were selling it to a Manchester firm (gang) in Risley Remand Centre. They took four gallons of the stuff on a promise they would pay up on the following Saturday. Credit's never safe in prison, as they could be moved and so on. This bunch of toe rags never had any intention of paying it back.

Three weeks later the wait was over. Tommy and me steamed into their cells and smashed them up with table legs. Funny enough they paid the following day, lovely.

Hutchy

I met him in Rampton in the 70s he'd been there a good 10 years before I arrived. Hutchy used to get one visit a year, which was from his mother. He used to get hyped up and all excited before this visit. On one occasion he went over the top and lost control – he punched both fists through a glass window and tore them to pieces. He cut one arm so badly it sliced the tendon in his wrist and sliced through the main artery, blood spurted up like a fountain, they had to get him to hospital fast. When his poor mother arrived she had to see him all bandaged up in the infirmary it must've been heart breaking for her. Weeks later I asked Hutchy why he did it, he said he really didn't know. That's what makes such places mad, there's a legend born every minute of the day in such places. I recall a time I punched my fist through a bulletproof window, I damaged my tendons, just a little bit, but it happens and you have to accept the consequences. Prisons are a depressing place to be but secure hospitals can be a bigger nightmare.

A-Z

Hygiene Man

I never realised there was an illness over one's own personal hygiene till I met this guy in one of the asylums. The Hygiene Man was so over the top with cleanliness it made him ill. He was so bad over germs that he wouldn't sit on a chair until he'd wiped it. He couldn't shake hands with anybody. He couldn't even use a snooker cue until he'd wiped it.

He was, though, a murderer and could turn very nasty. His eyes would glare at anybody who coughed and sneezed. He once punched a fellow lunatic when he seen him picking his nose. Then he ran into the recess to wash the fist he punched him with, as time went by he became worse.

I remember vividly the day he lost it altogether. Someone had spat at him, I don't know why, but one of the lunatics just did it. That was the Hygiene Man's downfall – he went berserk. He smashed tables and chairs; he pulled out the radiator from the wall and screamed blue murder. The white coats carried him off to the 'silent room'. He remained there for a very long time but I had to smile at the thought of all those hands grabbing him. I bet he took a week cleaning off all those germs – a definite legend in his own crazy way.

Issy the Bear

LEGENDS

There've been many convicts over the years that go under the name of 'bear' - I personally know several. But for me there's just one true bear and that is this guy - Issy the Bear.

He weighs in at 19 stone and he's totally covered in hair, with legs like tree trunks, a neck that makes Tyson look skinny. He's from Leeds and very well respected plus he's a good friend of mine.

The following event took place in Frankland Prison some years ago. The Bear's a Jewish man and some idiot kept putting slogans outside the Bear's cell door and they naturally upset him. The slogans were typical mindless crap from a pea brain that it all came on top for. He actually got caught doing it! So the Bear went into a rage, he picks pea-brain up like a sack of spuds and carried him off to the bathroom where he filled a bath with cold water and slung pea-brain in it. He washed pea-brains mouth with carbolic soap and left him trembling with fear.

I can honestly say that the Bear is 99% a calm character and a very decent honourable man. But people like pea-brain push people too far.

Jacks

I've put this guy in legends even though a few years ago I put a frying pan over his crust, but that doesn't say that I don't respect the guy. Jack knows why I clocked him one and if he were man enough he'd admit he was out of order.

Jack has spent his life locked away; he's in his 40s now but still has roof top protests. He spends most of his time the same way I do - in solitary.

I really do admire Jack even though I won't apologise for cracking him one. My best memory of him goes back to Full Sutton Prison block in the 80s. He's  always up to something. He somehow slung a load of papers from his cell window into my cell window when I was asleep. Unknown to me he slung a lighted bit of rag towards the paper. I awoke with a fire half in my window, smoke and flames were spreading all over – I couldn't believe it. That's what he's like – mad but I love him.

A-Z

J.B.

Johnny and me go back some years, he got life for chopping up a tramp - he used a chain saw! JB was to spend years fighting the penal system. I suppose the main incident was the hostage siege in Parkhurst Prison in the early 80s. Johnny and another convict took a governor hostage, armed police were brought in but it ended peacefully. JB received a further 10 years added to his life sentence. He escaped in '92 and as far as I'm aware he's still free. You beat the bastards JB and made my day.

J.K.

It was in Gartree Prison when I met up with JK in the 80s. Only weeks after my release in late '87 he escapes in a helicopter. The first and only escape in a helicopter in the country. Him and another friend of mine had flown out of Gartree to the cheers of the cons.

I was arrested January 7th 1988 over an armed robbery on a jewellers shop. I was quizzed over JK's dramatic escape. Probably because I'd only been released weeks before as a high-risk category 'A' prisoner from where they flew out. It was soon obvious that I had no part in it.

JK's now serving a 35-year sentence. When they caught up with him they added a lot more on top of his original sentence. The other guy who was with him, Sid, is still serving a life sentence. Andy Russell was given a 10-year sentence for kidnapping the pilot. It was the greatest escape of all British jails.

Joe the Greek

He got a life sentence for robbery and shootings. Plus he got an extra 10 years for running a blade down a jailer's face in Bristol Prison. Joe later got extradited back to Greece to serve his sentence.

I was in several prisons with Joe. He was a lively character and was only 5 foot 4 inches tall, a small man with a big heart - totally fearless.

Somebody once told him if he acted mad they'd send him to Broadmoor asylum where he'd get a television in his cell! So Joe

LEGENDS

got a razor and cut his stomach, he cut so deep that his insides were showing. Only God knows why he cut his stomach open, maybe he thought he'd get certified mad. Joe left plenty of memories behind for me.

Jon Jon

I met this con in Wakefield Prison punishment block in '93. We were both in the cages, there were only two cages in Wakefield (Monster Mansion) and we were in them. Jon Jon became a legend when the Strangeways Prison riots went off. He was one of the last off the roof. For his part in this dramatic siege he received 10 years but his legendary status hasn't stopped there. Whilst the trial was going on at Manchester Crown Court he escaped! That's what you call a legend. The courthouse was crawling with cops and prison guards and Jon Jon vanished but sadly he was arrested some months later.

J.P.

This guy's from my hometown – Luton. A really likeable fellow. I first met him up in Frankland Prison in the late 80s. He started off with a 10-year sentence then whilst in Wakefield Prison he stabbed to death a fellow convict and for this he received a life sentence.

Then some six years later he stabbed another con to death, this time in Parkhurst Prison, which he got his second life sentence for. The odds are not good for JP getting released. Yes it sounds as though he's a dangerous man but in my opinion he's the complete opposite in fact I believe that he's a gentleman. It's just unfortunate that he lost his cool on both murders.

I know what it was about as I've spoken with JP and witnesses. Prison is, after all, a violent place but outside JP would've walked away from it, but how does a man walk away in jail - you can't. I'm not saying it was right that he stabbed those cons but I'm not saying that it's wrong. He did what he chose to do and what he believed was right at that time.

A-Z

King Kay

In another attack on the Yorkshire ripper, Peter 'fuck face' Sutcliffe, this man, King Kay, is king to me in fact he was nearly a god as he nearly took the monster's eyes out. King Kay became a legend overnight behind those walls of Broadmoor – well done King Kay.

Mac the Knife

Mac was serving a life sentence in Monster Mansion when he ended up killing one of them dirty low down sex cases – for this they gave him a life sentence! Obviously he was put into isolation where he remained for several years but you know Mac was always good for a laugh even though he was given two life sentences and he always helped his fellow cons along. Nothing was too much for Mac.

I suppose Mac could be seen as a 21st Century superman, as lets face facts – he killed a sex case, he destroyed something evil. Nobody likes a sex case only another sex case. I personally know Mac and I would bring him into my home and I know all of my clan would be safe. He could be released today and the fact is he wouldn't ever re-offend but the system will want its pound of flesh as usual. The insane fact is why did the system put Mac in a position where sex killers surrounded him? They do the same with me, the system's gagging for it to go off, they'd love me to kill a nonce but they'll have a long wait. I'm gonna be free one day.

Monster Mansion (Wakefield Prison) is a notorious dumping ground for bad crimes and sadly some convicts will end up there amongst the scum of the criminal fraternity - sex cases, grasses and old women beaters. Mac the Knife may well be branded a mad psychopath but to me, and lots like me, he's a good man and has a heart of gold.

LEGENDS

Mad Bob

Bob's the longest serving 'solitary' prisoner in the country! He's in total isolation and has been constantly isolated since 1978, which is 22 years alone, no wonder he's mad.

He killed a fellow inmate in Broadmoor asylum then two years later he killed yet another two inmates in Wakefield Prison – both in the same day. Since these incidents he's spent the rest of his time in solitary confinement.

Bob must go in this book of legends – simply as the number one solitary man. I do not particularly like what he's done to the inmate in Broadmoor, as I know the gruesome details, which were unnecessary. My total isolation time is now coming up to 23 years but it hasn't been continuous so I award Mad Bob the 1st Prize.

Mad Dog Williams

I met this lunatic, and when I say lunatic I mean just that, in Broadmoor. In the 70s he was driving along a road, he just suddenly stopped, got out and started shooting at people in their cars. He was shooting innocent people dead in cold blood. He killed four or five; if he'd had his way he would've killed hundreds. I asked him, "Why?" His answer: "I don't know." He just never knew why he'd done it, he sure took the biscuit. I couldn't ever work him out but I suppose it made him a legend in his own insane world. One thing's for sure though and that is he'll die behind that 25 foot high wall, some will say sooner the better.

Malteser Man

Now this guy was a character, I met him at Broadmoor in the 80's. I don't wanna be nasty to him – but the only way I can describe him as is a 'RAVING NUTTER'. He used to have a crap in his pot and roll up little shit-balls the size of Maltesers, and roll them across the floor. They really did look like Matesers.

Malteser Man had been locked up for most of his life, a funny looking geezer, always smiling – that's life in these places. I've never known anyone to do what he did, and now you too know. You get to see the whole world pass you by if you look for it.

A-Z

Midge

I first met this guy in the 80s in Full Sutton Prison; he got a life sentence for shooting at some cops but on appeal he got it down to 18 years, still a long time for a young lad. I liked Midge from the day we met. He had great qualities. I next met him in the block in Albany Prison after his rooftop protest in Parkhurst. He arrived with another con all smashed up and covered in bruises, I went mad. I demanded they both got photographed with their injuries or I would smash up the block. The Albany screws were in fact disgusted at their condition obviously they didn't want any part of the injuries so they eventually got the camera down. I told Midge and the other con to call me as a witness when the case came up.

Midge is a legend in the system over his constant battles against the shit rules. He's earned a lot of respect in his own right; he's a good friend.

Odd Job

This freak I met in Rampton, he was a ringer for the James Bond character. They say he nutted a man to death in a pub fight, he was sectioned off under the Mental Health Act. I never had much to do with him, as I never liked him too close to me. It was his little piggy eyes I didn't like. I saw him get upset one day and he nutted the lockers they just buckled in. The dent is probably still there today. It was like a mallet smashing into it; on another occasion he smashed the recess door and smashed it off its hinges. He was the sort of guy you'd have to go all the way with if he took a disliking to you – I was always aware of his location in readiness.

Old Sydney

I met him in Ashworth asylum in the 80s. He was well into his 60s and had been locked up for some 40 years, most of them spent in Rampton (for the criminally insane). I loved Sid and used to get him out on my visits, both my parents liked Sid a lot and they used to fetch him a present up with them. I only stayed in Ashworth for six months, as I ended up cutting a lunatic up but soon after I left Moors Murderer Ian Brady arrived. Sid smacked him over the head with his walking stick. I was so proud of Sid I sent him a little

LEGENDS

parcel to help cheer him up. Even after 40 years Sid still kept his principles and was the same rascal as when he first started out.

Olly

I met this old boy in Full Sutton Prison in the late 80s; he used to be a pro soccer player, which's why his feet were all messed up with arthritis. The prison doctor had promised to get him fitted up with special shoes but Olly got so depressed over it. I think the pain was bringing him down. He finally lost control and set fire to his cell; then the legend was born. I managed to get his cell door open and drag him out and took him to another cell and made sure he was okay. I actually got a commendation for this from the governor, not that I wanted any praise for this, as Olly's from the old school. He'd just taken enough, more than enough I'd say. Truly the doctors in these places don't care however this act of madness must've done some good as a chiropodist soon arrived to take a look at his feet. He had a smile so big he could've put a banana in his mouth sideways.

One Armed Bandit

I met this guy back in Risley in the late 60s; considering he only had one arm he wasn't a bad grafter. He got himself lifted over a warehouse full of booze that went missing. I can't remember how long he got but it wasn't too long. I remember the day he lost his temper and smashed his artificial arm over a con's head. His arm just broke up. The con's head wasn't much better either. I can still see it now even though it's over 30 years ago it's as clear as a bell. The One Armed Bandit lives on in my mind but I've never seen him since that day.

Peter the painter

I met Peter in Full Sutton maximum-security prison. The guy was an absolute one off; I loved him at first sight. He was serving life and he served it his way and nobody else's way.

He painted the most fascinating pictures – a pure genius. He was also a fitness fanatic – yoga and a Buddhist all rolled into one unique specimen. He was a loner till I came into his life and we

22

became close; just like brothers. I learnt so much from him, he taught me how to relax properly – the breathing techniques and how to sit correctly.

The day I will never forget was the fly! I walked into the recess (toilet area) and there was Peter by the sink. He had a fly on his finger, which he'd found in a puddle of water in the sink. The fly looked dead to me. Peter blew on the fly several times and then he pulled a tissue from his pocket and put the fly on it over the radiator. Then Peter started blowing on the fly again and sure enough the fly moved slightly. Peter had brought it back to life, a bloody fly. At first I thought he was off his head. The fly then flew off and Peter smiled and said to me, "It's only a fly Charlie but it's a living creature!" In all my life I had never seen nor heard anything quite like this. Peter showed me something I'd not really seen in other men and he gave me an insight into something called humanity, something I ain't been shown much of.

Pebbles

If this guy wore a skirt and stockings he would look better than a page three model. He had the walk, the talk and the femininity. Everything about him was a woman; he was a woman trapped inside a man's body.

In the 70s and 80s he was a regular inmate in Wandsworth Prison. This was a tough disciplined prison; it caters for the hardcore convicts. Sometimes he would get into arguments with the jailers and he would blow them a kiss and wiggle his arse at them, it was his way of mugging them off. He stood no shit from anybody.

He would come down to the punishment block where I was held and talk to me through the window. We'd have a chat and he would tell me stories and jokes to cheer me up. He had real principles and he stuck to them. I've had many a laugh with Pebbles, as he's such a character. Pebbles is a unique character and it can't be denied. I've not seen him in prison for many years. Maybe he's given up crime and found himself a nice husband.

Psychotic George

George arrived at Broadmoor from Feltham Borstal in '79. He got certified mad for smashing somebody over the crust, he was young and full of beans, I took to him straight away, he was a breath of fresh air to me, as he was like most prison characters – good company. George had to be in my top 10 of violent men but unlike most violent criminals George was totally unique, he was unpredictable and dangerously out of control. He soon lost control in Broadmoor and stuck a pair of scissors into a fellow inmate's body a dozen times. Later I asked him, "Why?" George said, "I was fed up, I needed to brighten the day up."

Psychotropic Poet

I met this character in Broadmoor asylum, where else, it was in the late 70s. He arrived soon after I did so we were in the same induction ward at the same time. Along with a score of other lunatics.

The poet would write beautiful poetry and learn it off by heart. All day long you would hear him mumbling on and on with his poems. Some of them I must admit were red hot. He was certainly gifted to be able to write such poetry. But when I found out what he was actually in for I ended up head-butting him in the face.

What a bloody hypocrite he was, all of that poetry about flowers, love and the joy of living and he'd been having sex with dead people. I couldn't believe it when I found out. It goes to show how insane the world really is.

I'm putting him in this book simply because he fooled me completely. I was bowled over to find out that he was not the poet he made out to be, he never did create those poems, he'd copied them from a book! Maybe I should've tried to understand his crime but to me it was abhorrent but then again it takes all sorts to make the world go around. We've got a code of conduct and a pecking order of acceptable crimes; his wasn't one of them we could overlook.

24

A-Z
Robbo

This guy got a life sentence in the 70s for kidnapping a cop in Rhyl and forcing him to drive his panda car to Blackpool. I met him in Hull Prison in the 70s he was the number one artist in the jail at the time and his paintings were works of art, I believe he only got life because he was an ex-Broadmoor inmate – he never hurt the copper so why should he have been given life. I've not bumped into him since Hull so I don't know the score on whether he's out or what? I do know Robbo's a legend, who else kidnaps a cop in a patrol car and demands a lift to Blackpool?

Rocky – R.I.P.

In 1986 Rocky was stabbed to death in the kitchen of Parkhurst Prison, stabbed in the back, that's where most men get it – in the back. Rocky was a lovely lad full of life, fit and strong. He wasn't the first and he won't be the last.

Prison deaths always leave a bad taste in my mouth. No man deserves to die from holes in his back, Rocky still lives on in our hearts and there he'll always stay. He died because of an argument over a pork chop – it's a crazy world this prison culture.

Rooky

Another Canning Town (London) guy. I first met Rooky 25 years ago in Wandsworth Prison, since that first meet I've bumped into him so many times I've lost count – sadly always meeting inside. He's one con I'd love to meet up with on the out; I've so much respect for him. On the eve of my release from Gartree in 1987 Rooky sent me down a roast dinner and ice-cream & fruit. I was being released from the punishment block but he still made certain I got a last meal that was worth eating. That's the type of guy he is, he's a blagger – got 18 years. That meal he made really made my day, a meal like that in a prison block is a meal to remember, I slept like

LEGENDS

a baby that night and flew like a bird being released from his cage the next day.

It's great to be free, your old china, Charlie, being freed

Sawn off Harry

I was in top secure hospitals in the 80s when I came across this fellow. He was forever going on about shotguns; he loved a sawn-off better than a woman.

I'd learnt not to take too many people serious in the asylums for obvious reasons. But Harry was a frightening character. He'd been found insane for shooting a couple of guys. He went on and on and on about how good it was to blow somebody away and this was no joke as you could see it in his eyes - he loved it. He would tell the doctors and nurses how he loved the explosion and the deadly impact when it smashed through the body of a man, how the blood and gore would drop out of them.

This guy must've been the original psycho. He had no emotion, not an ounce in his whole body. I don't believe that he'll ever be released but maybe he doesn't want to be. If he keeps talking the way he was there's not a chance in hell that he'll ever get out.

Skinhead

I met young Kirk in Woodhill Prison in '93 he was on remand for beating up some Pakistanis. We were in the block for three months until I got moved on for the Andy Love hostage situation. Kirk was only 23, a big guy, shaven head, heavily tattooed, fearless and he hates blacks. I said to him one day, "Kirk, what would you do if a beautiful black girl walked into your cell with no clothes on?" "Fuck off Charlie, that would be bestiality," he replied. He really meant it he never joked but I told him

that one day he'd grow out of all of that. There's good and bad in all races. I liked Kirk he really cheered me up over those three months but what made him a legend was the day he started training with me on the exercise yard. He earned my respect how he worked his balls off on that hour a day exercise, we became good friends and will always remain just that.

Smelly Arse

This loony I met in one of the asylums; he was a right nutter. Until I came across this guy I thought I'd seen it all – one day we were all queuing up for our dinner and we got a strong smell of shit, everyone was looking at each other, no one knew who the fuck it was. I knew it wasn't a fart as the smell lingered on far too long. Then it happened, this loony went to walk towards the feeding hatch and shit was coming out of the bottom of his trouser leg. Dirty Smelly Arse was taken away and slung in the block and given a pile of fresh clothes. I gave my dinner a miss that day. Ga'wd streuth could you Adam and Eve it?

Smiley

I met this legend in Ashworth in the 80s he lived 24 hours a day smiling, he couldn't help it. Somebody had cut him with a Stanley blade across the mouth, what an ugly Mars bar (scar) but a lovely smile.

Son of Lucy

This loony I met in Parkhurst prison in the 70s and he had '666' tattooed on his neck. He was an original satanic worshipper; Satan was his hero. The prison chaplain stayed well clear of him.

LEGENDS

I met up with him again in Rampton asylum and he'd finally been certified insane. I believe that the authorities were too afraid to let him out into society. I don't know if he was mad but I do know that he was a strange one.

I'll always remember how he once picked up a pigeon on the exercise yard; the pigeon had a broken wing and looked half dead. I watched him stick a needle in its eye and as he done it he smiled with delight. He done it dozens of times and he enjoyed every minute of it.

I personally never liked him but I suppose he's a legend in his own circle thankfully not mine.

Spider

I met this inmate in the 80s and I last saw him in the early 90s up in Durham prison.

Spider was always up to something and forever being sent to the block. This particular occasion he had a plan to go through his cell wall, he happened to be in the next cell to me in the block. He asked me to keep ear out for the screws. So I told him, "If you are making one (escaping) I'll have some of that."

So the plan was he digs through the back wall in his cell then when he's almost through, I come through our adjoining wall and slip out with him. The first night he got four bricks out, he then patched it up ready for the next night's work. Spider went out on exercise with me and the screws spun his cell, unfortunately it never was to happen. Spider was a trier.

Days later I chinned a screw and we were both moved on. Last I heard that he'd got released but then returned on another sentence.

Stan the Man

I first met this guy more than two decades ago in Hull Prison and from the start I had the utmost respect for him. He'd received an extra five-years for his part in the Parkhurst Prison riot in '69.

It wasn't till the 80s that Stan made his scar on the system by his dramatic escape from a high security unit in Brixton Prison along with big Ron Moody and Gerald Tuite. But what made it so famous was the fact that Stan's trial had ended and the jury were out that night he'd escaped. Whilst he was on his toes the jury found him - 'NOT GUILTY'!

That's what makes a true legend, it's as if he tempted fate! The real legends just seem to be born to make history.

Steroid Steve

I met him in Ashworth, loved himself he did. After lifting weights he'd run to the mirror to check his hair. I must now say it's true, there's a rumour that steroids shrink your dick. Well after we all seen him in the showers it proved it, if it was an inch it couldn't have been any more, "Oi, look at Steve's dick," I said to the lads. "What's fucking up with it?" He said. "What's fucking up with it," I said, "...mine was fucking bigger than that at 10 years old." All the lunatics laughed, well...apart from Steve. If looks could kill I'd have dropped dead every day after that. He never did come in the showers again with us lot. He would wait till he left the gym and shower on the ward. But he made it into legends even though he had a tiny dick. See it shows I never hold grudges.

Squeak

I was up on the wing with this guy in Full Sutton Prison, Christmas 1990. Squeak's another Londoner who got 18 years; I've a lot of respect for him. In '93 he got a 'not guilty' for attacks on screws in Long Larten. I used to turn the recess into a sauna by turning on the hot taps and the showers it used to steam up lovely. Squeak and a few others used to come into the Bronco sauna, only the legends were allowed in, well you can't have any old riff raff coming into a sauna can you.

'T'

I only met this con about five or six years ago in the block at Lincoln Prison. He was only a young lad, 23, but I was quite impressed by his conduct. I had in fact heard about him from other cons, about his constant battle against the system. One in particular – a siege that I was quite impressed with. I've taken a few hostages myself, as you've probably heard, so I can understand 'T'.

He'd taken a few fellow convicts hostage whilst in Lincoln and

LEGENDS

barricaded up the cell.

His hostages were big guys and 'T' tied them up and wouldn't let them go till the prison doctor gave him what he wanted. At that time he was on a lot of drugs but I'm pleased to say that he's no longer on drugs and trains hard every day in his cell. He looks fit and well and I'm proud of him.

The Bull – R.I.P.

I met this guy in Hull prison in the 70s; he was a Leeds man, well respected in his own circle.

We had words with each other that ended up in a punch up. He caught me with a tremendous right cross, which almost blew out my lights but he made the mistake of not following it through and left himself wide open, consequently his lights went out. It was probably the best punch I'd ever slung in my life.

Later we became friends and had some good laughs together. He was always up to something. Like the time he went into a sex case's cell and set fire to it and shut the door with the sex case still inside of the cell. Sadly the screws saved the sex case.

The Bull, some years later, got stabbed to death outside a nightclub in Leeds - stabbed in the back by cowards.

The Cat

I met this guy in Risley Prison back in '69 and he ended up getting an 8-year sentence for a burglary on a big mansion. I suppose he was the first real cat burglar I'd ever met. I'm aware that he was a burglar but he didn't do it to people other than those with plenty of money. He was a pro, especially to get such a high sentence.

He unfortunately got shipped out to Parkhurst Prison just before the riots in '69. He was never what you'd call a lucky man. I remember his last words to me before he went, "Box it clever and remember what I told you, if you're going to nick out make sure it's worth nicking." Looking back on it I seem to have been influenced by a lot of guys from the old school and I think that's where I get my values. I never did see him again nor have I heard anything. It's possible he's lost his nine lives but I'd like to think he's running some pub or club somewhere.

A-Z

The Cream Man

This guy only gets a mention because of the pure madness of his ways. He was a black con, he hated everybody and had a chip on his shoulder so big it weighed him down. He could suck on a lemon and still not pull a face! His face was permanently cringed up. He was forever upsetting fellow cons with his weird ways.

The crunch came at Parkhurst Prison on the Isle of Wight in the 70s; he took a liberty and upset the whole wing. It was a Sunday, 'apple pie and cream day', and he ran his finger over the top of all the apple pies on the tray. He scooped up dozens of blobs of cream and ate them all! He was a filthy animal.

Some just never learn. The Cream Man nicked his last cream. He survived but he disappeared. No one ever got nicked for the stabbing, as nobody ever talked in Parkhurst, it was a cons jail while it was a high security prison way back then, now it's a 'B' category prison – softer and easier regime. People like the Cream Man would never be accepted for the likes of what he did. I often wonder if he learned his lesson?

The Egg Man

I met this character in Long Lartin Prison. He was serving 20 years, passing his time painting beautiful pictures onto the shells of all types of eggs. Chicken, duck, goose and he even had an ostrich egg!

He used to send away for these eggs and turn them into beautiful works of art. Some eggs he would decorate with jewels and would sell for a good few quid. Only once did I ever witness the Egg Man lose his temper. It was the day a screw went into his cell to search it and accidentally knocked over a prized egg!

I actually felt sorry for the screw, as he was one of the decent ones and it was a genuine accident. The Egg Man soon realised it was a real accident and later came back down to earth after ranting and raving. I did ask him later in the day if he fancied an egg sandwich but he was too busy. I recall a time I was shipped out of a prison and my belongings were sent after me. When I opened my bag of stuff there it was – a picture of my mum torn up, but the Egg Man's case was a pure accident.

LEGENDS

The Head

I met this strange guy in Rampton in the 70s. His head was twice the size of a normal head if not three times as big. From the first glance it reminded me of a giant pumpkin and his eyes were wide open, as if in a trance. I don't know why the Head was sent to Rampton but he must've been criminally insane, as we were all there for one thing or another. I was sent there for attacks on screws and the stabbing of a con in Parkhurst.

I often wondered what the Head had done to end up in this maximum-security hospital; he probably looked into somebody's window and frightened the bloody life out of them, ha, ha. It's characters like him that keep us all sane and happy. When it was boiled eggs for breakfast I used to tap mine on his head and say, "Nice one Head." He would smile and say, "Yeah, nice."

I often wondered what happened to the Head, oh well he's just another legend in my eyes.

The Human Dustbin

This guy I met in Wandsworth jail back in the 70s. I've never met such a fat, ugly, lazy bastard to come a good second, as the human dustbin was at number one.

He was a good 20 stone and all fat. He received a three-year sentence for stabbing a barman in a South London pub. We used to watch him go wobbling down the landings towards the dustbin outside the recess. He'd lift the lid off and dig his big sausage fingers into the waste and pull out old food. Bread, spuds, buns and whatever he could find and eat. Nobody wanted him around; he just wasn't fit to mix with humans. I was in the recess this day and an almighty crash went off. I turned a bit lively to see the Human Dustbin falling over by the sink. Somebody had smashed him over the head with a metal mop bucket and others were hitting him with mops and brooms. If it wasn't for him being such a monster, I may have stepped in to help him but he just had to go. I've never seen or heard of him since that day in the recess, not that I want to! I guess he's a legend in his own strange way. Make of it what you will but for me the bizarre has become a way of life and I don't really know what's sane and what isn't – it's an unreal world inside these dustbins of life.

A-Z

The Human Slug

This con used to make me puke; I've more respect for a cockroach. I met this vermin in Woodhill Prison; he was a disgrace to the human race. If he had the decency he would've hung himself. He stunk, his cell stunk and he moaned and cried the whole day away.

I tried to help him but it was useless, I spent hours trying to educate him, telling him to clean up his cell and himself and to stop moaning and face up to reality. I made him aware that he had his body and eyes and how lucky he was to have them, some people are crippled and blind. But it was all a waste of time.

He was a young man of 22 with a backbone of a six-month-old baby. A complete mummies boy – my advice is give it up. He's a legend in his own league, as I've never met such a useless, fat, lazy, smelly toe rag as the Human Slug.

The Key Man

I first met George in the 80s in Winson Green Prison; he's always trying something. They caught him with a homemade key and gave him 14 days punishment, but the Key Man just laughs it off like the man he is. George never fails to amaze me and that's why he's a legend in every sense of the word.

I remember when we were in the same punishment block we used to pass stuff to each other on a bit of string known as a 'line'. I sent over some drawings I'd done so he could see them and they fell off the line, but the key man being a wizard soon came up with an idea. He tied a blob of margarine on to the end of his bit of string and tossed it towards the drawings and 'plop', it landed on them and he fished them in safe and sound. The Key Man never let me down.

The Kite Man

I met this lunatic in Broadmoor, he really thought he could fly, he somehow scaled a building and got 20 foot up, he stood up and opened both his arms in mid air and guess what – he broke both his ankles! The Kite Man never tried it again. Such places reveal the other side of life and best you don't get to see it too.

LEGENDS

The Landlord

Simo ran a pub in Cheshire; in the 80s he got a life sentence for a murder he claims he didn't do. I met him in Armley Prison, Leeds. What makes this case so legendary is that a body was never found. This is one of a few cases in history where a life sentence is pronounced without a body. Simo continues his fight to clear his name it's definitely a case that will never be forgotten and it will no doubt become another embarrassment to the judicial system. I fancy the landlord will be pulling a few pints in the future.

The Mad Pope

This guy was the original lunatic, straight out of the Cuckoo's Nest. I met him inside a top secure asylum way back in the mid 70s. He blessed me every day for the six months I spent on the same ward as him.

He'd killed his uncle with a pickaxe, so I don't think he'll take over Pope John Paul's place. I remember the day he walked into my cell and got down on his hands and knees and kissed the floor! Then walked out as though it was a natural thing to do.

I miss the Mad Pope; he gave me some laughs and cheered the days up.

The Maggot

I don't know why I'm even putting this guy in my book???? I suppose cos I've never come across another like him. He came into my world in Rampton, he used to go through the bins for bits of grub – he was an ugly little maggot, he never spoke words just made noises. One day I saw him pull out some chicken bones and start sucking the bits of meat off it. I shouted at him, "Oi, you fucking maggot," and that name stayed with him forever more. But he made the legends simply as I can't forget the horrible dirty maggot!

I'm a clean and tidy person and that's the way I run my ship and as I steer through life I can gauge myself against others and based on the Maggot I know I've got morals and to see someone fall into something unrecognisable is sad – he was a sad case.

A-Z

The Mummy

The asylum characters are always the best to write about, as they remain inside one's mind forever. Take 'The Mummy', this geezer actually killed two people to end up in the asylum, but it was his behaviour inside that was the real problem.

He would disappear into the recess and lock himself in one of the cubicles. Then, without warning he would begin his mummy walk through the corridors of madness. You'd see him wrapped in toilet paper, from head to foot, and walk around like a zombie.

When I first saw it I felt very wary. But over the months and years of living with such lunatics it truly becomes a part of life inside a cuckoo house. The Mummy actually brought me a lot of smiles.

When I look back on those times with The Mummy and others like him I sometimes wish I could see it again - the walk, the slow speech. The toilet paper tearing off as he moved. The hysterical laughter of a madman. It was eccentric without a doubt. Madness without a doubt!

But characters actually make an institution. Without guys like The Mummy these asylums would be graveyards. I often had the urge to set fire to the paper as he walked by me, so as to see him running around on fire, but I never did.

For me The Mummy deserved a bit of respect. I only hope he still continues his marvellous act. Long live The Mummy!

The Pie Man

This guy was wasting his time in jail; he was a master chef. I met him up in Frankland Prison in the 80s; he made pies and sold them for tobacco – apple pies, plum pies, strawberry pies, cherry pies steak & kidney pies, beef & onion pies you name it he done it!

Bloody hell I'm starving just thinking about those pies; they tasted so delicious. A good pal of mine made sure I got a couple of pies every day from the Pie Man. Sadly it never lasted too long as I was moved on but I say to the Pie Man get out and open up a pie shop and you'll be a millionaire in no time at all. Prison brings out a man's talents yet society overlooks such skills from cons as being a gimmick or an attention getter. We've all got an angle but the Pie Man has my respect for being the best. ·

LEGENDS

The Praying Mantis

This guy's a human stick insect 6 feet 6 inches and about 9 stones in weight, I met him in Long Larten Prison. The way he walks is good to see, he seems to stop with every step, once he stepped right in front of me as I was walking back to my cell with a mug of hot cocoa. It went all down the back of his legs, he moved a bit that day, it was a genuine accident.

Days later I was in the recess shaving when I clocked the Mantis snooping, he had a razor in his hand and I really think he was planning to stripe me so I followed him to his cell and shot in for a chat. It turned out not to be what I thought but you can never be too safe in jail especially with a stick insect.

The Renegade

I met James in Brixton in '88 he was lifed off with Charlie McGhee; he lived in my hometown of Luton. In '94 James escaped from a van going to Wandsworth Prison from Whitemoor Prison. As far as I'm aware he hasn't been seen since — you stay lucky old son. It's lovely to know he's out there — try and win like Ronnie Biggs did.

The Sweet Man

I met him in the intensive care unit in one of the top secure hospitals, he was a strange one alright, every time he looked at someone it was with a cold hard stare, ice cool with a smirk. He was a frightening character but it was his strange behaviour that made me aware of him! He was always alert, his eyes, his movement, the sound, the smell — he was a natural survivor!

He always had a bag of hard-boiled sweets, and he always offered the wardens one. (But never the inmates.) I watched the Sweet Man for many a month before I gave him a pull. I asked him straight out, "Why do you always give sweets to the wardens and not us?" He answered: "I don't like the wardens!" The answer puzzled me even more, "If you don't like them then why do you give them sweets?" I asked. "Simple," he said, "I buy sweets and stick half a dozen up my arse every night and then in the morning I wrap them back up and give them out to the wardens!"

The Sweet Man had been doing this for years before I arrived

36

there and no doubt still did it for many years afterwards. It was a brutal place where the wardens were evil and nasty. For me the Sweet Man was a classic legend in his own right.

Tiger Tim – R.I.P.

I still don't know why they called him Tiger and I don't suppose I ever will now, as he's long dead.

I met Tim in Risley jail way back in the 70s; he was a timid lad and very much a loner. I ended up having him as a cellmate and it was like being padded up with a cardboard cut out. He had no conversation at all other than "What time is it?" Or, "I hope my visit turns up, or "What's for tea?"

He was in for forgery, chequebooks and stuff like that. We used to play lots of games such as chess, draughts, cards and such but he became depressed. I tried to get him out of his shell. I would let him sit on my back when I done push-ups. Then he would sit on the bunk as I used the whole bunk as a bench press machine.

He was never good for a laugh. He ended up going to court and getting remanded into the hospital wing for psychiatric reports. A week went by and he hung himself in the hospital wing. It really hit me and I was very cut up about it for a long time afterwards. I felt that I should've done more to help him but sometimes all the help in the world just ain't good enough.

Tight Arse

I met this character in Wormwood Scrubs Prison some years back. In my life I've never come across anybody so mean! He's a lifer and a very bitter twisted man. He's so tight if he had a band-aid plaster, he'd sooner cut himself and use the plaster himself rather than give it away.

He used to save up all of his sugar ration for weeks and weeks, then sell it for tobacco. He would also pick up all the dog ends and save them until he had a tin full, then sell the tin for civvy fags. He would truly take some catching up so I must make him the meanest bastard I've met.

Personally I never did like him but neither did his family, as he killed his wife. He probably killed her to save giving her money.

LEGENDS

Tiny George

I first met George in Broadmoor in the early 80s, he was sent there over his violence – no jail wanted him. He hated nonces and grasses. Eventually Broadmoor moved him to the 'Psycho' wing in Parkhurst Prison where George stayed for years. He got life over a stabbing in South London. He was then sent to Broadmoor from prison over another stabbing. George always said to me, "I can't fight my way out of trouble because I'm too small, so I stab my way

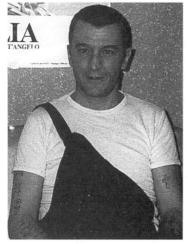

out." I later had the privilege of sharing a few months with George in Parkhurst on the unit. He's one of the all time prison characters I've met. Sadly some toe-rag upset George and rather than see George stab him up, I chinned the con in his cell and told him he was lucky that I'd given him a slapping otherwise George might have used a blade on him, lucky I came along when I did – because of that I was moved on to another one of Her Majesty's hotels.

George's philosophy was, "I can't fight so I'll stab," and stab he did. He's now doing well after being de-categorised and he loves a cup of tea, I gave him a teapot years ago and he still uses that teapot today. At least he never put it over anyone's head. He's left a few Mars bars on his victims over the years but we all mellow with age and George's doing just fine.

Tony the Terror

This guy's serving three life sentences but he's never killed. I first met him in Wandsworth Prison segregation block in the 80s – the youngest ever con to be put there. He'd kidnapped a fellow con and bashed him to bits with a chair leg at Chelmsford Prison, then he took a teacher hostage at Gartree Prison then he plunged a screw. Tony's done it all, roofs, violence, sieges, shit-ups the lot but he's legendary over pulling out his own teeth. Yeah, his own teeth! To pull out your own teeth is the ultimate challenge, could you do it, I couldn't but then again I wouldn't want to.

A-Z

Webber

Big Web's a lifer; he must have served a good 25 years. He once said it's his ambition to be the longest serving lifer of all time. Not a lot you can say about that is there, but like I say legends are unique people, they often blow your socks off when you least expect it.

Werewolf

Here I was in one of the top security hospital in the 80s and I stumbled across this lunatic. When I say lunatic, I mean lunatic.

Every full moon he would be up at his cell window howling through the bars. Sometimes when I felt in the mood I would howl back at him. He would howl back and I would return the howl until I got bored, as it sometimes could go on for an hour or more. In the morning he'd be all excited telling everyone that a real wolf was close to the asylum. I told him it was quite possible, as there's a lot of forestry. He was made up.

I don't know to this day what the wolf man was in for. I thought I best not find out. I also used to tell him that wolf footprints had been found by the outside wall and droppings had been taken away to be forensically tested. It kept the wolf man happy.

No doubt he's still howling out of his window, as he'll never be released, imagine having him as your next-door neighbour!

Whicker's World

Eddie I met in Winson Green Prison in '93. He was nicked over some guns but the charges were slung out and he went home – only right too. He came to my trial at Luton for the Andy Love and Governor Wallace hostage taking incidents – made my day. He's a proud cockney with solid principles but he does have some strange ways, when he was inside he used to wake up early and sing a song through his door and wake the whole bloody wing up. My favourite was *Green, Green Grass of Home*, he has a good and powerful voice but at five fucking thirty in the morning it's a bit out of order

LEGENDS

but we all missed him when he went. It wasn't the same without Eddie's early morning call.

White Mamba

This guy is a true East Londoner from Canning Town. I first met him in Brixton Prison in the 80s but the story I write is of Christmas '94 in the punishment block of Full Sutton Prison maximum secure unit. The White Mamba was in the cell above me so I thought I'd test his reflexes, I called him to the window, "Here, Mamba, catch this," I slung him up a raw egg. I expected to see it fall down to the concrete ground below but he caught it. Another con shouted, "It was only luck, a fluke." "Okay, pal," replied the Mamba, "I'll do it again, sling one up Chas." This time he caught it but it cracked in his hand. The whole block erupted with cheers. It's no wonder he's a great blagger with reflexes as fast as his.

Woody

I met this guy up in the block of Frankland maximum-security jail; he's a big man, 18 stone and legs like tree trunks. He's a biker, a real Hell's Angel, a legend in his own circle. He got involved in a big fight and was given a life sentence. He hates, despises, loathes and gets angry when a sex case is anywhere near him. He tore one up into little pieces at the Scrubs. To all sex cases - take this advice: stay clear of Woody or you could be next.

Zipper

This man may come across as a funny character but I assure you, the reader, there's nothing funny. He first entered into my world over 20 years ago at Parkhurst Prison. Since then our paths have met up at various prisons and asylums. Zipper is in fact a living legend amongst the prison population. 'A lifer' who is still caged up after 22 years and a dear friend who I love like a brother.

Zipper got this name from swallowing objects. He would get depressed and swallow things like glass, razor blades, bedsprings, tins and money. Some of these items were impossible to come back out nature's own way, so he would have to go under the surgeon's scalpel.

A-Z

Zipper done it so many times it became a regular occurrence for him to be rushed out to a hospital. On some occasions he almost died. The surgeon told him if he continued to do it he may well have a colostomy operation, as there was no skin tissue to keep sewing up his stomach. But the surgeon cracked a joke and said, "I can also put a zip on your scar so as to stop cutting you open". Zipper was created.

I am pleased to point out that he hasn't swallowed anything for many years now. I think the colostomy bag may have made him think twice before swallowing again.

I've actually been in the same prison when Zipper's been rushed out to hospital. I've prayed for the man, as I feel for him. Depression's a terrible illness but I knew in my own heart that Zipper would survive. I'm sure that one day in the future he'll walk free.

I often look at objects such as what he's swallowed and thought to myself, how could he swallow that? The thought of a bedspring sliding down my throat just sends a bolt of fear into my veins. I couldn't even attempt it. A razor blade is beyond my imagination.

Zipper is no doubt a worthy character of this book. I guess we must thank the surgeon for the creation of Zipper.

2

Icons of Icons

RONNIE BIGGS

Best known of all the great train robbers and maybe even better known than Pele the Brazilian football player. Ronnie's been on the run for 37 years since escaping from Wandsworth Prison. Biggsy's fought extradition from Brazil to the UK and successfully claimed to be the father of a Brazilian child, which prevented this 'dodgy' application to get him back to the UK cos nobody wants old Biggsy back in the slammer, as he's an icon.

When he escaped he had a face-lift and succeeded in evading capture but whilst in Australia he had a narrow escape from the police. It wasn't until some journalist discovered him in Brazil in 1974 that the world and his friend found out where he was.

Jack Slipper of Scotland yard tried to get him extradited and there was even a plot by a TV company in 1981 to get an ex-SAS guy to kidnap Biggsy and even though it happened Biggsy had to be released back into his playboy lifestyle when the kidnap was ruled to be illegal. Then in 1997 he defeated the UK government's attempts to have him extradited – clowns tried and failed, leave the guy alone cos he's a status symbol of struggle and strife. He fast became a celebrity and has remained in that status ever since. No one goes to Brazil without seeking out Biggsy for a photograph or two.

Front and reverse side of a spoof monopoly note - Autographed

Recently though he's had a stroke and it looked a bit iffy for a while but he's pulled through like a true legend. I was sent a little present from Biggsy; it's here for you to look at, like it? A true icon – long live Biggsy. **Website: www.ronniebiggs.com**

Legends

MARTIN CAHILL 1949 -1994
'The Irish Godfather'
R.I.P.

Four shots to the body and one to the crust ain't no way to end a man's life; in a typical drive by shooting Martin Cahill was killed while waiting at a road junction in his car on 18th August 1994, in the Dublin suburb of Ranelagh on his way to return a videotape to a hire a shop. Martin was known as 'The General' and was a charismatic man and in no way deserved to die the way he did yet it was somehow inevitable that this should be a fitting end to his life of crime. The man's profile was a one of mixed ideals and his chameleon like ways were part of his character.

He made it up the ladder from the Dublin ghetto to a position of almost celebrity status and became more than just a legend - an Icon. He was only 45 years old when he was murdered and had plenty of good years ahead of him as Ireland's ultimate warrior and gangland boss. When it came to dishing out the punishment he didn't discriminate against anyone – all those that went against him were equally punished regardless of their religion and on top of that he hated the Gardai with all of his soul. He'd spend hours planning ways of upsetting them with his shenanigans.

The General was the ultimate gang boss that no one was able to stop, except for the IRA! It was they that lay claim to this infamous murder, a murder not out of political reason but out of old scores to settle. As what usually happens after such a death there's the fight for the vacant territory but it was already carved out and the lion's share went to a guy called the Monk, then came a guy called Maradonna and some other guy called the Penguin, fucking hell we just need some geezer called Batman to come along and we'll have a house full of them. But none of them could match the General. He was a unique icon and will never be forgotten.

Cahill was so clever he even raided the Gardai's weapons store for confiscated weapons, then he blew up their forensic laboratories and to top it all he stole a whole bundle of criminal files that were classed as Top Secret. Cahill was dicing with death and there was only gonna be one ending for this guy – the morgue, I say that cos I know people who told me about this guy and they said he was the best but he didn't know the word 'stop'. For 20

Icons of Icons

years he kept his identity secret from the media but everything he did attracted the press's attentions.

In 1970 Cahill was to get a taste of prison, a four stretch, for nicking fags and he'd served his time the easy way, got to give him credit there. He says he handled his time in prison by priming himself up and when the screws shut his cell door at night he - in his head - was locking them out. He came out after serving three years and as usual there's always a copper waiting to stick to you like glue and the copper in this case was called Ned Ryan, Inspector Ryan. For over 16 years Ryan and Cahill were enemies and Cahill used to take the piss by blanking Inspector Ryan and his fellow coppers during interviews.

It wasn't long before the muppets in the law machine were trying it on with Cahill and he was up in the dock in November 1974 on a blagging charge. I'm known for my funny ways and I once blacked myself up with boot polish from head to toe when I went to court on a robbery charge, as a co-accused of mine was black, he got bail and I didn't so I thought if I was black too then I'd also get bail – did I fuck though!

One reason the General wouldn't do a job on the mainland was his fear of being fitted up by the English police – too right! He had a secret respect for the Gardai as he knew some of them were at least reputable guys being of Catholic upbringing and wanting promotion without a blemish on their characters, so London and Manchester were a no, no for him and you've only gotta look at the way all them other honest Irish (and English) geezers were fitted up by the English coppers to see why Martin wouldn't carry out robberies in England.

When the General was in the dock with two others they all covered their faces, what a guy and I class him as a true icon. His case was slung out due to lack of evidence, as it should've been. He kept his face covered at all of his future trials; he even wore a wig, false tache and glasses at one of his trials. That's why we haven't put a photograph here – out of respect to the General.

The General's territory was Hollyfield, a rough old area but full of good down to earth people, he never forgot his roots and for all the millions he had he didn't go over the top although he loved powerful motorbikes and the odd curry takeaway. He was the typical understated gangster, no flash Harry here just a solid staunch guy. To look at him you'd have to look twice cos he didn't

Legends

look like the typical gangster. Instead of Armani suits he wore a leather jacket and jeans. Instead of steroid pumped up arms he had a natural curry eater's body and his hair was brushed over a bald pat and he loved pigeons – the sport of pigeon racing that is, not pigeon pie.

When they pulled the Hollyfield Buildings down it was the General's place that was the last standing – the General's last stand. The thing is it was the sneaky way they went about pulling the estate down and it was during a time he was in prison in 1978 doing a four stretch for, would you believe, receiving a stolen motor, what a liberty!

Police and all sorts of other clowns evicted the last remaining residents off the estate when their appeals against eviction failed and when the General got out of jail in 1980 it hit him head on that his was the sole property left intact! He slugged it out with the council, his electricity supply was cut – he reconnected it himself and almost electrocuted his mother in law. His wife couldn't take it no longer and moved out - the General stayed put. While he was out one day, he was late in getting home; they'd pulled his place down - behind his back! So he put up a little shack out of the rubble and they took that away too. So he put a caravan there and it was burned out. So he set up a tent! Whatever they did he'd always have an answer and would go one better.

Eventually the Lord Mayor came and pleaded with the General to make peace and he promised the General a new home nearby when they were built and with this the General was happy but the way he fought against the council won the hearts of all the people around the area. Hollyfield Buildings was the place where the General had his heart. He later opened a pool hall and all the local tearaways would spend hours at the place, this man was your typical do-gooder gangster. It's estimated that during his criminal career that he was responsible for £40m worth of property and money being robbed! That was a conservative estimate!

There was a film made about his life and even that was ending up in a battle when two companies were fighting over it and in the end it was made but in black and white – they'd only gone and spoiled a good fucking film, I mean the only one made in black and white to have ever made it in recent years was *Scheindler's List*, don't even know if that's how you spell it but I sure know that *The General* should've been in colour but I heard somewhere that it was gonna be remade in colour.

To show you how clever Martin was when he was being tailed by a police surveillance team he led them a merry dance and eventually after hundreds of miles of travelling through and around the territory of Wicklow he stopped by the side of the road – he was low on fuel and obviously so were the police tailing him. He pulled out a five-gallon can of juice and filled his Mercedes up, smiled and drove off!

There are hundreds of stories just like this to tell about the General – there'll never be another like him, God bless the General a Chara (Gaelic). **Website: www.martincahill.com** (Was not active at time of print)

DAVE COURTNEY
'Dodgy Dave'

Legends

One flash bastard – but you gotta give it to him – a face in the criminal underworld. Had some close shaves when he was up against it and looking at big bird, mostly fit ups.

Then mysteriously pulled out and stopped all criminal activities and went straight, as he says; "Stop the ride I wanna get off." (Same as his book title.) He's the boss of a massive security network in the London area. Clubs, gyms and all sorts of straight things, he does it all and he does it best. Nobody can take it away from the guy. Didn't he do well but he's still a flash bastard but an Icon and must be in my book, a top legend at that. Any man who can stop the ride and get off and still win has my utmost respect.

Dave was made famous by the documentary *Bermondsey Boy* and was an associate of the Krays, former debt collector and yellow pages of crime. 'Dodgy' Dave moved into rave and was voted Rave promoter of the year in 1999. His most famous claim to fame was on a curry night out when he chopped and finely diced five Chinese takeaway workers for taking the piss out of one of his family. Dave decided to give them a carry out – five carry outs to be exact, all special died rice.

Well done, Dave, you deserve it and let's not forget it, it was DC who done a lot for Ron Kray and organised his funeral, didn't Dave look like a lord with his flash gear he was wearing, I know he's the face of modern crime and he's sometimes looked on as the new boy in town but I would ask that he now can be classed as part of the furniture. Fucking hell I mean if Dave's even passed his motorbike test so as he can be street legal it's gotta say something of his strength of character. Last time  I was out and rode a motorbike they was all BSAs and the like, flash, shiny chrome and reliable – same as Dave. Yeah Dave made it to the top – just make sure you don't fall.

Icons of Icons

Websites:www.crosswinds.net/%7Edavecourtney/dave.ht ml & www.davecourtney.com & www.davecourtney.org.uk

FREDDIE FOREMAN
'The Managing Director of British Crime'

If they invented the T-shirt just for Joe Pyle then they sure as hell invented *The Long Good Friday* for Freddie. Don't tell me none of you know what I'm on about. If I was to say Bob Hoskins played the part of a guy that didn't 'arf go as a ringer for Freddie then you might know what I'm on about if not then...well I'm not gonna say you're a clown cos that would be an insult to a clown. It's the only damn thing what's come near to being as real as it gets and now I hear they're gonna make another one – *Long Good Friday* 2. Sometimes a masterpiece is best left alone for fear of damaging it but so long as Freddie's got a role to play in it then it's gonna be a winner.

Freddie mentioned me in his book *Respect*. Said I was nicked

for tearing council house roofs off. The roof part was right but not the council house bit but someone like Freddie can be allowed to get it wrong as he's got my utmost respect and anyone invited to be a pall bearer at Ron's funeral (Ron Kray) has to be a staunch solid guy. Freddie and Tony Lambrianou have a book coming out called *Getting it Straight* and if anyone can get it straight then these two sure can, make sure you get it. Brown Bread Fred –

49

Legends

'TheUndertaker' was portrayed in the *Long Good Friday* and it must rate as second only to *Get Carter* as an all time great for being realistic. Freddie even had to show Bob Hoskins his mannerisms so as to get it right. One of the most respected underworld figures around today is our Freddie.

Although Freddie's admitted to a number of infamous murders in a TV documentary it might well be this was just a good piece of marketing, as *The Long Good Friday 2* is rumoured to be hitting the big screen and there's nothing like a bit of publicity to lift it and anyway so if he did kill Tommy 'Ginger' Marks and Frank 'The Mad Axeman' Mitchell, he was only doing what would've been done by someone else.

Mitchell was a gruesome character and a giant of man who was uncontrollable. What the Krays had unleashed on the world by breaking Mitchell free from Dartmoor then it was, so it's claimed, just Freddie putting it right again. What you gotta remember is that in crimebizz a lot of things are blown up out of all proportions and at times people are pushed into a corner and have to go along with the hype.

The TV Company who'd put the documentary together should be hammered for taking the piss out of the public in that a number of scenes just couldn't have happened; anyway it all made for good TV and hype - till the end Fred, Charlie B.
Website: www.freddieforeman.com

BILLY GENTRY

Anyone that's done big bird don't really need me to say who Billy G is but I will for those who haven't heard of him. Billy's one of the pure old school villains, a man who lives by a code of honour. I haven't seen him for a long, long time but the last time was in Parkhurst in the late 80s, what a gentleman. He pops up in all the crime books simply as he's London's Mr Crime (or was). I'd like to think Billy's now free, as he's in his 60s now. It's time he settled, got a club and raked some big bucks in. Billy once told me some years back, "Look if you're gonna be a criminal do it big time, don't fart about but you must be prepared to take the consequences, as it can be awesome." Billy must've served three big sentences that I know of. I'd say he was unlucky but I still say a great man, a man I admire – a credit to all legends.

Icons of Icons

VIV GRAHAM 1959 -1993
'Simply the Best'
R.I.P.

Viv's life came to a violent end on New Year's Eve 1993 – he was shot and later died in agony with half his insides hanging out. He managed to crawl a good 50 yards from where he was shot back to the pub he'd just left. When his friend, Terry Scott, rushed out of the Queen's Head pub Viv's main concern was that his wounds should be covered over so that no one would be shocked, that's how much of a gentleman he was! Viv was as hard as nails but at heart he was a big softy.

His rise to crimebizz came after he stood up to a local hard man, Paul Ashton, while working on a club door. A local hard guy pointed Viv into the direction of Newcastle and told him he'd find the streets paved with gold for such a man with his fighting skills learned from his junior boxing days. Viv quickly progressed up the ladder and eventually became the number one hard case of Newcastle. He started to make it big but he ended up being used by a lot of people and ended up serving three years for an unprovoked assault on another club doorman. Viv had been well and truly used and he knew it.

He came out of prison a changed man, a family man with old school values – now he set about building his club door security business up, only one problem and that was the council had outlawed anyone with a criminal record of any involvement with running club doors. Viv started to spread his wings and ran his business under his own flag away from the centre of Newcastle but he was always an influence in the city and it led to a few attempted murders against him.

One incident involved a shotgun being fired at him through the rear window of a Nissan sports car. The man who did this later ended up with a life sentence for killing an old man, left him for dead all trussed up after robbing him and turning off the electric supply in the winter, the guy, a war hero, froze to death! Viv, in a press interview, told them he didn't need guns, he'd use his fists but his old school wisdom was no match for those weaker than him who'd use a tool or a piece at the drop of a hat. Already a power struggle had developed and people were beginning to sense he wasn't the main man in Newcastle. When a guy from

Legends

Middlesbrough, Lee Duffy, challenged Viv to a fight and winner take all it was a difficult thing for Viv to do in not turning up for the fight but to have done so might have led to an earlier ending, as he feared even if he won then his rivals were going to use that setting as a murder plot against him. Duffy was to end up dying from knife wounds after a fight in Middlesbrough in an unrelated incident.

Another hard as nails man from Sunderland, Ernie Bewick, had involvement in running Sunderland's pub and club doors and his rivalry to Viv's status was always hanging in the air and in a nightclub confrontation with a rival from Newcastle it was to be Viv who would intervene when, in a straightener (rematch), Ernie was getting the better of this man. Bewick was to later receive a six-year prison sentence for manslaughter when he went too far in a brawl outside of a pub in Sunderland. One national newspaper, the Star, estimated Bewick to be the hardest guy in the UK after he was said not to have lost any of the 100 or so bare knuckle fights he'd had.

Soon Viv's name was used in just about every North East pub

Icons of Icons

and club if there was trouble then people used to say, "Call the 4th emergency Service, call Viv." The police would even pass his number on to pub owners that were being hassled by low life scum. He was a bigger deterrent than the police ever would be, his name had them running away for miles.

His tentacles of power spread as far as Tenerife, in the Canaries but he turned down the chance to take control of the lucrative time-share market over there. The man who made it big in Viv's place was later to be murdered in Tenerife!

Viv was opposed to drug dealing and wouldn't allow it in any of the pubs and clubs he had control over. When security firms tried to muscle in on his turf, one of them a company from Birmingham (Higgins), he soon sent them packing and the club doorman of Newcastle had Viv to thank for his intervention and saving their jobs, that's the type of guy he was.

In another incident Viv knocked a 7-foot tall USA Navy Boxing Champ out cold with one punch after the giant was becoming difficult to handle on the streets of Newcastle. A confrontation with *Heartbreak Hotel* actor, Tim Healey, ended up with Viv shaking him about when he mistook him as part of a rowdy group chatting up his girlfriend but he soon realised he had the wrong man. His best ever tally of knock outs on the street was four men, equally as big as he was, and within 30 seconds they were history, one needed over 40 stitches to put his jaw back in place – none of the men pressed charges because they knew they were in the wrong – Viv detested bad manners.

Gazza, a famous UK soccer player, was severely injured in a barroom brawl in a Newcastle nightclub and it resulted in his kneecap being shattered – as soon as Viv was murdered the press gave him the blame for this attack but Gazza being the man he is stood up for his dead friend and even contributed a foreword to one of two books written about Viv as a mark of respect. *Viv (Graham) – Simply the Best* and *Viv – and the Geordie Mafia Vol. 2*

"Viv no more, '94" This was rumoured to have been chanted by his killers in a celebratory drink after they'd killed him on that New Year's Eve. Although many people were suspected of the murder no one's been charged. Many reasons put forward including one that will go down like a lead balloon was that Gazza had hired some Italian hitman to finish off the hard man, which was invention by the press to hype the whole thing up. It's suspected

Legends

that the same people who killed Viv also had a hand in the murder of a pizza delivery driver, Paul Logan, from Shotley Bridge, County Durham. Logan, another local hard man, not in the same league as Viv but certainly a hard man was murdered only a few days before Viv met his untimely end!

Viv predicted his own end when he said in answer to a question about why he didn't save some of his income or invest it, "It's better to live for today, as tomorrow I could be dead." The web of corruption involved in this whole case has hampered a positive police investigation into both the Viv and Logan murders. Viv left behind three children, his insurers withheld payment saying his death was 'Self inflicted' and family and friends were lost without his guiding wisdom. Viv Graham – Simply the Best.

DONALD HUME

I met this legend in Broadmoor in the 70s. I can't understand how they haven't made a film about him, maybe he's been caged for so long that people have forgotten – that's sad. A legend must never fade away, a legend must always live on and a legend must live up to his or her status.

Let me tell you a bit about Donald and then you'll see why he's in this section. This guy was one of the first bank robbers to mix brain with brawn. He used aliases to keep on the move; his first alias was Pilot-Officer Don Hulme, DFM. He used this name in 1949 when his Cadillac car was used in a carnival in Torquay. Not one to shy away from publicity he signed the hotel register as Captain DB Hulme, DFM. He then changed his name in 1958 to plain old Donald Brown but he wasn't happy with this so he matched up the identity of a dead guy, whose details were stored in Somerset House, to his and took on the identity of John Stephen Bird. Maybe cos he'd done bird he wanted the name 'Bird'. Then when he went to Switzerland he used the name John L Lea and if that wasn't confusing enough he became 'Johnny Bird the fighter pilot' while in Switzerland.

Donald would practice saying, "This is a stick-up," after listening to movie star Jimmy Cagney say the words in films. (My favourite saying from Jimmy Cagney was, 'I'm on top of the world, ma!') He used to go and watch gangster films to sooth his nerves before doing a job. In 1958 he went to the USA to eye up a job he want-

Icons of Icons

ed to tackle and this was on a payroll wagon in Los Angeles but he gave that idea up when he seen what he was up against. I reckon he used to go and watch the gangster films so he could live out his dreams of turning over one of them cash vans in the USA.

Hume was one of the first International Hoods and for that reason he warrants a place amongst these Icons. He was based in Switzerland and would travel to other countries to do his work. One of the bank jobs he did in England was the Midland Bank, in Boston Manor Road, Brentford, London. He slipped in at one minute to noon and was locked in with the last customers before dinner closing. He had to shoot one of the clerks in the gut, as resistance was put up but he still got away with £1,500 cash.

He had to tell his girlfriend while in Canada that he was working undercover for the CIA, as she was getting a little bit suspicious as to what he was up to when he disappeared. What she didn't know though was that Donald had confessed to a newspaper that he'd killed car dealer Stanley Setty back in 1949. Donald had been nicking cars for this geezer Setty and way back then they were matching up the logbooks of written off cars to nice clean motors freshly nicked by Donald.

A fight broke out and Donald used an SS dagger to kill the man with the same initials 'SS'. What should've been a frightener ended up in death and later on the story was to be sold to a Sunday newspaper, yeah they was even selling Sunday newspapers stories way back then. Anyway it all ended when he was nicked for a bank raid in Switzerland and he was charged with attempted murder, armed robbery, threatening life and breaching this that and the other regulations controlling foreigners.

At the trial Donald was a little less well behaved than I was at my last trial at Luton Crown Court, where I gave my word to the judge that I'd behave – and I did behave. At one point Donald said to the interpreter to tell the judge, "If it comes to a slanging match, I will rip him to bits physically," luckily for Donald the interpreter didn't tell this to the judge. When the judge said to Donald that the raid was doomed to failure he replied, "I didn't want my conscience to brand me as a coward."

I can sympathise with Donald cos the Swiss psychiatrist who examined him before his trial said, "Hulme was incapable of normal sympathy and relationships with other people. During the whole examination he only showed deeper emotion when he talked about acts of violence. If he started to talk about these acts his face took on an expression that was so evil I often had shivers down my spine. He is incapable of love, he can only hate." I've had the same problem over the years and that's how I've been branded the most dangerous prisoner in the system but they, the doctors, were all clowns and muppets trying it on. I've not had many decent shrinks do reports on me.

Donald had shot a taxi driver while trying to escape and during

the chase it was a 16-year-old bank clerk who'd acted out the role of hero, he could've been shot. Anyway at court Donald praised him but knocked the rest of the bank staff for being cowards. The trail ended with Donald being given life with hard labour, this was back in 1959. Would you believe that while he was being led down from the dock in chains he tried to kick a newspaper photographer and it took a few guards to get him away into the van taking him to prison.

Straight away, into his sentence, Donald began it with three months in solitary at the toughest prison in Switzerland - the Regensdorf Prison. Would you believe he had the same traits as I've got. During a church service he started throwing pebbles at the priest. I hate those fucking sky pilots, most of them are paedophiles anyway, I mean look how many've been collared wearing women's clothes under their cassocks, look how many've been up for sexual offences against young 'uns so I can't blame Donald for that.

While banged up in Switzerland Donald wrote a thriller novel but

Icons of Icons

it hasn't been published, we've all got it in us, maybe I was lucky in having my work published but Donald could've made it big as a writer. He was kept in chains for 10 years in this Swiss jail, they were terrified of him and he was classed as the most violent man in their penal system.

It was in August 1976, after serving 16 years that Donald was released by the Swiss. Well he wasn't released, as we know it, he was chained and put on a plane under guard. Would you believe though that the Swiss had been begging the British authorities to extradite Donald but not surprisingly the British government refused. After he landed at Heathrow airport he was examined by two shrinks and escorted under heavy guard to Broadmoor where he met me.

Don was knocking on a bit when I met him, his hair was grey and he'd slowed down and accepted his fate. But Donald Hume remains a legend and will always be a respected man amongst the criminal fraternity. I used to tell the asylum loons to look on him as somebody very special and I'm certain one-day there'll be a film about this legend. Maybe it'll come when he dies but it's sure to come. I rank this man as one of the best and I leave you with a quote from Don. *"If you have an enemy who destroys your equilibrium – get rid of him. I believe in self-preservation, survival of the fittest, might is right."*
DONALD HUME

CHARLIE KRAY 1927 - 2000
R.I.P.

I met Charlie in Parkhurst many years ago when he used to visit his twin brothers and then I used to meet him in Broadmoor when he used to visit his brother Ronnie. Charlie used to always leave me some meat pies, just like his mum Violet used to do, with the Broadmoor nurses, I used to look forward to them and I've never forgotten it. Charlie's most certainly a legend and he was a very proud man, a well-respected man. He served 10 years for nothing just because he was the brother of the Kray twins. We all loved Charlie, he was from the old school and my respects come from my family along with me.

Charlie served a 10 year prison sentence, he got out and picked up the pieces but it all went pear shaped for him later on and turned to mush when he was convicted of drug dealing – all for a few grand up in Newcastle! Everyone knew it was a stitch up cos the deal Charlie was accused of putting together was so impossible, he was to have supplied a few £m worth of drugs over a period of time.

Henry Cooper (2nd left), Charlie Kray, Reg Kray and Freddie Foreman

The real story is he was just using the Kray name to make a few quid out of a possible deal in which he'd be a middle man, anyone in the underworld will tell you that it wasn't a likely thing to happen but the law in its infinite wisdom decided to believe a load of plonkers.

Sadly it came at a bad time for Charlie and when he was banged up in Durham Prison in '99 he suffered an illness and was moved to Parkhurst, which was now a category 'B' prison and more relaxed for him. Charlie had to be moved to St Mary's hospital on the Isle of Wight, as he declined in health.

He passed away in the hospital on the Isle of Wight in 2000 and once again Reg had to attend the funeral of another member of his family. Charlie was and always will be Ron and Reg's big brother – God bless you mate, a dinosaur.

Icons of Icons

REG KRAY

They sent Reg to Parkhurst SSU (Special Segregation Unit) in the 60s where the Richardson's were - they were rivals! They, the authorities, had hoped they'd all kill each other, that's how evil prison H/Q is. They want blood but it was obvious to them what was going on and they agreed that their inhumane sentences were enough to handle without more trouble. I last saw Reg in Gartree Prison in the 80s. It was through him that I got involved in the unlicensed fight game. Reg helped set up my first fight on the Paul Edmunds (R.I.P.) show. (Can be seen on my video documentary, 'Sincerely Yours'.)

I've got some good memories of Reg, I remember the time he knocked out O'Rooke in Parkhurst with one punch. I later stuck a sauce bottle in O'Rooke's face. Reg has a heart as big as the sky and it's a fact he's helped many a con out of trouble. He's taken weapons off young cons and given them good advice, he's sat down with cons that've given up and he's even prayed for some.

Reg's taken a lot of bad press over the years. A few years ago it was stated that Reg was taking drugs, well that's a load of rubbish. He trains everyday and he's 64 years old and has the body of a 30 year old, a man on drugs couldn't possibly be in such good shape. Reg watches his diet, he's a fitness fanatic, he despises drugs and I know it saddens him to have to read such lies. The propaganda machine of the Home Office is busy working away putting out their lies while Reg rots away inside.

Legends

In 1962 their hands on approach to everything they did foiled a number of assassination attempts against Reg and Ron. Reg married Francis Shaea on 20th April 1965 and they lived below Ron in Francis Court. Francis was Reg's love of his life. Later when Francis was to commit suicide at the age of 23 – she took an overdose; it really knocked the wind out of Reg's sails and it was said that he wasn't the same man ever again and to some extent he was quite depressed when Nipper Read of Scotland Yard arrested him.

Although a number of gang fringe members tried to hold it together it seemed Reg had accepted the inevitable and he'd hoped to accept some deals just on the violence side of things but too many members of his gang had fallen so it was that a recommendation of 30 years was passed and now that tariff's been more than met it would seem that the British Government have lied to him and failed to carry out what one of their representatives said more than 30 years ago.

Reg's served nearly 32 years, 32 years of shit to get where he is today – in a semi open prison! He's done no wrong, he's a well-respected man and he's been proven sane, saner than you or I cos he's had all them tests. He's helped this one and that one, supported charities, as he used to even when he was free, helped little old ladies, supported boxing clubs, used his influence to protect those who are weak and unable to defend themselves, followed all the rules laid down and yet he's still being treat worse than some greasy fucking evil paedophile, is that right?

I bet if they asked the public whom they'd rather have out living next door to them between some stinking child killer like Victor Miller (he killed a paper boy and attacked 29 other boys) or Reg then Reg would win hands down every single time. It stinks, let the government know it stinks, write to the gaffer of the Home Officer and tell them that it stinks. Reg has a campaign for his release but because its been going on for years it's become a bit of a regular thing like the annual ball and that's the problem – too much of a laid back approach by his supporters. Reg's gotta say if he wants to come out and if he does then they've gotta work their balls off to get him out – no more messing about, get it done, take it to the European courts!

Website: www.thekrays.co.uk &
www.crosswinds.net/%7Ethekrays/RRMainPage.html

60

Icons of Icons

Eddie ? Ron Kray, George Raft, Reg & Rocky Marciano

RON KRAY 1933 - 1995
'The Colonel'
R.I.P.

On the 17th March 1995 I woke up like any other day, I ate my porridge and went out in the exercise cage for my hour's exercise, the air was fresh and the sky was lovely; even the sun shone – I was in Frankland maximum secure block. That day hit me like a sledgehammer on the back of the head, whilst out on the yard I lost one of the greatest friends I ever had – Ronnie Kray passed away, I'm now gonna put the record straight once and for all, as during the first few days of his death I heard maggots going on about how mad and bad Ronnie was. The press and radio ripped him up, even John McVicar jumped on the bandwagon, well both the twins despised him as all he is is a joke, he couldn't even clean the shoes of the twins.

Ronnie Kray was a special man and he had the biggest heart of any criminal I've ever known and there won't ever be another like him, I'm gonna tell you something now...Ronnie Kray was a

61

Legends

legend, he was born a legend, lived a legend and died a legend. Reggie will continue, Ron wanted for Reg to go free and he will. A week before Ron's death he sent me £25, he looked after me - he loved me.

Reg Kray, Henry Cooper and Ron Kray

When Ron liked somebody it was total loyalty, a man of great feelings and great warmth. I can close my eyes and drift to over 2.5 decades ago to when Ron walked into my cell at Parkhurst. I knew from our first ever meet that he was a special friend, a hand shake like a grip of steel and eyes that were full o f s t r e n g t h ; h e conducted himself inside no different than he did outside – with dignity.

When Ron spoke people listened, I learnt so much from him, he was always polite and respectful and never spoke of crime or violence, he lived by a code of honour till the end. Sure, Ron was violent we all know that but many only knew that side of him, they didn't get to know the other side and that's why I'm gonna tell you.

I got certified a year before Ron so we met up again in Broadmoor. We both suffered mentally so I feel it brought us closer, Parkhurst made Ronnie very ill, violence breeds violence with violence and it's a place of violence that can only ever bring violence. Ronnie was a target but once in Broadmoor he quickly settled.

In the 15 years he was there he had very little problems, which only proves what I say. Parkhurst made him ill but Broadmoor suited Ronnie. Once you're insane you're always that way but drugs helped keep Ron stable. Did you know what Ronnie done for most of his 26 years caged up, I'll tell you, he helped people, he'd read a newspaper, let's say a little kid had an illness or an old lady got mugged then Ron would straight away try to raise money to help them. He'd paint a picture write a poem or organise a charity do all to help the sick. He literally gave away thousands of pounds if not a million.

All his life he gave and he actually cried over tragedies especially when kids were involved. He despised child abusers. Ron was always first to go and help the underdog, he never done it to boost his ego or to be the big shot, he done it for one simple reason and that was he couldn't help it, he was ruled by his feelings. I want you to know something about Ronnie, he looked after so many, he never stopped helping, it's why he's so special, so loved and will never be forgotten by so many.

Ron and Reg had a dear friend who's close to them, she wrote to me saying that Ron wouldn't want me to be upset and that he loved me a lot, Ron always got upset when he heard about my constant battles against the system. He used to write to me - when I'd been up on a roof or taken a hostage - telling me to slow down or I'd never get out. He cared about me and understood me and I read his words like they were from my own father. Steph says Ron's free and he's now with the only woman he ever loved. That about sums up Ron Kray, Steph's wrote it in once sentence and she's so right, 'He's with his beloved mother, Violet, the only woman he adored'.

17th October 1933 in Hoxton, East London was the day Ron was born. Ron was the second born of the two twins. Violet said of the twins when they were born that they were 'so lovely, like two little black haired dolls.' Ronnie was always polite but he held the upper hand when it came to Reg fighting others, as if Reg was fighting and he backed down then Ronnie would know and it was said that Reg said, "He'd be a sort of conscience and I found it hard to face him afterwards." Ron was born ten minutes after Reg but it seemed he wanted to lead the way.

Legends

This could've had some bearing in the Jack 'The Hat' McVitie murder when it's alleged by a close contact that when Reg pulled the trigger and the gun he was holding to McVitie's head didn't go off that it was his twin, Ron, who came in with four male dancers in tow and he handed Reg a knife and told him to 'do him'. Obviously with a room full of people standing about it wasn't gonna be easy for Reg to back down and lose face so he had to go through with it cos otherwise he'd find it hard to face Ron afterwards.

Ron   Violet (Mother)   Reg

The first appearance of the twins was at the Old Bailey back in 1950 and the case was thrown out for lack of evidence when a 16-year-old lad was beaten up with fists, boots and chains. They, Reg and Ronnie, both turned pro-boxers in 1951 and started out as lightweights but Ron wasn't as skilled as Reg in this noble art of pugilistic skills.

Their first HQ was a billiard hall and from there they started up 'the firm'. Ronnie got his nickname 'The Colonel' after being dismissed from the army. Their reign spread over all of London but they still had run ins with other up and coming firms the most notorious being the Richardson gang.

Ronnie loved to dress like a gangster and he even had his own barber but even though he was tough maybe we see a little bit of

Icons of Icons

the fear we've all got within us when I tell you that he used to sleep with the light on; showing that he was just as vulnerable as the next man when it came to trying to conquer his inner fears – we've all got our own battles going on inside of our heads; Ron was no different.

A docker who claimed Ronnie had shot him later went on to pick him out of an ID parade. Ron went on the ID parade and it seemed to sort the situation out after he said, "I'm not Ronnie Kray, I'm Reg, I wasn't no where near when this bloke was shot." After it was all dropped Reg wasn't too happy with Ronnie saying, "You must be raving mad, you shoot a man and leave me to clear it up." Ronnie spat back, "All you're fit for is clearing up, you couldn't shoot a man if you tried!" Maybe this was what motivated Reg to pull the gun on Jack McVitie so as to show Ronnie he was able to shoot a man, but if the truth was known Reg would've walked away from it until Ron came in and from then on Reg was caught in a trap – no way out.

This rivalry seems to have followed through to the end of their days on the streets of London. Reg was put in a position of not only having to keep face with the crowd at the private party where McVitie was stabbed to death but to keep face with Ronnie and for this reason it has to be looked at in a different light that it was obviously a kind of duress that led to the situation. Maybe that's just a guess, only Reg can answer that but if that was the case then Reg should've been walking the streets years ago. Now he has to carry the flag of honour on his own shoulders since the loss of Ron and Charlie.

Ronnie received a three-year prison sentence at the Old Bailey on 5th November 1956 for a wild slashing attack with a bayonet against Terence Martin, Reg had nothing proved against him and this proves to some extent that Reg really isn't a violent guy but was pushed into a corner by a set of circumstances.

The most famous club owned by Ron and Reg was called 'The Double R' in Bow Road, London. The Double R was doing well and was heavily populated by celebrities. Ron though was still in prison and he had bouts of depression, which led to him being declared insane at the age of 24.

February of 1958 Ron was sent to an asylum but soon made a recovery and it was during a Sunday visit that Reg swapped over with Ron and eventually was captured. When Ron was released he

Legends

came out a changed man and looked different to Reg, the time behind bars had taken its toll on him and now something had changed, maybe being apart from his other half was to blame but it looked like Ron would have to carry the scars of his own mental torment.

Ronnie was fast starting to become difficult to control and Reg, it was rumoured, wasn't too pleased about the situation. Reg had to go away to serve time and when Ron took over the reigns of The Double R club it seemed to go downhill and Ronnie wasn't ashamed of his sexuality, which at this time in London wasn't too fashionable but he always kept his dignity by maintaining he wasn't a 'puff' but that he was 'homosexual'. Ronnie was at least man enough to accept what he was long before we had the famous 'Naked Civil servant', Quinten Crisp, parading his weak kneed act to TV viewers portrayed in *The Naked Civil Servant*. No limp wristedness was on show here and at least Ronnie set new standards for others to follow.

Everybody knows the story of the shooting in the Blind Beggar pub, Ron shot a guy called Cornell cos he called Ron, "A fat puff." Nobody could remember what went on or who did it – bad memories were a good thing to have back then. Lots of people went missing, lots. Only them what deserved to go went and it would seem that the Krays did every crime in London but in reality they did more good than bad.

I met Ronnie in Parkhurst and later on in Broadmoor (More details in my autobiography, 'Silent Scream'.) and as usual he was the perfect gentleman. He stopped me from sorting a few eggheads out. Ronnie's most famous saying to me was, quote: **"Madness is a gift of life, it's how you use it that counts."**
Ronnie Kray

CHRIS LAMBRIANOU
'The General'

Here's an interesting point for you to take note from, Chris Lambrianou was the guy Vinnie Jones took off for the character he played in the film *Lock, Stock and Two Smoking Barrels*. Chris was a force ten storm when he kicked off and he sure could give it some. But an even more interesting thing that also happened is this, Steve Richards interviewed Chris's brother, Tony, for the video

Icons of Icons

documentary on me, *Sincerely Yours*, and promised he'd put flowers on the grave of Tony's mum when he was next up north – I leave Steve to tell you the rest:

It just so happened I had an unusually strong urge to go and get some flowers and visit the cemetery where Mrs Lambrianou is buried. So off I went and bought a nice bunch of mixed flowers and drove out to Shotley Bridge, County Durham. My PA (Personal Assistant) was with me when we interviewed Tony so I asked her if she wanted to accompany me and maybe give some directions.

I was reminded that the cemetery was to the rear of Shotley Bridge hospital, so round and round I drove, no sign of the graveyard anywhere? New houses were being built so I reckoned that they might have built over it, and then I thought to myself, "No way would they build over a graveyard". Further up the road we found the cemetery and drove into it.

I didn't think it was going to be so huge! It was going to be a difficult job finding the exact plot, but I gave my word to Tony so my PA and I walked back and forward looking at row upon row of headstones until I became blinded by looking at them and couldn't make out the names on them without having to concentrate.

We'd both been doing this for about an hour when I noticed this group of people sitting by a grave. A woman with blonde hair was sitting by a grave with a young boy; an old lady and a well-built man were standing next to them. I worked my way towards them, looking this way and that and I'd gone further on when the man in the group shouted something. I was so deep in concentration that I didn't hear the exact words he was saying, he came closer.

He said, "Can I help you?" I explained that I was looking for a particular grave. He then went on to say, "It's Catholics over this side..." as he waved his huge hand to point in that direction, "...and it's Anglicans over that side." "I'm here to put flowers on a grave on behalf of a friend in London, Lambrianou's their surname," I said. With that I noticed a quizzical look on his face, but before I could say another word he said, "I'm Lambrianou, Chris Lambrianou!"

Well, you can imagine the total shock we both had at this remarkable coincidence, just out of this world, unbelievable! Tony's dear old mum must have set this meeting up, that's all I can say, what else can explain it? I said I was looking for the grave of Lilly Lambrianou. The sun was shining so I guess with my shades on I looked a bit suspicious eyeing up the graves.

Chris and I shook hands and he pointed to where Lilly's grave was, which was some way further on, I didn't ask what they were doing further down the cemetery (but it turned out he'd only just discovered the graves of his grandparents) and by this time the old lady had walked off. The woman with the long blonde hair and the young boy had joined us and Chris introduced the lady as Sharon, his wife. I shouted to my PA to join us, she was a long way off busy looking at headstones. I needed to explain to someone that this was Chris Lambrianou and for him or her to witness this remarkable double coincidence. I was in a state of euphoria and also full of sadness that we had to meet under such circumstances.

I walked to my car and drove over to where Chris had his car parked and we talked a while. Chris said, "My dear mother died on Friday the 13th!" The thing is this was Friday the 13th, the anniversary of her death, eerie and uncanny are the only two words I can think of to describe how I felt at this meeting and when you consider that Chris had travelled all the way from London just to lay a wreath it makes my spine tingle. Chris went on to say, "We're here on the anniversary of her death, she came back to visit her native North East after 25 years and died the same day!"

I'd not intentionally set off because it was the 13th, maybe subconsciously it had played on my mind, maybe something that Tony had said but even if that was the case how could I have timed it to coincide with a time of day that Chris was visiting the area? Although it was a sombre time Chris still raised a smile.

Chris and his wife, Sharon, had travelled from Oxon and stayed in Yorkshire over the previous night and had travelled on from there that day, so how could I have anticipated

Icons of Icons

that and be there at the very same time? My head was spinning! And the strange thing is the headstone didn't give the name 'Lilly' it was 'Elizabeth', maybe I'd have made the connection and maybe not, but Chris was there and that's all that mattered.

Sharon, Chris' wife, said that she'd mentioned on the way to the cemetery that she had a feeling there would be flowers on the grave and here was I with flowers!

To mark the occasion I we both took photos, Chris shook my hand when we parted and it was only then that I realised his hands were larger again than I'd first noticed; huge shovels that swallowed my own size 11's up. We all parted on a laughing note and I remarked that maybe I shouldn't be laughing and to excuse me since of where we were, but give Chris credit he said it wasn't a sad time as he only had happy memories of his mother. He followed me for a few miles, as I said I'd direct him to the A1 and the last I saw of him was his enormous hand waving from the window as he shouted, "I still can't believe what happened back there!"

Chris has written a book called *Escape from the Kray Madness*, which was a best seller and can be picked up at most good book-shops. He's currently working on a book and if it's half as good as that one then it will be a winner.

People seem to think that once someone's a gangster then they're always a gangster but Chris has done so much work for charity over the years, he's helped drug addicts get back on track and he's a genuine 100% born again Christian. He found this in prison and he's continued it through. Chris could have been a top underworld figure and his violent traits were picked up on by Vinnie Jones to help him portray his character especially the way doors were kicked open, Chris was legendary at doing that sort of thing and he was a dab hand at handling guns and other weaponry.

If the truth could be told, as they say, then I believe Chris's transition from gangland enforcer to God's talker is nearly, but not quite, as unbelievable as our meeting in the cemetery.

What a wonderful guy Chris is, just like Tony to talk to and so easy going and so calming. Nothing has been quite as unbelievable as the experience that happened on Friday the 13th at that cemetery. Nothing has ever made me feel so bowled over, not up to now anyway. When I asked Chris's permission to use the photo he recalled that unusual day immediately.

Legends

TONY LAMBRIANOU

Dave Courtney, Tony and Joe Pyle Jnr.

Tony has to be one the most sensitive of the chaps around today. You can see his soul if you look into his eyes, I met big Tony up in Hull and he's a guy that a lot of people have got respect for, okay he was part of the Kray firm and he even wrote a book called *Inside the Firm*, I've read it and it makes for sensitive reading – straight from the heart and that's what makes me know Tony's an old romantic at heart regardless of his past for which he had to serve 15 years.

The story goes that both Chris and Tony Lambrianou had to entice Jack the Hat McVitie to a private party held in the home of Carol Skinner. The twins were gonna be there and it was Reg who put the gun to McVitie's head and pulled the trigger, click – nothing happened; the gun failed to go off, was it trying to tell Reg something? McVitie made a run for it but Reg got a knife and stuck it into McVitie's face and stomach and so ends the history lesson that I'm sure you'll all have been taught.

It brought the downfall of the Krays' empire and it also brought down a lot of other peoples' empires. Alan Bruce Cooper, an American, who was already a registered informer working for a copper called John Du Rose was one of the first to make a statement. Cooper would've been charged with offences had he

70

Icons of Icons

not of been a registered informer. Then there was the statement of a man called Paul Elvey a bag man who used to run dynamite from Glasgow to London in a briefcase – he was nicked for this but had to be used as a witness when his connection to Du Rose was pointed out to Nipper Read of Scotland Yard. The dynamite was obtained from coalmines in the Glasgow area hence the connection between Glasgow and London when it comes to hard cases.

May 9th 1968 was the turn of Nipper Read to have his day when he arrested most of the Kray gang members and charged them all with 'conspiracy to murder persons unknown' - a holding charge. It was while the gang were locked up that it was possible for Read to work away on potential witnesses and he came up trumps when people felt safe enough to come forward knowing that the Krays were safely locked away - Freddie Foreman was also arrested as well as Charlie Kray but being the true staunch people they were nothing could be extracted from them. There was more chance of extracting information from a disused coalmine than these two.

Billy Exley at the edges of the firm offered evidence and a surprise witness was gang member Albert Donaghue. Donaghue had no reason to feel any loyalty to the gang, as it was Reg who'd shot him in the foot in a barroom argument. Ronnie Hart was another gang member who stood in the dock pointing his finger at Ron and Reg – their fate was sealed.

Anyone who was anyone was connected to this trial and it all ended with the streets of London being cleared – for a short while. Now the streets of London are jam packed with people wanting to speak with Tony and wanting to get his latest book, which he's working on with Freddie Foreman (*Getting it Straight*). Tony's settled down quite a bit and found love again when he was freed, must be his Latin charm. Tony – thanks for appearing in the video documentary and saying it like it is – CB.

HOWARD MARKS
'The Welsh Mr Nice'

It was in the 60s that Howard made his mark - pardon the pun. He was a well-educated guy and was bringing tons and tons of marijuana into the UK up till the mid 70s. He became known as

Legends

'Narco Polo' and he handled up to 50 tons of weed in one go and had over 40 different names, that's 38 more than me! Now anyone who knows me knows I don't agree with drugs but when you get to speak to Howard then you'll know he's not the sort of guy to bring down a whole housing estate with a liking for the stuff. The drug was starting to come into this country and Howard jumped onto what he seen as 'an earner'.

London 2000

Howard's connections went as far as the IRA, the PLO, the CIA and the Mafia. In 1988 the reign of the king of cannabis smugglers, Howard Marks, was to come to an end. He started handling small amounts of dope in Notting Hill and then Brighton. He replaced a friend on a smuggling route and went on smuggling a few hundred pounds in weight of the stuff and then it went into tons of the stuff. But like anything else they wanted more and more so they looked to the USA for bigger bucks.

In 1973 Howard was waiting for a big importation of happy baccy to arrive at Newport Beach, in USA. He saw the details being broadcast on TV and made a sharp exit. His reign continued but it wasn't long before the old British government wanted to recruit him into MI6 and he used this ploy of being an MI6 agent when he was lifted in Amsterdam and was bailed.

Icons of Icons

Howard was later lifted again in 1980 in Suffolk and a subsequent trial crashed when he was able to produce a Mexican Secret Agent to back up his story of involvement with MI6 and he walked. This led to his downfall, as the law were really upset by his book of memories *Howard Marks – His life and High Times*. Although the book was initially a flop it lit the fires of the law and they were now gunning for Mr Nice – Howard Marks.

Howard was now based in Majorca and he had contacts with high society in the UK. Manila grown marijuana was going to be upgraded in quality by Howard and d u r i n g t e l e p h o n e conversations that were tapped by the UK police all the details were recorded. The problem here though was that some of the people Howard was tied in with were also wanted just as much by Scotland Yard who were chasing a commercial fraudster.

Howard's number was nearly up and a member of the gang was pressurised into spilling the beans by Scotland Yard. Moynihan was the guy to bring it all down when the police wired him up. The end was near and with the evidence at hand Marks was arrested in Majorca and extradited to the USA and to top it all he had to plead guilty when he knew his partners were up against him – he was given 25 years!

The thing is it turned out that all of the people in the same boat as Howard pulled the plug on him, he could've turned the tables with all of the info he knew but he didn't – too nice of a guy for that though.

He served 7 years in a USA prison and he's now back in the UK selling other types of stuff demanded of him by the public – talks and book signings. And that, as they say, is how Howard Marks became a legend in my book, not because of his drug dealings but because he was able to turn his charm and charisma on to another commodity – fame. Howard, good luck – Charlie Bronson.

Legends

LENNY MCLEAN 1949 – 1998
'The Guv'nor'

One of the hardest legends in this book but sadly died at the age of 49. It happens to the best, considering he was as hard as he was he was a deep down loving family man who worshipped his own – and he stood loyal to his friends. There are millions of stories on Lenny to be told but few ever portray him, a gentle giant of a man, with good honest morals and values to life, as this sort of person.

He never done a lot of bird but the bit he done he left his mark like the time in Wandsworth Prison he put his fist straight through

the toilet door cos the con inside was taking too long. Imagine sitting on the bog and all of a sudden a massive fist comes through the door – then you see the Guv'nor, veins in his neck bulging – that would make you shit yourself! "Oi, hurry up!" He booms out – Lenny was a bit hyper – electrifying to have around. Well missed – but never forgot. My respects to his wife, Val, and his kids Jamie and Kelly.

£14.99 by Blake Publishing

**Website:www.geocities.comsithomas316/&
www.lennymclean.com**

JOHNNY NASH

What a guy he is; he's been around since the year dot and he's still going strong with the heart of a lion. People call many of these icons 'gangsters', well if the term can be used in the proper context then fine but many people try to twist the name and bastardise it into something dirty. When someone fights their way up out of it then they have to have respect and Johnny has mine. Back in the 60s he had string of West End clubs under his protective hand and

Icons of Icons

back then it was well worth having someone like Johnny on the team cos they was muscling in from all over the place. Johnny liked to be known as 'The Peacemaker' and who's gonna argue with that.

Back in '59 Johnny helped stash away a pal of his, Ronald Marwood. Ronnie was wanted for stabbing a copper and was later sentenced to be hung, how true this is I don't know but when you've got someone like Johnny as a friend you'll always be well taken care of. Johnny hasn't got through it all without the odd skirmish and one of them was when he was charged along with Charlie Richardson and John Lawrence for a shooting incident, which was later slung out of court when one of the women witnesses couldn't remember much. That's the way it was back then.

The connection to other icons was solid and when clubs coughed up for security services it usually went three ways: the twins, Freddie Forman and Johnny Nash, which is no different to Group 4 collecting from banks for handling their cash. They had a job to do and clubs were thankful to have such people around them. I know whom I'd rather employ for security services if it was back then.

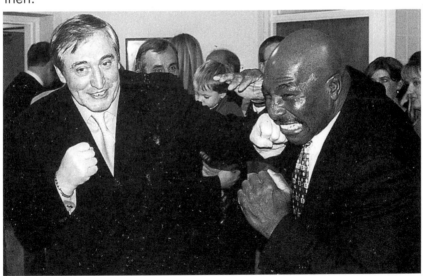

Johnny shows Ernie Shavers how to do it, in a friendly way of course!

Sometimes friendships were strained and when Jack 'The Hat' McVitie was snuffed out it brought some friction as he was related to Johnny's top man. A story was put about that Jack had blown

Legends

himself up when some dodgy gelignite had blown up in his car – this was to soften the blow for when the Nash brothers heard about his death. That all seems like a long, long time ago but it'll all go down in folklore and be remembered forever and that's what makes Johnny an icon.

Johnny was one of the pallbearers at Ronnie Krays' funeral showing of course how what I say is true - a legend will always remember a legend.

KENNY NOYE

I met this legend up in Frankland max secure back in the 80s. He's doing life just now for that headline grabbing road rage situation. The old bill just want Kenny in a hole, they'll never be happy until he stops breathing, as he's done one of their own – the old bill never forget. Kenny is just a very shrewd businessman who's earned his cash the hard way. It's sad how it's all ended up on some motorway in a roadside fight with some young 'un who to all intents and purposes was a bit of a ruffian himself and fancied himself as a bit of a kick boxer.

Kenny tried to walk away from him, witnesses seen it, they seen the young guy corner Kenny and when Kenny's cornered what's he supposed to do, let himself get kicked about the hard shoulder of a motorway? You must ask yourself this, does a man in Kenny Noye's position go around pulling up in front of battered old vans and then stab the driver just for the fun of it. It's like me sniffing old ladies bicycle seats, it just don't happen. Then they claim Kenny's turning into a supergrass, I'll believe it when I see the statement's he's supposed to be making, all propaganda put out to camouflage the facts.

Kenny's always been under surveillance from the law and that

76

Icons of Icons

sort of thing is pressure in itself. One day a copper was hiding in the bushes in Kenny's garden and after a confrontation the copper was dead – Kenny walked out of court a free man and from that day on the law haven't ever forgotten it. But what about when the law kill people in custody and get off with it? Kenny's had contact with anyone who's anyone in the crime world and his status has always been high profile so when he went to court on the road rage charge it didn't ever look too good for him.

The newspapers say he's trying to buy his way out by dropping high profile people into it but maybe they want him sorted while he's in prison and don't want him ever coming out but until he tells me or I hear of him spilling the beans he remains an icon.

It was a summer's day the last time I saw Kenny out on the exercise yard I said to him and a few of the other chaps, "Don't get involved," as I went and grabbed the governor – it must've been the sun beating down on my head.

JOE PYLE

Joe and Roy Shaw at Joe's book launch Nov 1999

Every now and then nature throws up something new, a one off and Joe is that one off. His connections are solid and when he says anything then people listen cos what he says is worth listening to.

Legends

A man of very few words so when he spoke up for me on the video documentary it was something of importance and that's why I asked him to write the foreword for this book.

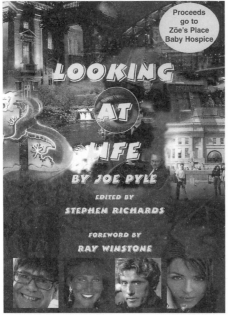

Joe's been like a father to me and I often call him dad, which's out of respect, he's my Icon of Icons. He's a man full of wisdom and lets his mind do the thinking before he lets his tongue do the talking. He's been there and back and just for the hell of it there and back again. Okay he did time, what self respecting guy hasn't in this modern day and age when you can get picked up just for stopping to fasten your shoelace. He's done more than his fair share of helping them that need help, he's helped raise over £20,000 for a baby hospice simply because he attracted stars from all over the shop and he gave up his royalty cheques from his book, *Looking at Life*, just so the hospice could get some extra dosh.

People want to get themselves to one of his boxing promotions that his son, young Joe, puts on – they'd see how much he does for them kids. He's been accused of all sorts of things but he hasn't been accused of the good things. Every time I needed a new set of special glasses it was Joe who got them sent in and we're talking hundreds of quid's worth of headgear here.

But that's not my reason for making him my Icon of Icons, he's gonna be embarrassed at all these good words cos when you've had so much bad shit said about you like he has then you become thick skinned to it all – I should know! Good words from me don't come cheap; talk isn't cheap in my shop. Joe can see through people with his X-ray vision he soon spots the fakes.

Joe's survived all what's been thrown at him – A TRUE WARRIOR. Everybody loves and respects Joe Pyle but if you don't then you're just a clown, you can't but admire this man. A very successful bizz

78

Icons of Icons

man, a man who's done his bird and gone out and made good – that to me says it all.

Joe's been around for a long time, done it all, seen it all – Hell they invented the T-shirt just for Joe. Anyway I'd like to take this opportunity to just say THANK YOU for being a good friend to me. As like my dad he too is called 'Joe' and like my dad I love him. Till the end Joe.

Joe and Harley looking at a manuscript

Website:www.joepyle.com

BRUCE REYNOLDS
'The Prince of Thieves'

Bruce got 25 years for his part in the Great Train Robbery; I met him in Parkhurst in the 70s, he was the library orderly at that time. He masterminded the job way back in 1963 and was nicknamed 'The Napoleon of Crime' and 'The Prince of Thieves'. After five years on the run Scotland Yard eventually cornered him. You'd see him walking about with a bag of books, papers and magazines. I asked him once to sort out some boxing material for me, to my amazement he got me enough literature on boxing to keep me going for years. Nothing was too much trouble for Bruce; he's an absolute diamond. Since then Bruce's went on to write his book *Autobiography of a Thief*. He's a regular on the underworld crime to books circuit and is one of the nicest guys you could ever wish to meet. Bruce is now well

79

Legends

sought after within the world of Crimebizz. Where Bruce leads others follow.

Website: www.brucereynolds.com

CHARLIE RICHARDSON

They don't come no more legendary than this man. Known as the torturer boss in the 60s he got 25 years for it, a sentence he served 17 years of. A sentence them days of 25 years was seen as inhuman, Charlie never killed nobody, how could they give him 25 years? Even by today's standards it would be seen as inhuman. Charlie being the man he is survived. He never forgot me at Christmas time either; his loyalties are second to none.

Also bear in mind that prison in the 60s is not like it is now – he had it hard whereas puppets like McVicar got parole, Charlie got nothing he done it all. Like all legends we rarely get anything off the system it's a fact. I always get good advice from Charlie, which I respect. I try to achieve it as well but it don't always work out. He knows what I'm up against cos he's had it all himself.

He's the elder brother of Eddie. It runs in the family – solid men. Yeah 17 years he served at a time most lifers were getting out after 10 years. I've always said and always will, they threw the lot at this man simply as they wanted to make an example of him. Charlie's a very shrewd bizz man and knows how to make a few quid or three. He occasionally drops me a line to let me know how the world's going.

There was a story going about that he held court and wore a judge's wig and gown, and why the fuck not. There were also stories going about that he sentenced people to torture and the likes, well that's nothing new, as the judge what sentenced me has done the same thing, the only thing is Charlie got time for it and the judges that's sentenced me over the years got fuck all. I've

80

Icons of Icons

nothing but admiration for the Richardson brothers and in the criminal fraternity they're myths. Charlie could have a right fight too – fearless. This book couldn't be complete with these sorts of legends, historical.

EDDIE RICHARDSON

This man I feel had a bad deal in life; he got 15 years in the 60s and his brother (also in this chapter) got 25 years then in the 80s Eddie got 25 years. It's as if fate had something to do with it, had he been a Joe Bloggs he'd have only got 15 years, being Eddie Richardson didn't help him. In the 60s he was as powerful in South London as the Krays were in the east. But that was then – let's look at now. What sort of judge or society can lock a man up for 25 years? It's an inhumane sentence; Eddie will be 70 when he gets out. I spent Christmas with Eddie up in Full Sutton jail – I love the guy. If it were humanly possible then I'd serve five of his years for him. That's how much I respect the man. He now sits in his cell and paints the most legendary paintings. He won a Koestler award for one of them and in years to come the paintings will become priceless.

Eddie was the most violent out of the two brothers and in an incident in a club called 'Mr Smiths', in Catford, when the Richardson's flexed their muscles, there was a Wild West shoot out. Eddie, it's claimed, laid the law down and sparks flew around. There was wars going on over the West End and everybody wanted a slice of it so it meant the Richardson's had to fight for it and there was often wars going on between the different firms. It was the Richardson's v The Kray's but the final confrontation never came off, as the Krays gang were hauled off and the rest, as they say, is history. The Krays had no competition with the Richardson's put away – could of had it all.

ROY 'Pretty Boy' SHAW

Roy became a boxer for Mickey Duff after he escaped from borstal. His first prison was Maidstone and then the fun and games started cos he smashed his way out of the cell. He was given 18 years back in 1962 for taking part in an £80,000+ robbery. He's been in with the best and was in Wandsworth Prison with Ronnie Biggs

Legends

and turned down the chance to take part in Biggsy's escape.

He chinned so many screws they nutted him off to Broadmoor

asylum but Roy survived it all, Broadmoor was the only place that the Prison Service could think of sending Roy to and he endured explorative brain surgery and of course the 'liquid cosh'. Roy's actually done a rooftop protest at Broadmoor and he was then put back into mainstream prison and shifted from pillar to post before being freed.

The real Rocky and I've always said the real Guv'nor. Hard as nails and bundles of respect got out and made it big time out of prize fighting at a late age. He fought Donny 'The Bull' Adams (King of the Gypsies) and beat him and he became king of London at the age of 42. He now has a number one best selling book – *Pretty Boy*. Roy, I wish you well mate and I'm pleased for you. You're a legend and always will be, a one of so few that managed to get into the 'Rip a Cell Door Off' Club – that to me says it all.

Roy ripped off a toilet seat in Broadmoor back in the 70s and broke a chief's jaw with it. That'll teach them not to fuck with the gaffa.

Roy came to court for me when I was up at Luton Crown on my St Valentine's Day trial in 2000, I was surrounded by half a dozen burly screws when I was in the dock. Roy and I looked at each other, he stretched his hand out to shake mine and the screws part-ed like the Red Sea for us two warriors to meet and join as one. Roy's just as fit now as he was 20 years ago and I reckon he and me would make a good tag team in the ring taking on Lennox Lewis and Mike Tyson, we'd kick their arses for them alright and still have energy to spare to go and watch a video of him beating half of London.

Icons of Icons

Andy Jones receives items for the Crime Through Time Museum from Roy

I'm gonna do my Michael Caine impersonation now and say "Not a lotta people know that but..." Roy's been let down by people when it comes to promises of being able to get him a copy of the Shaw v McLean fight, the one out of the three fights he had with Lenny that he won. Roy's still a champ in my book and when his film comes out there's gonna be a lot of people realise what he went through in life.

Incidentally Roy's looking for a copy of the fight in which he beat Lenny McLean, although Lenny won the other two, which have been traced, he'd like a copy of the one he won. Can anyone make his day by supplying a copy, if so please forward one on to the publisher, address on back flap of this book. Roy – box it clever, your old china Charlie Bronson.
**Website: www.prettyboy2000.freeserve.co.uk &
www.royshaw.com**

ALEX STEIN
R.I.P.

I'm gutted I never met this legend; he died in '98. Joe Pyle and Ron Kray told me all about him. He always pops up in books and he always wore dark glasses. A well-respected man in the boxing scene and a man well missed. The stories I've heard about this man are all honest, he was an honest legend and honesty paid off for Mr Alex Stein.

Legends

Joe Pyle, Roy Shaw and Alex

ARTHUR THOMPSON 1931 –1993
R.I.P.

Arthur Thompson was born in the Provanmill district of Glasgow, the third eldest in a family of four brothers. The first year or so of his life was spent living in a tenement building before the family were re-housed in the 'slum clearance' district of Blackhill, where Arthur then stayed for most of his life.

Managing to avoid the pitfalls of approved school and borstal as a youth, Arthur grew into manhood with a growing reputation as a fighter. It was this reputation, and confidence in his own strength and abilities that made Arthur decide that the quickest route to riches was to take over from the reigning gangsters of that time.

In 1955 he tried his hand at bank robbery, attempting to blow open the vault of a bank in Beauly, Invernesshire, along with his safecracker pal, Paddy Meehan. They were both captured and Paddy, because of a long list of previous convictions was sentenced to six years. Arthur, whose record was comparatively mild, got a three. In his entire career Arthur served only four prison sentences, the longest of them being four years for reset (receiving stolen goods). But the failure of the bank robbery taught him a salutary

84

Icons of Icons

lesson, and when he was released he decided to turn his proven talent for violence to profit from protection rackets. He did this by making a frontal attack on the two top men of the day in Glasgow.

Although he always denied it, Arthur was 'credited' with the shooting of Glasgow gangster Teddy Martin and the beating up of the feared Algie Earns in the city centre.   Both of these men ran protection rackets in pubs, clubs and street bookies and now, with their demise, Arthur was 'The Man'. He was never charged with either of these two incidents, but anyone 'in the know' was aware that Arthur Thompson had made a decisive leap onto the criminal ladder. Unopposed, Arthur took over the protection rackets and moved into the drinking club scene, opening The Raven Club and becoming part owner of the Hanover Club in the city centre and it was from these two places that he ruled his growing empire.

These two clubs were very successful but the police viewed them as criminal hangouts and strove to close them down. After a particularly serious assault, where a man had been slashed repeatedly about the face, the police used Fire Safety rules to shut the doors of both clubs. Arthur was charged and appeared at the High Court for the assault, only to have the case dropped through lack of witnesses.

After the closure of his clubs, Arthur opened up an illegal street bookmaking business.   He did this quite openly yet the police decided not to arrest him for it. A senior policeman said that Arthur actually *wanted* a conviction for running a bookmaking business, as this would explain away any large amounts of money he might be found with in the future.

Of course Arthur had his rivals, and for years conducted a running feud with the Welsh family, also from Blackhill.   This feud finally came to a head in 1966 when Arthur rammed a van off the road, imbedding it in a lamppost and killing its two occupants, Patrick Welsh and James Goldie.   Arthur was charged with the double murder and tried at the High Court, where he was found Not Guilty. Three months after the van 'accident' a bomb meant for Arthur went off under his car, missing him but killing his mother-in-law. Later, the two Welsh brothers, Martin and Henry, were acquitted at the High Court of murder and the bombing of Arthur's car.

In fact there were three serious attempts on Arthur's life. The first one was the car bomb, which had such tragic results. A few years

Legends

later an 'unknown' assailant shot him in the groin, but he had the bullet removed and claimed that he had injured himself with a broken drill-bit.   The third attempt was later in his life when a young man, a friend of his son, ran him over with a car.

By 1972 Arthur owned two public houses in the city: the first one, The Provanmill Inn, being the premier pub in his own Blackhill area.   The second pub, The Right Half in George Street, was close to the city centre.   Success followed success, and Arthur was reputed to have a finger in most criminal activity in the city.   He moved into demolition and the scrap metal trade and was doing extremely well in legitimate business.

Of course, like most serious criminals in the late 70s and early 80s, Arthur found himself drawn irresistibly into the burgeoning drugs trade. It was his son, Arthur Jnr that took the lead in the drug business, unashamedly capitalising on his father's reputation and wealth to do so.   But although the profits were huge, it was their involvement in the drugs business that was to bring heartache to the Thompson family.

In 1991, young Arthur, who was on his first Home Leave from

Glasgow Herald & Evening Times

prison after serving six years of an 11-year sentence for drug dealing, was shot and killed outside his own house in Provanmill Road.   Arthur Jnr had been vociferous in announcing that he would soon be out for good and would "take over" the drugs business.   But others had moved on during Arthur's long absence, and although all old pals, there was no love lost between drug dealers.

Four men were said to be involved in the "execution" of Arthur Jnr: Paul Ferris, a lifelong friend, and accepted into the Thompson family as practically a son, Joe (Bananas) Hanlon, Robert Glover and a fourth man who's identity is unclear.

Icons of Icons

What is known is that on the day of Arthur Jnr's funeral both Hanlon and Glover were found shot dead in the back of a car outside their local pub. To this day no one's ever been charged with their slaying.

Paul Ferris, once the best friend of young Arthur, was later charged with his shooting, but after the longest murder trial in Scottish History he was found not guilty.

Some 18 months later, Arthur Snr, a man who had survived a bomb, a bullet and a charging car, died peacefully in his sleep from a heart attack. A legend was dead.

VALERIO VICCEI 1955 - 2000
'Gi Gi – The Wolf'
R.I.P.

Known to his friends as Gi Gi and also the Wolf. I am honoured to have beeen a friend of this man.

I first met Gi Gi in Brixton Prison on the maximum-security unit way back in 1988. He was on remand for the Knightsbridge Safety Deposit Boxes Robbery, the biggest robbery ever at £60 million. A robbery every criminal dreams about. I was remanded for a robbery on a jeweller's shop and was locked in a cage cell. Owing to my unpredictability I was not allowed out of my cage when the other dozen cons were out.

Every day Gi Gi would come to my cell and play chess with me

Legends

through the bars. He'd bring a table and chair and he'd play chess and help pass away many hours like this. Sometimes I would point through the steel bars and say to him, "Who's that coming?" As he turned to look I'd pinch one of his pieces. Most of the time he wouldn't realise and when he did I'd convince him how I'd won it earlier in a move.

Sadly he ended up with 22 years and had since written a book and been extradited back to Italy after only serving three years over here in England. It was thought he'd use his influence to get an easy time of it over in Italy – well...money talks. They only ever got £10m back from the heist and even £60m might have been a low figure put on what he got, as most of the boxes were never even reported as being opened, as so many were owned by criminals. Gi Gi was a great help to me and through his friendship it helped me get out of the cages. If he were able to have read this before his death then I'd have said to him, with all due respect, I'd still have beaten him at chess even if I hadn't of pinched his pieces, but I can tell you that no man can ever beat his charm and charisma that he held.

Over my 27 years within prison I would class Gi Gi as one of the most decent, honourable villains I've ever come across and believe me I've met them all.

Gi Gi was finishing off his time, in Italy, and he was getting back on his feet, under Italian laws he was entitled to work out of prison during the day and return on the night to serve his time, he had himself a little business and was setting his sights on getting through his last few years. Sadly though he was mysteriously shot, 8 times, when he had some sort of meeting on a county lane with an underworld figure when the cops pounced. The police

Icons of Icons

indicated Gi Gi was on his way to do a robbery, as it was claimed he had a weapon and a mask in his car – bollocks is what I say to

that. He was set up if anything and had 8 shots pumped into him when a police gun accidentally went off – so it was said. This man was a thinking man's criminal; a methodical planner, a lone wolf so when you hear things like I've just described it just doesn't seem possible that he could've been on a job cos that just wasn't Gi Gi. The Wolf isn't forgotten and he'll live on forever. Here's something he wrote to me in '88:

Written to me on 15th June 1988

'Friendship is usually a matter of time...the time it takes you to do a thoughtful and generous favour that wasn't expected of you. The time that it takes just to answer a call to let someone know that you're there. Friendship is really a matter of time...the time that you take when you care - **Valerio Viccei**

3

Prison Directory

Abouzuz

Tahir, I met in Gartree Prison in the 80s, he was from the Middle East, and was always getting involved in things that used to end up in him having a punch up so they put him in the block with me for a spell. I only had a month before my release so I was in strict training. I asked the screws if Tahir could train with me out on the caged yard.

My request was granted so we trained together but one day our sparring got out of hand and he ended up being sparked out. Then another day he caught one in the eye and that was it he never came out with me anymore but I love the guy and he loves me. I believe he's since been extradited back home to the East. I hope he remembered all the moves I taught him?

Ronnie Abrahms – R.I.P.
'The Screaming Skull'

Anybody who's been in a maximum-security jail in the last three decades would've seen 'The Screaming Skull' or heard about him. He's serving a life sentence. He shaves his head and does yoga exercises for the duration of six hours per day. He weighs in at eight stone and must be the fittest and supplest man I know.

I find it difficult to actually pinpoint a story of 'The Skull', as there's many. To most cons the Screaming Skull's a lunatic and a complete eccentric. He does his sentence his way.

I remember some years ago in Parkhurst, he upset a few heavies. They were wary of him over his unpredictability until one

Icons of Icons

con broke the Skull's jaw in three places. I actually saw it as bullying but the Skull got his jaw wired up and carried on as normal. It would take a lot more than a broken jaw to stop him.

It was soon after this that a homosexual made an advance for the skull. This time it was the homosexual who ended up with his jaw wired. Both of them were now wired up.

I'm sad to say that he's died since I did this write up. They found him stiff in his bed up in Frankland max secure jail; he'd served over 30 years, who said they stopped the death sentence?

Neil Adamson
'The White Shark'

I met Neil in the 80s at Parkhurst Prison; he received a life sentence in the 70s for killing a cop. He spent some time in Broadmoor after pulling a blade out in the doctor's office in Parkhurst Prison. Whilst at Broadmoor he cut up a guy so bad that the guy's insides were hanging out. Neil had to be one of the top 10 most violent men in the system in the 70s and 80s. With age he became more manageable and mature. I'd like to think he was in some place that was less secure and more pleasant.

Dave Andrews

In the 80s the cops shot him five times, yeah five times! So I say Dave's a legend, what a fighter to be shot once and to survive is a fate but to have five bullets smash into your body and survive is just incredible! I met Dave at Parkhurst and I just totally admire the man for his sheer grit. We all see it in films and read about it in books but Dave Andrews is the living proof of a legend. I can't praise the man enough, those cops who filled him full of holes tried

Legends

to blow him away, what a bunch of wankers. For me he's a born winner and a smashing guy.

Dave Anslow

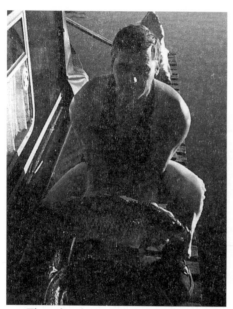

I first met this guy over 25 years ago in Armley Prison, in Leeds; at that time he was serving 12 years for armed robbery. Dave's become a life long friend and so have his brothers, John and Eric, they're all good loyal men.

I've many memories of Dave but the best one is when we were in the block in Armley and we were both making our way through the cell doors, I managed to get through my metal door, they had to close those cells down and we both ended up in 'strip cells'.

They had to call in reinforcements and a score of screws, some with dogs; they were all right outside our cell doors waiting for us – our plan obviously never worked.

Eric Anslow

Another one of the Anslow brothers, I met Eric down in Parkhurst in the 70s at that time I'd say Eric was, without a doubt, the fittest con in the jail. Nobody could keep up with him; he served his sentence well and was a respected man – long live the Dudley boys.

Prison Directory

John Anslow

John's one of the Anslow brothers from Dudley, a true warrior. I've been in several jails with John; he's served a 10 for a blag.

Sadly when John got out he lost a leg in a motorbike accident. Like all the Anslow brothers John's a good breed – fearless. John once had words with the man himself, Paul Sykes! When Paul knew it was an Anslow brother he walked away cos you just don't mess with an Anslow brother if you want to stay healthy.

Ian Ball
'The Royal Terror'

In the 70s Ian Ball almost pulled off the kidnap of all kidnaps - Princess Anne. It happened in the strand he just attempted the impossible, alone, and he almost pulled it off! Sadly for him he was certified insane and he's been in Broadmoor ever since.

I met him in the early 80s, quite a nice chap but I think he knows they won't ever set him free. The Royal Terror terrified the wrong family, I guess it's a fact of life if you bite the hand that feeds you then you'll starve to death.

Harry Batt
'H'

I met 'H' in the Scrubs (Wormwood Scrubs Prison) in '85; he was Sammy McCarthy's co-defendant; he got 18 years on a blagg. We later done a spell down at Parkhurst, as I got moved out of the Scrubs a bit livo – I demolished the seg unit and tried to strangle a governor...well he did upset me! Harry was in his 50s and a pure old school East Londoner.

I loved to listen to his stories, at this time I was in love with Jennifer Rush; she had a song in the charts – *The Power of Love*.

Legends

Once when *Top of the Pops* was on I got so emotional over the song I slung a chair at the TV.

A week or two later Harry called me in his cell after I'd finished my chokey for smashing the TV and he gave me the Jennifer Rush LP. Harry wasn't to know that I didn't have a player; I was soon on the move again, as I chinned a kanga.

He must be nearly 70 now; I haven't heard from him for years, I've some fond memories of the legend. I hope I get to buy him a pint like I'd do for all legends, I'm sure I'll bump into him later. Legends like Harry aren't too common in this day and age and when they've all gone it's gonna be full of smack heads.

Phil Baxter
'The Axe Man'

There's been several 'Axe Men' over the years but my buddy, Phil Baxter, is my number one when it comes to axe men. Phil got sent to Ashworth asylum in the early 80s. He ran amok in Brighton, England. He never killed but the whole of Brighton shit their pants.

When Phil loses it, be sensible keep out of his way. He once demolished a whole ward in Ashworth; it looked like a disaster area, like a bomb had hit it. Phil's a big powerful gentle giant and a lovely guy and a dear friend.

Frank Birley – R.I.P.

Frank was recently shot; he died from a wound to the neck. He was a tough guy alright, from Leeds. We'd done time together and

Prison Directory

shared each other's company in some of the hardest conditions in prison. He was always kept under tight conditions but he never lost his smile or happy outlook for living in the fast lane and that continued when he got out. He run parts of Leeds and he often had to battle to regain his territory and if that meant hurting other people involved in that side of life then he done it without fear or favour.

He was only 34 when he passed away, same age as Viv Graham (Icons of Icons chapter), maybe all hard men are destined to die young, Cahill, Graham and now Frank Birley. He spent time in Amsterdam, some say he was there doing a hit but if I know Frank

Photo taken inside high security prison

he was there enjoying himself and he comes back to England to regain territory and he gets himself shot. How it come about I don't know, but he's buried now so they must've cleared up how he died. Some say it was an accident while he and his pal were running away from a shooting incident, some say he was shot in the head while sitting in a car but however it happened it resulted in him losing his life.

A hard man's hard man and a legend in Leeds – Frank's been taken from us – God Bless his soul.

Wayne Black
'Strongman'

This guy pulled a nice one on his way to court from Belmarsh maximum secure unit. What made this special was that he was a high-risk con and he had it off (escaped) and went through a hatch in the top of the van.

The category 'A' vans have a special steel cage in the back where the con's locked inside and there's no escapee. So Wayne came up with a great idea and hit the jackpot! Unfortunately he was captured a month later and is now doing bundles of bird. Not

Legends

many make it to complete freedom, the only ones I've seen make a success of escaping are the rich – them that never get to see the insides of prison cos they buy their way out of trouble.

Danny Blanchflower

Danny was only serving a small sentence when he lost the plot and caved in the skull of a prison worker. I think he knows he'll never be set free. I feel sorry for Danny, as he was only young when it happened. These things just happen on the spur of the moment, it's never planned – 'boosh' and it's done; brown bread! (Dead) It could happen to any one of us. I think Danny should write a book, as it would benefit a number of would be criminals. Once you realise the dangers of prison life it really isn't the place to be in to win.

Tony Boldon

Once Tony was high-risk and almost escaped from a van on the way to court. He used some gas and sprayed it in the old bills' faces, he got a right beating for it but he almost got away. For that attempt he was nicked for 17 assaults, yeah that's legendary or what? That's what I call awesome, Tony's a proud North Londoner respected by many, he often pops up in books and magazines, he lives fast and furious, but he's not flash nor does he look down on anybody. I've been in a couple of jails with Tony, sadly on our last meet at Wakefield seg unit he told me about his wife being murdered whilst he was inside. I'd heard about it from others but hearing the details from the man himself was something else. It was a terrible shock, a sad story but Tony Boldon will return.

John Bond – R.I.P.

John got life in the 70s for killing his girlfriend but I'm gonna tell you all now he loved her and he was in mental pain every day since he killed her. I don't know the ins and outs of the case and I don't wish to know, I only know John Bond. I can only write on what I know – he suffered terribly. He was a fitness fanatic, some days we trained together. He could do press ups like no man I know and he was also a very clean and tidy man, always cleaning his cell it

Prison Directory

was the cleanest cell in Parkhurst you could eat off his floor, everything was in place like a military set up.

John's downfall was that he suffered with chronic depression; he got so bad at times he would go and bang himself down the block. All the cons tried to help John come to terms with his situation although he never moaned or cried but you could see the pain in the man's eyes. He could never relax or stand still. He finally cracked and hung himself in the block in Parkhurst.

I believe John actually died the day he killed his girlfriend, I believe he loved her so much he killed her rather than lose her and then he couldn't live with himself – sure he survived a couple of years more than she had the chance to but did he, I don't think so. I personally liked John and felt a lot of sadness for how it ended up, maybe they're now together – yeah that would make me happy.

John Boyle
'The Don'

I met John in the top secure unit in Brixton in the 80s; he was a yank charged with a multi-million dollar drug ring, mafia connections were brought out at his trial, he received 20 years. I later bumped into him up at top secure Frankland jail; he was busy preparing for his appeal, which he won. He was flown back to the USA as an undesirable alien of the UK but I've always remembered one thing he once told me, quote: "Charlie, you're never dead until you're buried."

'B' is for Bang-up

Don't think I'm stuck in a cell with a 32" colour TV set and a video recorder, that's only for paedophiles. Right now I'm on a 'Riot Unlock' it means I've got six to eight riot shields poked into my face the minute my door's unlocked. I've got bullet proof glass in between me and my visitors and I'm not even allowed my art materials whilst here at Whitemoor (August 2000). Wanna swap places? I don't know what kindness is anymore, especially after being on riot unlock at Woodhill Gestapo Headquarters for 14 months of inhuman torture.

All I know is the rock and a hard place, nothing in between. Comfort's something you put in your washing machine or give a

Legends

baby – me I get none of that. I'm not complaining so long as them paedophiles get the same treatment I'd eat shit but as long as they've got comforts and sympathy, oh yeah the Prison Service give 'em plenty of that, then I demand the same – at least!

Bradley Brothers

They're my favourite brothers in Luton. They all love me as their own blood! They're all legends in their own rights, salt of the earth – men of steel.

Chris Brand
'Brandy'

Chris Brand got 2½ years; whilst he was serving it he killed a fellow con and got life! 21 years later he's still inside and out of that time he's probably served half of that in solitary. He's had a rough ride and has had a lot of problems on the way.

He's been nutted off twice and gone to Broadmoor and Ashworth asylums. The con he killed he drowned him in the bath. (Few ever go into the bath when Brandy's about! Would you?) There's not a lot this guy hasn't done and I mean everything.

Roofs! Hunger strikes! Shit ups! Violence! Murder! And it all began as an 18-year-old lad with a 2½-year sentence…so let that be a lesson to any kid out on a life of crime. Brandy will tell you himself how easy it is to get trapped in. But he's a legend and a

Prison Directory

legend he remains! You can't take it away from him – mad maybe but a one off for sure.

Kev Brown

I first met Kev in Wandsworth Prison when he started a 17-year sentence in the 80s. We were destined to met up again several times after this.

Kev's a block man and he does it easy, he just fights on. I suppose he made his mark at Wandsworth when he almost escaped with a JCB along with another three cons. There must've been a hundred cons watching it happen but unfortunately it was an escape not meant to be.

I bumped into him again in Winson Green Prison and he still looked fit and strong. He's one man who doesn't kid himself into thinking about parole or getting released earlier than his date. He knew from day one he'd never get anything from the system. Kev plods on in his own little way; he's done all of his time the hard way. There's two ways to do something in life: The way others tell you to do it and the way you WANT to do it - Kev does it his way.

Eddie Browning

Eddie got life over the murder of Marie Wilkes. It was a brutal, inhuman, senseless murder that shocked the nation, whoever done it should be put up against a wall and shot or better still they should let Marie's family get a hold of them.

I met Eddie in Full Sutton in the 80s, he was fitted up, he didn't kill her. I read all his paperwork and his appeal papers, I claimed all along he never done it. He was finally cleared of the murder at the appeal court and he was freed after six long hard years for a crime he didn't do nor know anything about.

A lot of cons made it hard for Eddie, he got beat up a few times, smashed over the head, spat on and burnt out but he'd never bow down, why should he, as this guy was a victim like the Birmingham Six. The cops fitted him up and they had to put somebody away for a crime that disgusted the nation. Eddie was the scapegoat.

Since he walked out of the appeal court I hear he was given a right few bob to compensate those wasted years. No amount of money could compensate what he suffered. The slags that allowed

Legends

it to happen have yet to answer to the judge – the ultimate judge. All those scumbags who lock up innocent people and lie on oath have it all to face; they have a worse fate than most will ever suffer on this earth. As that famous dead homosexual once said, "There's nothing worse than the felon but the man who turns the key to lock him up."

Kenny Carter

In the 80s this guy was doubled up with another con in Durham jail, when the screws unlocked the door Kenny's cellmate was hanging from the bars; he got life for it but says it was a suicide. Since that life sentence Ken's been fighting his innocence and a few years ago he climbed up a security camera pole to protest his innocence.

I don't know how strong his appeal is but I do know he'll never give up fighting to clear his name. He's in my book of Legends solely for his determination to fight to the end – he won't ever give up.

Nobby Clarke – R.I.P.
'The Silver Foil'

He went to Broadmoor in 1969 after the Parkhurst riot for stabbing a Greek Cypriot. While there in the 70s he was charged with murdering a fellow lunatic.

Nobby chose to defend himself, he was the first certified madman in Britain to defend himself in a court of law and he fucking won. Obviously he was supposed to be insane and here he was defending himself and beating the prosecution!!

But the question is how could a certified lunatic defend himself on a murder charge? From that day I've always said that you're only insane when it suits the system and this one incident proves my point.

It was in Parkhurst when we first met in 1975; I got on with him as he always had something to have a conversation about.

He used to collect old packets of tobacco silver foil. He never told anyone why he wanted it, but this collecting went on for many months.

We watched as he picked it out of the bins, he would ask the other cons to save it for him till finally he'd a box filled with the stuff.

100

Prison Directory

He then stuck it on every brick in his cell and even covered the door. His entire cell was decorated with this foil and it was named the Silver Cell.

Nobby later died in his cell; he lived in prison and died in prison. You just don't get to hear about such legends, until now that is! To die a free man is something but to die whilst in prison...well that's something else!

Tommy Comerford
'The Boss'

Old Tommy Comerford, Scouse Tom, 'The Boss' – what can I say, the man's been around so long he could well be immortal but he's eaten too much porridge. It breaks my heart to keep seeing this man inside. Boss, slow down! God let me buy you a pint one day, Tommy we all love you.

Paddy Conroy

Paddy's record reads like an A-Z guide on crime and his past record weighs in at the top end of the scale but when you look at how he was fitted up for an assault on a copper when he got five years for a section 18 assault and won his appeal it makes it less than favourable to see that he's now fighting against his 11½ sentence for torture and escape from prison custody. Paddy's from up north, Newcastle to be precise, and they breed 'em tough up there. Cos Paddy's got an appeal in with the CCRC I can't go into things too much but what I can say is that my lawyer, T, is working on his case and if anyone can prove he was fitted up then he can.

Paddy and his co-accused made one of the most daring escapes from a prison van taking them to court and within a few days Paddy was abroad while his co-accused stayed in Newcastle dressed up in women's clothes.

It later came out that his co-accused was a police informer and that the escape might not have been as well planned as it first seemed! I mean you don't use a mini bus to transport two of the

101

Legends

north's most dangerous cons around, do you?

When they was recaptured months later there was high profile security – guns, helicopters and dogs. So it was a bit suspect on how easy it was for them to get away from custody in the first place, don't you think?

Paddy's story is covered in one of the chapters in *'Viv – and the Geordie Mafia (Vol.2)'* and it sure makes some accusations about his charges and those involved. It all started with a dirty little granny basher damaging Paddy's late father's headstone.

While this goes on Paddy's been stuck in Cat 'A' status since '95 fighting for the truth to come out and it all revolves around six minutes of missing audio tape that the judge at his trial wouldn't allow in and then said it hardly contained anything of any interest, I say let's get that fucking tape and get it played – good luck Paddy, your old china Charlie.

Bertie Costa

I met Bertie in Hull Prison back in the 70s, he had a bad time in the Hull riot, the slags beat him black and blue and he lost two years remission. The screws dished out some beatings back then but you could give as much back, now though it's all one sided. Bert always bounced back as the man he is. Last saw him in Parkhurst it would've been about '78. He looked in great shape and he was looking forward to getting out and spending some time with his family.

I've never seen him since so I hope life worked out for him. It was a great shame Bertie ever took up crime as he was a great boxer and had the ability to get to the top.

Jock Costella
'The Ripper's Reaper'

To many he remains a saint. The 70s and 80s was a violent era in HM Prison Parkhurst. I weighed in a screw and a con, Ronnie Kray was forever attacking screws, Dougie Wakefield killed a con, John Paten turned out a con so did Rogers there were sieges, violence and all sorts going on but the best ever act of violence was Jimmy's when he ripped the Ripper.

70+ stitches in the monsters boat race, it was beautiful – now

Prison Directory

see why we love him. I bet the victims' families of the Ripper love Costella too, we all love him but sadly there's a real price to pay for justice it cost Jimmy more years inside and through it he lost his wife.

The Yorkshire Ripper, Peter Sutcliife, met his match in Parkhurst hospital wing with my little friend, Jock Costella. Sutcliffe was in the recess slopping his piss pot out when Jock gave it to him with a coffee jar (see photo in the Monsters chapter). He tore the Ripper's face to pieces; sadly it cost Jock five years added to his sentence, he should really have got a medal for it not five years. Jock spent some tough years away nearly always in the dungeons. He's a free man now and has settled right down. The Ripper will carry the reaper's scars forever.

Courtney

I met Courtney in Gartree in the 80s then later at Long Larten, he's got a great sense of humour this guy. He loved a drink and he was always brewing up a bucket of hooch, he always made sure I got a bottle or two. He got out and sent me this magic photo. I've never heard if he stayed out but I hope he's okay and doing well just like Rumpole's right now.

Les Cromer – R.I.P.

I met Les in Walton Prison block a few years back, he looked after me with a lot of magazines and papers. He's a typical scouser with a good sense of humour. He told me that this was his last ever time inside, he would get out, settle and never return. You hear this all the time but this guy meant it – you could see it in his eyes. He just kept on about his family, how he was to make it up to them, I liked Les a lot. He made it out but a short while after he died in a car crash. I know this blitzed his family, as it did many legends. There's so little that words can add to such a tragedy, only, Les Cromer is never far away, a great guy who meant well to all.

Legends

Del Croxen – R.I.P.

I met Del in Wandsworth Prison in the 80s I used to walk around with him on the yard. I then bumped into him in Belmarsh Prison in the 90s he was a strong man, fit, powerful and full of character, he oozed out strength – he was respected by both cons and screws as he conducted himself as a real man. Whilst I was at Belmarsh a screw unlocked my door and hit me with the biggest bombshell I'd ever know, the screw was Mick Reagan, and I could see by his face that something was wrong. "Del's dead," Mick told me. He'd just been found in his cell. Later at the inquest it was said to be drugs, what a shock what a waste, he was 38 years old, had a lovely wife and children, he'd trained all his life and we all loved the guy.

Dessy Cunningham – R.I.P.

After serving the best part of his 17-year sentence, and he done it hard with lots of chokey. For some strange reason he hung himself on 1st January '99 in his cell a Whitemoor Prison. A sad day for all the Londoners as Dessy was a respected villain with a solid background. It's no secret that Dessy and me fell out some years back in Parkhurst but I gotta take this opportunity to say I was gutted and very upset over his action. I still can't understand why he did such a drastic thing but these jails turn any man's head inside out. I hate it when good people take their own lives. Dessy was a legend and remains a legend, he'll live on but I do wish he was still with us.

Tony Cunningham – R.I.P.

On the 14th December '85 I was walking around the exercise yard of Wandsworth Prison with Tony and Noel Travis. It was bloody freezing, Tony was telling us a few jokes; he had us laughing. The very next day he hung himself in his cell. He really broke my heart, he was a great guy, I liked him – it should never have happened! He was only serving 7 years; he was so young and had a great life ahead. Why, can we ever know why, does it ever make sense, it just doesn't make sense. He chose to tell Noel and me his own jokes

Prison Directory

rather than his problems, for that we must respect him but I wish he'd told us, I only wish.

Vic Dark
'The Real McCoy'

Another true East-ender – not those muppets on UK TV. Vick got 17 years for an armed robbery, he's one of the hardest cons in the system, disciplined in martial arts and he could bench press over 500 pounds! I've been with Vick in most of the top secure jails. This guy became a legend outside and he earned my utmost respect. Armed cops were after him in a car chase, his pal caught a bullet. Vick crashed the car and run with his mate across his shoulders, yeah, real Hollywood stuff, eh? What a hero and what a legend. Vick Dark is the Real McCoy

Frankie Davis

I first set eyes on Frank through the spy hole in my cell door in Wandsworth Prison block. His cell was directly opposite mine, the screws went into his cell and grabbed him so I started banging on my door and shouted, "Leave him alone," they did. This was back in '76 when Frank had just got 21 years for the Spaghetti Siege in Knightsbridge, London. The siege went on for almost a week. Tony Monroe and Wesley Dicks both got 15 years each. They had eight hostages inside the basement of the Spaghetti House Restaurant. I'll always remember Frank's face when the screws used to pile spaghetti on his plate. I had a lot of respect for the man, as he was a born fighter. He'd already served a sentence for armed robbery.

Bobby Dew

This guy got a 17 stretch, what a great legend. The old bill shot him in the arm, almost blew it off, he was in a terrible state but he fought back to health and like all legends got back up. I remember Bob in Gartree jail, he made his son a fort; it took him months but what a fort it was. Bob lived for his son, worshipped him. He served 12 years and got out and I've heard no more of him but Bob told me once, "Chas, when I get out I'm never coming back to this shit."

Legends

Johnny Dillon

I met Johnny in Risley in '85; he was only a young con then and fearless. He's been involved in riots, violence, you name it and he's done it. (A good scouser.)

But his greatest feat was the day he was escorted to court from Risley and a car stopped the van and a load of masked guys got out and took off with him! That's what makes a legend – a legendary escape. I later meet up with Johnny up in Full Sutton jail; they'd captured him and given him an extra five years but he was still bouncing about. Guys like JD won't ever lie down. The Scousers can be proud of this guy, a living legend.

Albert Dryden

This poor guy got life, what for...I'll tell you what for, for being a working class man all his life, for building his mother a bungalow with his bare hands and then some arsehole from Durham County Council's planning office with a 10 gallon ego says, "Pull it down – you don't have planning permission." The bungalow was built below ground level; you couldn't see it!

So Albert warned them all off, "Leave me alone, I'm a happy man, I don't want any aggro." They kept on at him, "Pull it down or we will!" BANG! One dead and one wounded when Albert was captured on TV, this was a full on confrontation, the planners knew there'd be trouble; they brought a high profile posse along, TV cameras, the law, the lot. Hell, he shot one copper up the arse; I've never seen a copper run so fast! They're okay when they shoot us in the back but the minute you pull a tool on them they turn into athletes.

Albert got life for protecting his own property, anyway I'd say to you all if there's one legend in this book that deserves some compassion then it's Albert Dryden – send him a card of support.

Prison Directory

Last I heard he was at HM Prison, Wakefield, England. He's not a criminal in my eyes and he only did what any man should do – fight for his castle.

Sid Earnshaw

What can I say about old Sid! What a character, what a legend. I met Sid in Ashworth max secure hospital; this was way back in the 80s, by this time he'd been locked up for well over 50 years! Yeah, frightening.

Sid's case was a typical case of what the authorities were good at – forgetting about people. It started with Sid when he was a boy, he was a live wire – he couldn't be tamed. They sent him to borstals, prisons – he had it all – torture, birching, solitary, starvation diets and drug control until they finally nutted him off!

For 20 years he rotted away in Rampton asylum where the  damage was done. Sid became institutionalised – like so many of the old boys I've met. But Ashworth tried to undo the damage. They treat him well, fed him well, clothed him well, gave him a TV in his room and started a rehabilitation programme to prepare him for the world outside.

After four decades of incarceration they sent him to a half way home, it was Christmas time; he was lost, depressed so he set fire to the Christmas tree. The van sped off with Sid inside. Ten years…he potters bout the grounds of Ashworth max secure.

There's no cure for this legend! He's kind of happy in his own way. They created the problem long ago and now they're stuck with it. Sid will undoubtedly die in Ashworth with a 25-foot high wall around him. He'll not be the first or the last but he's a legend.

Ronnie Easterbrook
'Semtex Man'

I first met Ronnie Easterbrook in Parkhurst Prison in the 70s.

Legends

Ronnie's the complete legend; there are so many stories to write about Ron that it's difficult to choose one. Ron was being escorted from the Old Bailey back to Brixton Prison in the 80s in a cat 'A' lorry with an armed escort when there was a massive explosion and the lorry's roof buckled in with the explosion. Ron was lucky to survive as he'd attempted to blow his way out of the moving lorry - miraculously he wasn't hurt.

He ended up with a life sentence for the robbery in which he was shot in the back from a cop and Tony Ash was killed. It was a liberty giving Ron a life sentence, a very unjust sentence, he's the ultimate man of pride and nobody could ever break this man's morals. His trial was a real farce and I believe he should never have got life.

The longest ever dirty protest was our Ronnie – 2 years. (In the 90s at Whitemoor Prison) This is a true old style con, a man who lives and dies with respect. Since '88 Ron's fought it with hunger strikes, shit ups you name it. Ron's now nearly 70 years old and it's taking its toll. He's currently in Belmarsh Prison hospital wing in a wheelchair. Send the man a card of support cos he's a legend.

Imagine it a two-year shit up protesting over a life sentence he shouldn't be doing. They've even still got this man, in a wheelchair, on category 'A' status – fucking clowns. He's an old man and they're treating him like a mad dog. A friend of mine tried this, he rang the RSPCA and told them that an animal was being kept confined in a concrete shed with only one hour of exercise a day and it wasn't given any sort of other stimulation. The woman at the RSPCA said, "Where's the place, as we'll send an inspector round straight away, as this sounds like an act of cruelty?" My mate said it was Whitemoor Prison and put the phone down. There's laws for dogs but none for us!! That David Ramsbotham Prison Inspectorate guy got fuck all done for me while I was at Woodhill – he's just a fucking muppet, how else did he get his knighthood.

It took me to kick off and fight off, not 24 as reported in a newspaper, but 60 screws, 60 of 'em to get a change of prison and end up at Whitemoor, Whitemoor of all the fucking places on earth, I'd rather have been put in the cage at Wakefield than Whitemoor! You don't believe it do you, you think I'm on one of my missions again, don't you; well let me tell you that I never lie! Two cons can confirm it one of them is a guy called Sharkie and the other's Keith Pringle. I was busy kicking in the door of this sex case, Victor Miller,

Prison Directory

after I'd just told the screws I wasn't going back into that concrete coffin – I couldn't breath in it, I was claustrophobic and near to losing it so when the door opened I had to get some air, eight screws scarperred – I'll tell you more about that later on in this book.

Now see the insanity of it all, it's not just the insane that are unpredictable and dangerous, it's them rats up in HQ who are the maddest. But they lack something we've got – bottle. They're really envious cos they're faceless gutless people.

Paul Edmunds – R.I.P.
'The Promoter'

Paul was a born and bred East-ender from Canning Town, a salt of the earth manor. I first met this guy in Parkhurst back in the 80s. He was serving 11 years for armed robbery. Years later he became my fight promoter. That's how insane this life can be; Paul was a

great guy and a man of honour. When I got out of jail he looked after me and so did his mother, I was only free for 69 days but I had three unlicensed fights and I won them all. Paul's a legend in and out of jail. When he served his sentence he raised a lot of money for children's charities by organising prisoner's art shows. Then when he got out he put on boxing shows for charity, he was probably one of the biggest hearted guys to come out of East London and I loved him as a brother and I love all of his family just the same, they're all salt of the earth people.

When the hang 'em and flog 'em brigade come out over villains they should look carefully at what guys like Paul Edmunds did. He's featured in the video documentary *Sincerely Yours*, directed by Steve Richards, and you'll see me in action in one of my fights. The other two fights I had were also videoed and anyone who can lay their hands on the other two I'd be much obliged if they could give the publisher of this book a shout.

The fight when I killed a Rottweiler dog was also videoed. Some

Legends

plonker's turned round and said they've never come across a 195 pound dog in that breed in their life. Well obviously the guy knows fuck all about fighting dogs does he, they pump them full of steroids meant for horses, put them on a treadmill for hours at a time and feed them full of chicken, if this geezer was to get the same treatment it would be nothing less than what he deserved for being such a clown. The only reason I killed the dog was cos I wanted to show the crowd that they were all losers but you can read about that in my book, *Silent Scream*, in more detail.

Paul sadly passed away at a young age and I hope for all of his hard charity work he's up there watching over us, God bless him.

Paul Flint

This guy got life in the 80s; he's a good guy, a solid cockney with plenty of morals. When I say a solid cockney I mean just that. Don't class him the same as some of them riff raff you get to meet that give cockneys a bad name. I first met Paul on the Lincoln special unit in 1990. He's a complete fitness fanatic and not many work out like this guy.

Paul Flint, your old china; Charlie and Tony McUllen (Hull Special Unit 1994)

Prison Directory

I've seen a pool of sweat in the gym when he's completed his workout. I next bumped into him on the Hull Special Unit. Even on Christmas day he went out for his run (We're allowed an hour on the exercise yard, so don't think we had some big fuck off park to run round in, we didn't!) and then he came in and went for an hour's workout in the gym. (Remember this was a very special unit, you don't get these facilities in any old lockdown jail – sadly the unit closed down.) Nothing or nobody stops him training that's why Paul's in my book of *Legends* – he comes second to nobody where fitness is concerned.

Stevie Gillan

I first met him some years back in Wandsworth Prison; he was category 'A' and just copped a 14-year sentence for a blagg. I next bumped into him in Full Sutton jail where he showed me the manuscripts of his novel; what a read it was brilliant, I couldn't put it down. Steve's just a pure born writer and why he's not had any of it published is beyond me. He had no need to turn to crime with such talent and such a gift of life. He can't have too much left to serve. I say to him now, pack up crime, get the pen out cos you'll earn more from books then you would from crime. I'd love to see you win, I really would cos legends like you should show the way; you're a big guy with a big heart, a true East-ender through and through.

Ron Greedy

Now this guy's a legend from his toes to the top of his crust. I met Ron in Broadmoor in the 70s then again in Ashworh asylum in the 80s, Ron's now in his 60s. He once got sent to a halfway house (a sort of hostel to get you back into society – something I've never had!) to rehabilitate him but Ron scampered off and stayed free for only three weeks; he spent the other 44 years and 11 months in Ashworth and Broadmoor. Not once did I ever hear him moan. All he ever did was to go out his way to help other guys, obviously he's totally institutionalised but he's a legend inside the asylums. I don't know Ron's ending but I would say it was time someone came up with something to get him out; only a legend could survive so long.
Ashworh Special Hospital, up in Liverpool, is the home of my

Legends

dear old friend Ron. A man with 40+ years of being caged up, 20 Of those years served in Broadmoor when it was a feared institution. Ron's rubbed shoulders with the toughest of the tough: Frank Mitchell, Roy Shaw, Marty Frape, Timmy Noonan, Nobby Clarke and Danny Clarke. All these men passed through Broadmoor in the years Ron spent there and these men were all feared beyond reproach but it was a respected fear. Poor old Ron's still in max secure conditions, he now runs a tuck shop in Ashworth and makes a tidy packet, which he puts back into the hospital fund. Ron's really just another 'old boy' who knows nothing else. Yes, I feel a lot of sadness for this man, as he's such a loveable character but he's well looked after by life long friends. For me he's like an uncle, I promised the old boy I'd take him into a restaurant for whatever he fancies, it's now his dream and he won't die till it happens. Unfortunately Ashworth wouldn't allow me to visit anyone when I was out as they felt I was a security risk. I just hope one day that I could make Ron's dream happen, it would be the greatest gift I could ever give him.

'H' is for Hangman

I see they've done away with the electric chair in the USA, Old Sparky, about time too. But what about the lethal injection. What about the Firing Squad still in existence in China. What about the

Prison Directory

chopping off of hands in the Arab states, just for theft! What about all those people proven to be innocent, after they were hung! You can't bring 'em back, can you? So if they've now discovered hanging to have been wrong then surely it will one day be proven that what the British penal system is doing to me and others is also gonna be classed as barbaric. But I reckon it'll be long after my time on this earth, think about it!!!!!!

Ritchie Halliday

I met Ritchie in Whitemoor segregation unit in '99, well I never actually seen him only heard him. He was in the next cell to me for a month. Crazy – only feet away from each other and we never saw each other in a month. He got four years in a stabbing over a kebab would you believe! I respect the guy cos he stood up against the brutal regime that's in Whitemoor and like myself he was on 'Riot Unlock'. Only the two of us was on this unlock out of the whole unit cos the other 20 or so swallowed a lot of shit so Ritchie earned my respect the hard way. He does his bird like a man. I can't forget cos on the 1st of April they steamed in and beat him up cos he wouldn't stand up for them. They put him in a strip cell. An hour later the governor went in and again he refused to stand up, why should he? So they beat him up again – madness but Ritchie just laughs at the clowns cos that's all what they really are. In all the time he was in the next cell to me not once did he stand up for them or let them get into his nut. We both stood firm and beat them.

Micky Hammad

Nigel Benn (The Dark Destroyer) and Micky Hammad

113

Legends

Micky sent me this photo only a few years ago of him in Nottingham jail with a visit off the Dark Destroyer (Nigel Benn), a boxer we all respect. Micky's been a close pal of mine for over 25 years; we first met up in Hull jail in the 70s. Micky later got out only to come back in again...for life! A great guy! A friend forever!

Well over 10 years had passed before I met up with him once more then in the 80s I bumped into him in Gartree jail where I found out about his life sentence. It was a sad time in his life as his father had just passed away – a man he idolised. It was a terrible empty existence for Micky at this period and there was so little anybody could do to help the man over it. But being a true fighter he's now doing well.

I always remember Micky for his curries up in Full Sutton; nobody makes better chapattis like he does. A legendary cook. I've seen Micky in all sorts of scrapes and I've never known or heard of him ever losing a fight – like Nigel Benn a born winner, stay strong Micky.

Johnny Heibener

Ron Kray (far left) Johnny Hiebener (2nd on left) Reg Kray (far right)

I met John at Parkhurst in the 70s; he got life and 25 years over a contract killing. He still says he never did it. John was a great boxer in his day, the Kray Twins used to go to his fights, he had it all speed, footwork, hooks, crosses and one hell of a punch. John

114

Prison Directory

was a potential world champ. He once knocked out three screws in one day in Albany jail on the Isle of Wight; they soon moved him to Parkhurst. At that time I was going through a bad patch in my life. I'd just been certified mad over a GBH on a screw; I was awaiting a move to Rampton. It was John who talked me out of smashing a guy's skull in with a lump of concrete, I've never forgot that and I'll always respect Johnny. 25 years on he was still locked up as far as I had heard but he was still super fit and hadn't lost his sparkle.

Michael Hickey
'Roof Man'

The longest ever roof protest in a British prison was at Gartree in the 80s by Michael Hickey. Michael spent three months on the roof in the wind, snow and rain. He was protesting against his conviction for the murder of Carl Bridgewater. Obviously he was getting food, water and blankets passed up to him, he even had a radio – the cons looked after him but just think about it, could you survive for three months on a roof? That's what makes the guy a legend. Now he's in top security Ashworth asylum. I must add he's still protesting his innocence and I do believe he got his life sentence for nothing. One day it will be proven that he's innocent.

Les Hilton – R.I.P.
'Big Bad Les'

I first met Les in Hull jail over 25 years ago; he had so many battle scars he was a walking myth. A lot of cons were afraid of Les; his size alone was at times intimidating. He could make a man sweat just by eye contact. Six jocks once burst into his cell and stabbed him up. He fought them all out of his cell, he then lit a fag and burnt each wound and patched himself up. That's what you call a real man. I used to play scrabble with Big Bad Les. I loved the guy. Some brave toe-rag stabbed Les in the back – he died in the gutter. I guess even this legend one day had to lose one battle.

Legends

Tommy Hole – R.I.P.
'King Tommy'

Tommy Hole was one of my best ever pals. I first met him in the top secure unit in Brixton Prison in the 80s. He ended up with 19 years and tragedy hit Tommy time and time again while he was on that sentence and it was so heartbreaking to look into that man's painful life. He found his son hanging in a cell in Parkhurst. Imagine that – no one can!

King Tommy had a wonderful lady, she kept him strong and he won his appeal for freedom. He was a strong man, a man I loved and respected. King Tommy is inside my heart and I was always on his side no matter where or when or whatever the odds I was always there for this guy. Tommy was shot in the back in a pub in 2000.

Eddie Holland

I met this guy in Full Sutton, he's a diamond of a man, we trained together for a spell. Eddie knows how to conduct himself and I later met up with him in his hometown of Leeds, he was working on a pub door. That first night he had to sort out a spot of bother, two right hooks was plenty enough for two troublemakers whose lights soon went out – all that training soon paid off.

'H' is for Hostages

I've gotta give credit to all my hostages so here goes and I wish them all the best and no hard feelings apart from Adrian Wallace cos he laced into me when I was held down after the event. They're not in any particular order cos time and dates don't matter; get the fuller details in my autobiography *Silent Scream*. My hostage taking days are over; okay I said it before, promise! I am not one to cry wolf, it's gonna take time for people to realise I'm a human being and not a god.

Prison Directory

1. **Andy Love** – Was prison librarian at Woodhill and I picked him up, slung him over my shoulder and ran for it, after 16 hours I released him with a hand shake.
2. **Adrian Wallace** (Hull Prison's Deputy gov.) He was by far the most ungrateful hostage I've ever taken.
3. **Phil Danielson** – (Civilian Education Officer) What can I say about this guy that hasn't already been written in thousands of column inches of newspapers. He was with me for 44 hours in Hull jail special unit. The Prison Service dragged it on and on and even Phil was pissed off at them for not even giving him a cigarette in all that time. He demanded that the governor be called, he even told them they were breaching his human rights, which they were and I hear Phil's claiming compensation from the Prison Service via the Home Office. Phil, mate, if you're reading this then if you wanna call me as a witness then I'll only be too willing to turn up for you. It was disgusting how the negotiators couldn't do anything till HQ had given them the nod. See what really happened, watch the video documentary and hear Phil telling them he doesn't want to press charges against me – Phil, don't let 'em grind you down.
4. **Dr. Wilson** - Winson Green, didn't come off too well this one.
5. **Robert Taylor** - Bullingdon jail was the scene for this brief encounter with a pen, a bit of a mix up really. He was a short stay hostage and I held him with a pen to his ear and threatened to push it into his brain. Sounds nasty but you'd have to understand the circumstances of it all and when you hear that Robert didn't press ant charges you'll understand how this was a bit of a misunderstanding that really wasn't his fault - one of the better hostages.
6. **Governor Masserick** - I wanted to have a chat with the governor so I picked him up, slung him over my shoulder and took him into the wing office for a cuppa. He was a bit of a weight though, needs to go on a diet!
7. **Mr. Jones** - Full Sutton; he was a probation officer.
8. **Hassan Sahib, Adnan Alharei and Jason Greasley** - all of Belmarsh jail. The first two named had been on remand for hijacking a plane at Stanstead airport with over 200 people on board. I was getting nasty looks from them and one day one of them bumped into me on the prison landing, didn't even say sorry or fuck all else. I followed him into his cell and that was it. (Full details in *Silent Scream*) I had all three of the named held hostage,

117

Legends

I was later to get seven years for this and the Iraqi hijackers only got five!!!!!!!!!!??????

Nissa Hussain

Nissa was the brother of Arthur, they both got life for the murder of Muriel McKay but her body was never found that's why it became such an infamous case. How can anyone get life when there isn't a body, but they both did?

I met Nissa at Parkhurst in the mid 70s, I'd say he was more of an acquaintance than a friend but he made the most delicious curry I've ever tasted. Lots of cons used to say that he and his brother had made a curry out of the body of the dead woman, some say the pigs ate her and some say she was buried in a flyover on the M1 – all rumours, all speculation as no body has ever been found. Nissa was released on his 20th year and he flew back to Trinidad and wasn't ever seen again. Poor Arthur though went mad and he was sent to the hospital for the criminally insane at Ashworth. But I often worry over that curry Nissa used to make, it did taste nice.

Colin Ireland
'The Fairy Liquidiser'

When I was in the cage at 'Monster Mansion' (Wakefield Prison) a few years ago I noticed a con walking around the punishment exercise yard, I recognised him as Colin Ireland – the homosexual serial killer. (He killed five gays.) So guess where they sent him, Wakefield (Monster Mansion) and it's full of gays...well most of them are gay. He lasted a short spell and then all of the gays were running into the wing office afraid for their lives. It's like the system wanted Colin to kill again.

Colin told me he was in the block for slagging a screw off up on the wing. The insane thing is that Monster Mansion is full of

Prison Directory

homosexuals and the Fairy Liquidiser was living amongst them all – I can never make this system out?

Personally I'm not a mate of this man and don't go a lot for him, but I guess he's a right to be here after all he's Britain's first serial killer of gays, nobody can deny it.

Roy Ivors

I first met Roy in the 80s and have since been in many jails with him. He's a legend in every sense of the word. Everybody respects the man. He once tried to have it off (escape) a van; he was up against six screws and almost made it! The van was almost demolished – he'd kicked out windows, buckled the doors and ripped out seats but they overpowered him and he got an extra five years added to his sentence cos of it. The photo shows Roy working with children that often visit prisons for therapy, it's sort of two sided therapy cos the kids you see benefit from the facilities and the cons benefit from a little bit of outside contact and can learn to be sensitive. Mind you only a con that's 100% gets to work with these kids; have no fears there. I've worked with such children myself and they were the best thing I had in my life whilst inside and that's why we're setting up a charity called *Bronson's Children* (The Humanitarian Relief Fund). It's not just for children but cos everyone sees me as a father figure we thought we'd name it *Bronson's Children*.

He was last serving 19 years in Parkhurst, I can honestly say he's one of the nicest cons I've ever met, keep strong, Roy and maximum respect.

Micky Jamieson – R.I.P.

Sadly he hung himself in Full Sutton Prison after serving a good 20+ years of his life in prison.

Legends

Ray Johnson
'Big Verne'

If you don't know Verne then you ain't done time in maximum-security jails. I met Verne (Ray Johnson) in Full Sutton and then later on in Parkhurst. He broke a screw's jaw in one of the London jails, he has a good punch on him but he's not a clever fighter. He knows how to survive. He does his bird easy, he makes the most out of a bad situation; I like him, as he's always good for a laugh. Sure he's violent and he can snap but it's mostly harmless it's in his nature and it won't ever change.

Ron Johnson
'Big Ron'

I met Ron Johnson in the block in Albany Prison on the Isle of Wight in the 80s. Ron got 18 years for bank raids; he's 6 foot 3 inches tall and got shoulders like boulders. He's a great guy and a good storyteller; I could listen to him all day long. He served his sentence and got back out, I hear he did well. What makes Ron a legend in my book is the day he slung his piss pot, full of body waste, under the door of a grass who was a couple of cells away from us.

Dave Kelly

I met Dave in Parkhurst C-unit. He'd come from Grendan where he'd taken another con hostage and the 'A'-Team blew a hole in the wall to get the hostage out. Dave's a lifer and a very dangerous man (when upset) so don't upset him – simple as that!

Alec Kessen – R.I.P.

Alec killed a con in Maidstone Prison years ago, he got his second life sentence and disappeared into the bowels of the system, he popped up at Parkhurst in the mid 80s. He was a strange sort of guy with his dark glasses and long hair and extra long fingernails. Once he told me, "Nails are handy for gouging out eyes." I knew that this guy had to be taken in small doses, not the sort of chap to take home to meet grandma. Sadly Alec died in Parkhurst, he knew

Prison Directory

he was never to be released so I guess it was a blessing. His favourite saying was "Trust me," he always said this with a smile and a twist in his face.

Mohammad Khan

This guy I met in Gartree Prison in the 80s. He got 18 years for a crime he says he didn't do. I read all his deps and appeal papers; it was obvious the West Midlands Police Force had fitted him up.

Some of them cops were charged with perjury. Mohammad couldn't have committed that crime, as the cops said he was seen running away from the robbery but only the week before the robbery he was charged with he'd lost a couple of toes!

It would've been impossible for him to be running one week after losing his toes. He was later to win his appeal and to be compensated. Those evil cops also fitted up other cases. It makes one wonder just how many more have been fitted up, how many were hung? How can they lie and put a man away for 18 years or life and not feel guilt? How many coppers stood back and watched innocent men hang? FOOD FOR THOUGHT!

Mark Leach

You can't but respect this legend, served 20 years in prison but made it work for him, he got out and became a lawyer, yeah amazing! His time in prison wasn't easy; he suffered a lot of brutality and had many moves. He wrote a book and he now helps so many cons. I never did meet Mark but I'm sure I will later.

Wally Lee
'Human Volcano'

I met Wally in Parkhurst in the 70s; he must've been the most explosive man I've ever met. The slightest little thing and he'd lose control; apart from his explosive nature and violence he was a very shrewd and smart guy. He made a blinding escape from Walton jail in the 70s by digging through his cell wall but Wally never stayed out too long and soon after his capture he got another five years for a hostage incident in Parkhurst. The Human Volcano deserves to have a place inside this book and I only hope he's cooled down a bit.

121

Legends

Ferdie Lieveld

Big Ferdie was in Woodhill in '99 and he was charged with stabbing a screw with a broom. He was in big trouble and looking at a life sentence. At that time he'd the same lawyer as me, Martin Oldham. Ferdie told me, "Chas, he's clown a right mug." So Ferdie sacked him and defended himself after Oldham said to him, "You haven't got a chance of winning." Well he fucking won and did it all himself. The main charge was slung out, I later sacked Oldham myself cos I considered him to be a rat. Oldham also told me I had no chance and I had best plead 'guilty'. I later defended myself and won two of the four charges! Let this be a lesson, a lot of lawyers are false with no balls and are hypocrites. Don't believe all they say unless you really know them well.

The QC Oldham got for me was Ed Fitzgerald, he's married to Lord Longford's granddaughter but I can't hold that against Frank (Lord Longford). Fitzgerald told me to go guilty on all the charges and he'd put in mitigation at court for them to go easy on me – "Not fucking likely," I said. I sacked Fitzgerald and had two of the four charges slung out!! I found out that Fitzgerald had an appointment the following week so he could go and defend Myra fucking Hindley at the House of Lords. What he'd wanted was an easy case with me and then time to pop off to the Lords – another fucking rat.

Mark Lilliott

Here we are waiting in the wrong hotel 9th Nov 1992

Prison Directory

I met this guy in Risley in the 80s. I'd just been badly beaten in the hospital wing. I saw him walk past my window.

He's a legend in his hometown of Wallasey. When he was a kid he was badly burnt, so bad that he'd lost some of his fingers and a lot of his face. For many years he had to have skin grafts to

rebuild his body and face. Obviously his fingers are gone forever.

We became friends and worked together in the prison gym. It was actually him and his girlfriend that met me when I was released from prison the first time.

The thing I most remember him for is in Risley when I started to go a bit crazy and out of the whole wing only he came to cool me down. He's not afraid of anything or anybody. He's just one guy who'll try and help anyone. I rate Mark Lilliot as one of the best humans I've ever met. The photograph of Mark and me was taken in the wrong hotel, how's that you say? I'll tell you why cos I was supposed to meet Frank Longford in a hotel with exactly the same name, Grosvenor, but in another area of London, stone the bleedin' crows, maybe next time I'll get it right.

John 'Alf' Lodge
'The Welsh connection'

This photograph was taken in the gym at Leyhill Prison in 1994 and would you believe the governor, Trevor Phips, took it. I believe Mr Phips was to have a bit of trouble himself later on. I met Alf in Long Larten in 1989; he's our Welsh Connection. I'm gonna let John explain a little about how we first met:

Legends

I was working at the time as a cleaner on A-wing with Johnny Walker of the Birmingham six. Johnny told me that after dinner we'd be having another cleaner working with us and that his name was Charles Bronson and that he was the most dangerous man in the country, it did freak me out a bit but Johnny said, "He won't hurt you, Alfie, you'll get on great." After dinner my cell door was opened and opposite me was a poster on a cell door it read: CHARLES BRONSON - DEATH WISH 7.

I didn't get to meet Charlie that day. The next morning I had just started sweeping the floor when Charlie walked across, there was no mistaking him, it was Charlie Bronson alright. As he walked across towards me he said, "What do I do, mate?" I replied, "After those screws have gone from down there you clean that part." Charlie started walking down the landing towards where the two screws were sitting and without warning he pulled them out of their chairs and almost chucked them down some stairs. I remember saying to Johnny Walker, "He's just chucked those two screws out of their chairs to clean his area!" That's how unbelievable it was.

After a while of working with Charlie JW and I got to like Charlie very much as he wasn't a bully. He used to make us laugh and most nights he used to call JW and me into his cell. On his locker was a stack of tins with no labels on, he'd shake each can by his ear and guess what soup was in the tin, as it was for our supper.

One day I had a bad belly, it must've been on a Tuesday night, maybe from drinking hooch, (prison booze distilled from various vegetables or fruits) with JW, as he made a wicked drink did JW. I was by my cell door, Charlie come by me and went and told a screw that if he didn't get a doctor to me within 10 minutes then they'd know all about it in the morning. It must have been about 7.40pm, 20 minutes to locking up time. I was starting to feel a bit better and told the screw I was okay, got into bed and went to sleep. The next morning I was getting breakfast with JW, Charlie was in front of us, he hit one screw with his tray and they all ran away from him. We could see all of this through bulletproof glass as we were on the stairs and all the remote control doors were shut. I could see Charlie hit a screw and a nonce (sex case).

After a while JW asked the screws to open the door and JW put his hand on Charlie's shoulder and asked him to come to his cell for a cup of tea. Charlie went with JW to his cell and I went off to make us a cup of tea. It was a Wednesday morning and we always

Prison Directory

had cornflakes on a Wednesday and usually we'd have loads of milk but there was only one carton left as Charlie had broke the rest of them.

The Governor, Joe Whitty, came into JW's cell and said to Charlie, "Charlie, please give me six months?" Charlie had to go to the block (prison within prison) and JW walked with him, Charlie spent a month there on punishment. Charlie accepted responsibility and when he got out we had a party. I remember waiting by the door of the punishment block and when I saw Charlie he didn't look like he'd been in the block a month, we had a great party with Charlie singing George Formby (Music Hall ukulele player and singer) songs, one of them was 'Leaning on the lamppost'.

I went on a programme with Charlie on Channel 4, a prison forum programme with Jimmy Boyle. The last time I seen Charlie was first thing in the morning, he came out of his cell with a broken bottle in one hand and a pointed sweeping brush handle in the other. He was naked and covered from head to toe in black boot polish and he was wearing a red headband. He shouted, "It's all over," and he went chasing screws that were running away from him. They shut the prison down and kept us in the gym.

Another day Charlie asked me to go down to the office with him, as our TV wasn't very good. He said to the screw, "If there isn't a decent TV in the TV room after dinner when we come out then you'll know all about it!" After dinner Charlie went into the TV room and come out with his hand on his chin! (We leave the interview there as the rest of it can be caught on the video documentary, *Sincerely Yours*. Wouldn't want to spoil it for you or anyone else.)

John 'Alf' Lodge was one of the most prolific post office robbers in Wales. When he was eventually caught in Barry, Mid Glamorgan by the No 8 Regional Crime Squad Alf was told he'd come closer to being shot than any man in Wales and they'd never shot anyone in Wales.

He wrote off over 30 post office robberies and 20 jewellery shop robberies when he was arrested and it was the start of a clean slate for Alf, he even got his sister to hand some of his guns in while he was in Long Larten and he was transferred from a category 'A' status to a 'D' status and finished his time off in Leyhill Prison, all at the stroke of a pen.

Alf had robbed nearly every post office in Gwent but only used

Legends

a gun in two of those robberies. He used a brace and bit and a pickaxe, as most post offices then had a flat chipboard roof and within minutes he was looking at the safe and if it had a brass handle then he was into it in minutes, as easy as that. Sadly though they've all got time locks on them now! Alf was also responsible for robbing most of the jewellery shops in Gwent.

Alf's longest sentence was 2½ years and then he moved into the big league and earned an 11 stretch for conspiracy to rob (armed robbery) and all in all he's spent over 20 years in prison and up to date this is the longest length of time Alf's been free since the age of 13 – he's been free for over five years.

When you hear how Alf was first put away you'll be left wondering how it all began. Alf had a dog, which he'd rescued from a dog home; he called it Rex. While Alf was in school Rex had managed to get out and had a fight with another dog and the owner gave Rex a kicking, naturally, Rex fought back and bit the guy. When Alf came back from school his mum told him that Rex was put to sleep by a local vet. The owner of the other dog had called the vet! Alf

Alf and Zak 1999

ran out of the house crying and called into a pal's house and borrowed his 4.10 shotgun and ran to the field where the vet kept his horse. Alf shot the horse twice; it didn't die but went crazy and ran into a hedge. That's how it all started and now Alf's a reformed character; he wouldn't even nick a bar of chocolate, as his nerves are shot.

Alf was once the most wanted man in Wales and it all ended when a man who was

Prison Directory

doing jobs with him acted as an agent provocateur, he'd a typical Welsh name – 'Jones'. Jones got £5,000 for setting Alf up but since Alf's living with a Jones they're not all bad. In all he got about £250,000 from the robberies but it went through his hands like butter melts in the sun.

The last offence Alf was charged with was 'Trespass for game' in the Forest of Dean (2000). When the police pulled him in and checked his record they said, "You really have retired haven't you." He was given a £25 fine by Gloucester magistrates' court and it would've taken them all day to read out his past record so it was dealt with quickly.

Micky Lowes
'Lucky Lowes'

I met Micky Lowes in Belmarsh Prison punishment block at a time when his world was falling apart. The slag that'd raped his sister was actually in the same prison under governor's protection. (If that was in Durham Prison now then the slag wouldn't have had anywhere to hide as the nice governor fellah doesn't allow protection and a few have been slashed because of it so I reckon we need to give this governor geezer at Durham jail a medal.)

But there was little any of us could do. We all knew what we wanted to do but in prison a lot of filth put themselves on protection wings for safety. I sort of kept Micky on top, cheered him up a bit. Then we both ended up on the same wing and Micky got a right result at court and a job on the hot plate. He put a stone on me in a week. Lots of grub! Always good for a proper chat and got a big heart.

I left Belmarsh a bit livo; they moved me out fast. I never got a chance to say cheerio to the lads especially my pal, Micky. I'll say now, from all of us legends, we was all proud of you Micky how you handled it. Only a legend could've coped with all that pain you had. All of us respect you and all of us would bust that rat's jaw on sight. Me, I'd have him turned over, he'd be pushing up daisies. We was all with you and you'll never be nothing but a legend. Anyone who'd been through what Micky had been through might not even be here today, it's testimony to his strength and that's what true legends are made of, tough stuff.

Legends

Peter Lovesey – R.I.P.

I met Peter in Broadmoor, he was a good lad and I liked everything about him – loyalty. He got 12 years for a bank raid but they sent him to Broadmoor when he refused to conform in Parkhurst. They put Pete on a lot of drugs, he slept a lot, he became overweight, I witnessed his deterioration but he survived it all, all 12 years of it then he gets out and dies from an overdose.

It always upsets me to hear it, sure that's life, we've all gotta die but when a guy survives so much and goes out and dies so soon it doesn't make sense.

Dessy Ludwick

We met in Belmarsh, he stood out from the rest, he was only in his 20s but he'd lived for a million years and he's left behind a lot of smiles. Des is a guy with bottle he'd fight a lion if he hasn't already. If he hasn't he will now.

I gave him a few bits and pieces, he got out and he wrote to me with these immortal words: *'Ill treasure these things you gave me, I'll have them buried with me.'*

John Marky

John Marky on the right

Prison Directory

John got out after 10 long hard years and made it in Milton Keynes by opening up a café called 'Sunshine Café'. Don't that say it all, what a legendary name all those wasted years rotting away in a stinking cell and now he's free and got his sunshine that sums up a legend for me. We all need to aim for the sunshine; the John Markys of the world always bounce back. John had some stick from the 'know it all' brigade in the local council, as John was sorting out grub for the down and outs. Why is it that when some genuine geezer comes along to help others that these plonkers always have to try and stop it, fuck knows? John, you've found a place in heaven – respect.

Terry Marley

That's big Terry sitting on Bill The Bomb's shoulders with all the chaps. I met Terry in Parkhurst some years back; he was one of the fittest men I've come across, for a big guy he could run but to see him on the bag was like watching a middleweight. After 10 X 3 minutes pounding away on the heavy bag he'd then do his skipping.

Terry Marley - sitting on shoulders

It's only sad he never turned pro, as in my books he was a potential champ. People like Bruno wouldn't have lasted one round with Terry not that Bruno could last much lately with all of the marital trouble he's been having, which shows the bigger you are then the harder you fall.

I've lost touch with Terry so I just hope he's doing well and still the fighter that I once knew, a great guy - one of the best.

He once told me: "Charlie, if you can't knock them out in the first round then why be in the ring at all?" Words well said and only a true legend could say that.

Legends

David Martin – R.I.P.
'Houdini'

There've been many escapologists over the years. Cons, like Robyn, Lee and JK – some legendary escapes. The one con I truly admire was David Martin. I met Dave in the block in Wandsworth Prison in the 70s; he was moved from Gartree after getting out of his cell and caught in the workshop. Whilst at Wandsworth Prison he cut his cell bars. He was forever trying to get away. He could make keys out of plastic knives, he was probably the most gifted of all the would be jail breakers I've ever met. He later became Britain's most wanted man after escaping from a cop shop. The cops shot him, he shot them. Later he was set up by a girlfriend and was caught in the London underground.

He received 25 years and finally hung himself in the special unit in Parkhurst. I could never work out why he decided to take his life, as sure as day turns to night my money would've been on Dave to escape again. He was born a legend, lived a legend and died a legend.

John Massey

I met John in Albany Prison years ago; he got life in the 70s. I lost track of him for a long time then I met up with him in Frankland in 1990, he still looked just the same. John hates anyone who takes liberties. The doctor was taking liberties with him so John gave him a good hiding, it was what the ignorant man had coming to him. They moved John to Armley Prison, Leeds and they beat him half to death. Later John had the last laugh – he escaped!

John Masterson

John's been free for many years now but he has to be a legend as he was the first con to go into the Wakefield Control Unit, which typical of Wakefield, it was a brutal and cold regime in fact it was inhuman, it's why it only remained open for one year. The unit opened in '74 especially for disruptive cons and was closed the following year as it got so much stick from the prison groups P.R.O.P and F.R.F.I. but guys like John survived it like all legends would. I can only hope John's freedom remains, as he sure earned it the hard way.

130

Prison Directory

Micky McAvoy

Micky copped 22 years for his part in the £26m Brinks-Matt Gold Bullion Robbery in the 80s; he's a diamond – one of the old school. He's done his bird like the man he is. I've got a pair of boxing gloves that he sent me for a present and those gloves will be with me all through my sentence – Cheers Micky.

Micky May

This photo was taken at Ashworth max secure hospital in 1993. That's Micky standing up, next to him is Michael Hickey (one of the Birmingham Four) and next to him is Jason Thorpe.

I met Micky in Broadmoor; his case is really a tragedy. He got sentenced in '77 to 12 months for a burglary but whilst in prison he attacked a con and a screw and got himself 'sectioned' off. Last I heard he was still locked up in max secure conditions – indefinite! It's really a disgrace; Mick's no more mad than any guy you meet in a pub or a club. He just likes to have a good time.

I remember the time we were both sitting at a table in one of the wards called Norfolk House by an open window, as we were chatting a bat flew in through the window and started flying around the day room. All the madmen were shouting and trying to catch it. The bat landed on a curtain and Mick went over and squashed it. He came back over to the table, lit a fag and carried on chatting.

Legends

For over 25 years they've had this guy caged up – it really breaks my heart cos it's so unnecessary. But like us all…he plods on and hopes and dreams that one day he'll walk free.

Mick's become a good artist; many of his works hang up in the asylums. It's something he can be proud of but the fact still remains – the system stinks. But legends have to suffer to become legends, how else could he be in the book of 'Legends'? Like Micky says - he don't cry – he gets on with it but he says, "As long as the sex cases serve as long as he has then he don't mind." But unfortunately they too often get set free long before they should and they destroy more kids' lives. You keep strong, Micky, my friend – max respect. PS And leave those bats alone!

Charlie McGhee – R.I.P.
'Red Nose McGhee'

In the 80s at Brixton Prison I met Charlie; he was on remand at the time for allegedly blowing a cop away on an armed robbery. He was later passed a sentence of 30 years for the offence.

He was given his nickname 'Red Nose' over a trial where he was acquitted, it was in fact red nose day for comic relief and thousands of people were walking around with red noses on. He pulled a red nose from his pocket and put it on just before the foreman of the jury said, 'NOT GUILTY'. I think that was a blinder.

On the 8th January '95 this legend was rushed out of Frankland maximum secure Prison with pleurisy and pneumonia he breathed his last breath in an ambulance going to an outside hospital, a heart attack took away Charlie McGhee at the age of 38, a man from my home town of Luton. He was a cop killer and armed robber; he got 25 years in '89. Charlie had a bar in Spain and was well known for his fast living. In '88 he was acquitted for the attempted murder of a bouncer outside of Hatters nightclub in Luton.

A legend in every sense of the word and he died a legend. Red Nose will be missed by many, both inside and out, a legend will always remember a fellow legend, they're engraved into one another's hearts, it's the death of a brother.

Prison Directory

Chris Moody
'Man Mountain'

I met Chris in Parkhurst in the 80s; he was 22 stone...of fat! I was with him on C-unit, he come down from Hull jail. I couldn't believe this guy; he was like a big spoilt brat. When he got upset he'd tear up his clothes and sling them out of his cell window. I gave him a big poster of Madonna and he tore that up too! I took him in the gym to help him lose some weight and all he done was moan, "My legs hurt, my arms ache." Man Mountain was just a useless big lump of lard. But he's still a legend in his own right, unique, a one off, not a great legend but one that deserves a small mention if only to help him come to terms with himself – keep trying Chris and maybe one day you'll become a great legend, a mountain to be respected.

Kevin Oates
'The Toy Man'

I met Kev in top secure Full Sutton in the early 90s; he's only a small

guy but a tremendously strong man. He can bench press the equivalent of a 17 stone man, phenomenal strength. Kev used to make a lot of furry toys for kids. Some days he would sew teddy bears then golliwogs and then bunnies, he just kept going and going; all for kids. For a small guy he's got a great big heart – until someone upsets him. One day someone upset Kev in Full Sutton; Kev just let him have it and the guy never upset Kev again. Best leave the 'Toy Man' alone and let him make the kids happy; he's a good man and a nice guy.

Legends

Terry Perkins – R.I.P.

I met this guy in Frankland Prison. A lovely sort of bloke, he just did his own thing and never bothered anyone; he'd been in the army and done jungle warfare. He always had a story to tell and I could've listened to him all day. He served his 10-year sentence like the man he was and within weeks of his release he died of a heart attack – the only consolation is he died a free man.

Stevie Peterson

When I met Stevie he was called Stevie Booth. I met him in Rampton in the 70s; we have the same explosive nature. Stevie actually had his name changed to Stevie Peterson in respect of me so we're brothers, maybe not in blood but most definitely in heart. I love Stevie like I love my real brothers; he's family to the end. My greatest memory I shall always have is the time he came back from the dentist with the two same teeth missing that I have missing. He begged the dentist to take the two teeth out, he only done it so he'd look like me. Call it madness call it anything - I call it pure brotherhood.

Sadly the authorities tried their hardest to stop our bonding even when I got out they refused me to visit him although I was only out for several weeks I tried desperately to get to see him. The doctors in the asylum thought I was a bad element and a visit was not acceptable. Stevie's been caged up since '72. He's never killed. He got sent to the asylums for a violent attack on a prison officer. It's a terrible injustice but Stevie was born a legend.

Tony Peterson

Tony's an old school sort, good mould of character, he goes back to the Parkhurst Prison riot in '69 – probably the bloodiest riot in British History. I bumped into Tony in '96 at Belmarsh and he was

134

still the same man he was all those years ago. Born men and they all die men.

Ronnie Pewter

I met Ron up in Durham Prison in the late 80s; he was given 16 years for armed robbery. He later became the first man to escape from Parkhurst and escape off the Isle of Wight. To this day no one knows how he managed it, some say he walked out disguised as a building worker, some say he climbed into the back of a lorry but it doesn't really matter how he did it the fact is he did. For a con to escape from a top security jail and for no one to know exactly how it was done is a fantastic achievement and it's also a total embarrassment!

Keith Pringle

What a blinder, this guy's good stuff. He was once on a shit up in the seg unit at Parkhurst along with the late Frankie Birley another solid guy I admired. Well the door sprung open, the MUFTI squad rushed in and they slung Keith into a waiting van. Keith was made up, as this is what he wanted – a move. But it wasn't such a great move, as the van only drove 100 yards to the hospital wing and there they slung him in the strong box. It's stories like that what bring a smile to my face. Even Keith will look back on it and laugh, sure it's not funny at the time but we all know nothing ever lasts and as sure as shit sticks to a blanket Keith will have the last laugh.

Big Pat Purcell

I met Pat in Full Sutton seg unit some years back, strange our paths have never crossed since but in one jail he sent a message to me to pull out of an hunger strike I was on. He'd heard I was deteriorating and he genuinely cared about my health, that's what a legend's all about, they care and don't forget about such kindness.

Frank Quinn

Frank's the first guy to escape from Frankland maximum secure

Legends

jail. He got clean away, a true East Londoner. Only a small guy but got bundles of bottle, he's done all his bird on high risk in and out the units. He does his bird well cos he does it his way and only his way. He don't go along with the sheep, he's his own man.

Chris Reed

I met this guy in Broadmoor and then later at Ashworth. He's spent 20 years inside the asylums but does it with the pride of a lion. As I was writing this life was looking up for Chris when he was moved to a halfway house to prepare for release, which is just the thing needed to straighten people out. Me, I was released twice from category 'A' conditions with no help whatsoever. So I know how good these places are, if run right and I know it benefited Chris as he moved on from there.

A certain geezer got Chris into a lot of trouble, the slag made a story up to help himself and damage Chris, I hope someone can make amends for Chris as the rat deserves teaching a lesson or two. Chris never deserved it. After so long away he was working to get out not stay in longer! But Chris has rode it out and he managed a spell of freedom but he relapsed for a little while but I hear he's out once more and now he must stay out in readiness for my coming out party and that one's gonna be big, really big. We'll have to get a marquee tent and put it up outside one of them big jails and invite all my Bronsonmania fan club members, maybe we'll have some dwarf throwing as a distraction, who knows and we'll have the Swellbellys band there to sing out the night.

Alan Reeves

In the late 60s Alan was sent to Broadmoor for killing a pal. Alan was 17 years old at the time, later he stood trial over the death of a Broadmoor inmate, which he was found not guilty of. Then years

Prison Directory

later he pulled off the greatest feat any Broadmoor inmate can ever achieve, he went over the wall in the 80s and he got clean away. He was on the ferry before they knew he was missing. Some six months later a cop, in Holland, shot Alan in the back but Alan spun round and blew the cop away – he received an extra 15 years for killing the cop. He served 10 and got released.

This is what makes Alan Reeves so legendary, he escaped from Broadmoor asylum and then shot a cop, then he got 15 years, then he got released. Alan beat the whole hypocritical system. One day he's insane, the next he's not, then he is! He proved what a bunch of mugs they are. This photograph was taken in 1982 when he was just married – stay free brother.

Mad Ritchie

I met Ritchie in Ashworth in the 80's, he's a big shaven headed six-footer who was forever listening to the Eagles (Remember them – *Hotel California*) on his walkman. He was also into religion in a big way. I don't knock anyone if they say they've found God – each has his cross to bear in this madcap world.

He was a frightening character if you never understood his ways. One guy came running up to me one day! He was white and trembling, his eyes looked like saucers. "What's up?" I asked. "It's Ritchie," he said, "He's gonna chop me up and put me in a curry!" That's just Ritchie's sense of humour! He just don't realise the fear, he at times, causes. I told the guy not to worry as Ritchie was only joking. I got on quite well with him, we had our fallouts but we always made it up later. Mad Ritchie will always be a legend in my

Legends

book, as he's a unique character. I don't know where he is now as it's been 15 years since I last heard. I'd like to think he's out but I doubt it very much – who knows, stranger things happen at sea.

Barry Rondeau – R.I.P.

I first met Barry in Gartree Prison in the 80s; he got a life sentence for stabbing a rival football supporter. He was only a lad when he got his sentence; I believe it should've been manslaughter not murder. Barry used to work out with me in the block; he was super fit and could leave me standing with his supercharged fitness. He almost made it off the van when he was being transferred to another jail. It was a brave attempt but it wasn't to be; the screws overpowered him. A couple of years later at Long Larten Prison he was found dead in his cell, he'd cut his wrists and his throat – he was 10 years into his life sentence. It was a death that shocked us all; he was the last person in the world you would've thought could ever do that.

Steve Roughton
'Hercules'

The strongest man I ever did come across in the asylum was big Steve Roughton – naturally strong!

I met him in Ashworth hospital in the mid 80s. He was an ex-pro rugby player, as strong as a bull. No man in the asylum could beat him in an arm wrestle – nurses or patients.

One day he escaped from the ward and ran around the grounds shouting and screaming, he obviously wasn't going anywhere, as there was a 25-foot wall around the asylum. So the nurses just let him burn himself out – they walked him back into his ward for a nice cup of tea and some cream buns. Sadly after I left the asylum Steve Peterson stuffed a china mug into Hercules' face. I don't know the ins and outs but if Steve decided he needed a china mug in his face then that's what was gonna happen. I'm glad to say they shook hands later.

Andy Russell

I met Andy in Leicester Prison back in the 80s; he's another

Prison Directory

East-ender (London). Nobody in the system's got more than Andy; he won't ever give up. In '93 he almost made it to freedom from top security Whitemoor jail along with five IRA men. Until you've seen the height of the walls, the security, the dogs and the cameras you can't ever realise what a feat it is to come so close to breaking out of a top security jail. Nowadays it's almost impossible to escape, I used to play five-a-side football in Leicester with Andy, he could've been a pro player but he choose to become a legend inside the criminal fraternity and part of my book – a chapter in my life.

Alex Sears – R.I.P.

This photo was taken in Full Sutton max secure in 1980. That's my oil painting in the background, not that you'll be able to make it out too clear, it's a great big tree. Alex is – 'was' – the No 1 blagger in his day, another solid East-ender (London) to the core. There are so many stories to write about this legend it's difficult to decide on a one but I've chosen one of his many escape attempts.

It happened at Long Larten max secure when Alex and six others made a ladder and went through the bars. They made across the prison grounds, they got through the wire fence with cutters but the ladder collapsed against the wall!!! While the others were trying to assemble it back together the alarm went off. Alex tried desperately to hold off the rushing screws but it cost him a big gash in his crust from a screw's truncheon! Nobody got out! But it was a near thing. Bear

Double lined security fencing - cut away!

139

Legends

in mind Long Larten's a maximum secure establishment –they done well even to get out of the cell window let alone up to the perimeter wall. This was only one of many daring legendary escapes for Alex.

He served his 19 years sentence all on category 'A' status and he served it his way so for that I had to make him a legend. Max respect to a legend that earned this write up with blood, sweat and brains.

Billy Skingle – R.I.P.

This guy shot a cop seven times in the crust whilst he was out on home leave. I met Billy years ago, he spent a good 20 years on the max secure units and he done it his way – the only way he could. He told me, "Hey, I never meant to shoot the cop, the trigger was faulty," that was Billy's sense of humour. He once told me he'd die in jail and come back as an eagle, "An eagle," I said, "Why an eagle?" He looked at me with that crazy smile and said, "So I can swoop down and peck the screws' eyes out. Billy died in Full Sutton jail in the early 90s so watch out screws cos Billy meant business.

Warren Slanney

I first met Warren in Long Larten Prison some years back; he got fitted up over a double murder. I'm convinced that in time he'll prove his innocence. Warren was born in good old East London but lived in Leicester for some years. He was on his way to becominga boxing champion, many say a potential world champion; he chinned a lot of screws over they years only because they pushed him into a corner. Warren's a man of strong principles no drugs, no fags and no booze. He lives for his son. It's never easy in jail but it's double bad when you're an innocent person, it must eat you up at times. It always saddens me when I see the injustice and nowadays it's 100 times worse than it ever was, also nothing ever seems to be done about it even when it's proved to be a fit up the police are never sent down over perjury and blatant fit-ups. They should have to serve the same amount of time as the person they stitched up. You'll win Warren.

Prison Directory

Tony Stabiello
'Bullet Proof'

I met him in Albany jail in the 80s; he's another one of my all time heroes. The cops' shot him four times and he survived! They gave him 16 years - he should be out now, Bullet Proof is immortal.

Paul Sykes
'Sykesy'

There's no other name for this man but Paul Sykes, a legend born and bred. All 6 foot 4 inches tall and 15$\frac{1}{2}$ stone. The man, who fought at the Royal Albert Hall against John L Gardner for the British heavyweight title, he sadly lost.

I first met Sykes in Liverpool in the early 70s and at this time he was probably the fittest con in Britain. A hard man from Yorkshire, a fighting man in every sense. A lot of people never liked him perhaps they even feared him but I respected the man for what he stood for. No matter what though he's a legend and if people are talking about him then I want him in my book.

Liverpool Prison still speaks of when the cat went missing. It was a big chubby brown cat that all the cons loved to watch through their cell bars when it pounced on rats. The cat was the best rat catcher in any prison. Cons idolised that cat and some would even give it their rations of milk. Then the cat mysteriously disappeared and nobody saw it for ages.

Word went around that a big fat rat had killed it. Rumours had it that a screw's dog killed it or even old age had crept up on it. But nobody knew the real truth until Sykes walked out of his cell with a Davey Crocket hat on! I don't know if he'd killed and skinned it but he had it on his head. This story is still being told now.

Bob Taylor

Bob's a lifer; I met him in Parkhurst in the 80s. He'd stabbed a con in the head with a six-inch nail whilst at Gartree jail so they sent him to Parkhurst. All he does is pick up dog ends, he swoops his life away dive-bombing for those fag ends. What a great artist he is, one of the best in jail. He could earn a good living from his art but he just keeps swooping, he's happy doing this and at least he keeps

Legends

the exercise yards clean – not a dog end to be seen.

Brian Thoroughgood

This guy's gotta be one of the unluckiest guys I know; he's done so much bird. His last sentence was 21 years knocked down to 18 years on appeal. But like the old soldier he is he plodded on – served 12 years of it and got out. Brian spent years up in Frankland max secure up in Durham. He was in fact the longest serving con in Frankland; I believe he spent seven years at the jail – all on category 'A'.

Brian always seems to get grassed up by women. He gives 100% but has very rarely got more than 50% back! He's a born fighter, fearless!

It's never easy to have to spend so many years inside but that's how it ends up when you keep trying for the 'pot of gold'. It's like a dream but you keep awakening to a nightmare.

Franco Vincitore
'Shotgun Franco'

It was in Woodhill segregation unit in 1993 Franco was allowed out on the yard with me for my one hour of exercise per day that I was allowed. I would lie on a mat whilst Franco would throw Bertha, my medicine ball, at me, I'd catch her, sit up and throw it back. Once I caught it and shouted, "Look at that," as I looked up in the sky Franco looked up too. Then I slung Bertha at 30mph, it hit

Prison Directory

him on the side of the head and almost blew him away.

Always keep your eye on the ball Franco, never take anything to be as it is, as it could've been a rocket, anyway Franco took it well and maybe I did throw it a little too hard. Great times brother! Fit days! Strong! Happy! Treasured memories and like all legends you live on.

Johnny Walker
'Innocent'

This is his real name and he's worthy of it, as you'll find out when you read on. Johnny was one of the Birmingham six whom I met in the 80s at HM Prison Long Larten. He was serving 21 life sentences for crimes he DID NOT commit. He was a legend when it comes down to making hooch (booze).

He could make a bucket of hooch as good as a pint of Walker's Ale. Johnny was famous for his many thousands of bucketfuls of hooch over his 16-year period of imprisonment. I personally helped shift many a pint with Johnny and every pint I ever supped with this man was in total respect.

Johnny spent all of those wasted years helping other cons around him; he was always good for a laugh and always took the side of the weakest.

I always remember the time a young con did something that upset a lot of the other guys. Violence was in the air it was electrifying but Johnny just went up to the young con and told him to pack his box and go – the lad did just that. I asked Johnny why he intervened and he said: "Charlie, I'm doing 21 life sentences for a crime I knew nothing about and I may die inside, but whilst I'm alive I'll fight my case and at the same time I will keep my dignity. I don't need violence plus it only spoils what I've got. I love my pint of hooch, it's really I'll what I've got inside. The lad's done wrong, he's gone now and he'll suffer enough without us hurting him." This man should win the Nobel Peace Prize cos he's got a sense of righteousness about him and he always believed in the truth.

Well, Johnny, my friend you impressed me many times over, you certainly are a legend and now you're a free one but I do miss your drop of hooch and I guess I can speak for hundreds of cons who drank in your company - I wish you well my friend.

Legends

Gary Ward

Gary's in Frankland jail at the time of writing this; he's in for murder. He was one of the youngest club doormen to work in Blackpool, employed by Sabre Security. He thought his luck had changed till he met James Docherty. Docherty ended up with a determinable prison sentence for manslaughter and by applying pressure to Gary he escaped a life sentence. Gary carried the can and now he's fighting for his freedom and trying to unravel the web of deceit that helped put him away for a murder he had no hand in other than to try to stop Docherty from going

Gary Ward (right) and his Dad George

any further till Docherty pulled a gun on him and he had to keep his mouth shut. When Gary was on remand his pregnant girlfriend was threatened and if Gary stepped out of line he was told she'd get it – he obliged and kept quiet.

When Gary realised it was all a plot to get him to carry the can he started fighting back even though it was late in the day. There's no evidence against him and in fact a set of teeth prints on the dead man's body didn't match up to Docherty's or Gary's bite imprint. There's now a big chance that he'll win through it all and prove his innocence. His story was written in one of the chapters of *Viv – and the Geordie Mafia Vol. 2* and it reveals how Gary had no hand in the murder of Mark White. Up to date a number of MPs, including Gordon Marsden, have taken an interest in his case and the CCRC (Criminal Case Review Commission) are looking into it, although they're sadly short staffed and overworked, which might in fact hinder his chances if not handled properly. Gary – good luck.

Prison Directory

Eddie Watkins – R.I.P.

He took an overdose 12 years into his life sentence but still the legend lives on we'll never forget him.

Dennis Wheeler
'The Sailor'

Dennis got 14 years for bringing over a couple of tons of cannabis. I met him in Brixton's Special Unit; he looked after me. Dennis had the most beautiful wife you could imagine and he lived the life of a film star. He'd travelled the world and lived everyday to the full. I later spent some time with him in Full Sutton jail.

One day I painted an oil painting and when I gave it to him his face said it all. It was as if though I'd given him a gold watch, he actually said he'd have it sent out to have a gold frame made for it. I said, "Blimey, Dennis, that's a bit over the top, ain't it?" A legend always comes up with some unique idea. He's out now and I often wonder if he did get that gold frame?

Eddie Wilkinson

Another born and bred East-ender is my old mate Eddie Wilkinson. I first bumped into Eddie 20 years ago and our paths have crossed

many times over. Eddie hasn't had much luck in life! The only result he ever had was getting his life sentence reduced to 14 years on appeal.

Eddie's so loyal it's unreal. A couple of muggy cons upset Ed in Wakefield jail some years back...they both ended up in hospital the day Eddie snapped. He steamed into them both with his meal tray.

Sadly latter Ed suffered a blood clot and

Legends

ended up paralysed. He spent a long time in hospital, he couldn't move for months and months. When I last seen him he was only 10 stone and had a bad limp – it upset me to see it. But Ed being the born fighter he is got strong; he fought it. He's out now and doing well - love ya to bits, Ed.

George Wilkinson – R.I.P.
'Big Wilkie'

If anyone done bird in the 70s, they can't but have heard of Wilkie – George Wilkinson.

I don't believe there's been a man since the death of Wilkie who terrified the screws so much. He was a big giant of a man and a Geordie. He started off with a small sentence and it got trebled for taking hostages.

I met him in Wandsworth Prison block in the mid 70s. He'd just been ghosted out of Parkhurst for taking a screw hostage. The screw retired soon after - he was a physical wreck.

I used to go on exercise with Wilkie, he was a man of few words, but I truly liked the man. But the screws were all on edge and tense whenever Wilkie's door was unlocked. He kept attacking screws and they kept attacking him. He went on a lot of drugs prescribed by the doctor to cool him down. The next I heard he's dead – a mystery death it was. They say he died in transit from Strangeways Prison to Walton jail.

He was a legend but he lived and died a lonely way. No man since Wilkie has brought so much fear - how'ay the Lads!

Billy Wilson – R.I.P.
'Punchy Wilson'

I met Billy in Full Sutton Prison; he got life in the early 70s. He was an ex-boxer a big man but an old man. I never knew at the time that Billy had cancer; he never told me or anyone else. I used to enjoy a pot of tea with Billy in his cell. On his wall he had posters of all the great boxers Marciano, Lewis, Dempsey, Johnson, Jeffries and Robinson he loved them all. The only fighter he hated in this era was Tyson.

Billy had cancer of the groin and was soon to die after I left but the day I will always remember with Punchy was the day he walked

Prison Directory

into my cell and handed me a paper cutting of years gone by and his trial, "I loved her, Chas," he said. He's kept that paper cutting all those years in a plastic folder, he'd killed the woman he loved – it was a sad story and a sad ending but Punchy Wilson went the distance.

Charles Wilson – R.I.P.
'The Gentleman'

I met Charles Wilson up in Hull Prison back in 1974. I've never met a con since who I can say could ever have the qualities Charlie had, he was an absolute gentleman, respectful, polite, genuine, and loyal and a totally lovely guy that we all loved. He was given 30 years for the great train robbery and he served his time like the man he was.

His cell was like a library, he had volumes of books, books of interest, books to learn from and he was always digesting knowledge. He was a clever man, a man that couldn't be beaten, a man who wouldn't accept defeat, a fighter all the way. Some arsehole shot him dead a couple of years ago by his swimming pool out in Spain. A right fucking liberty and a great loss to all who knew this man – a contract killing. Whoever paid did so with blood money and is a despised son of a bitch and will never be fit to clean the shoes of Charles Wilson.

Reg Wilson
'Silent Man'

This feat of strength was done in Frankland max secure jail in '93. In all my years inside Reg's the only man I know to achieve this feat. He can hold this position for 30 seconds. I only met Reg at Wakefield seg unit in '97. Sadly he was in the next cage to me but we got to see

Legends

each other on exercise. I'd heard a lot about the guy over the years like the time he got out of his cell in Frankland and made a ladder and got up on the roof. He's a silent man and says very little. He's serving natural life but I admire the guy for his mental and physical strength no drugs, no booze and no fags – hell this guy don't even look at newspapers or a fanny mag.

He trains hard everyday of his life. Even Christmas day in Wakefield he was out on the yard doing his hour-long exercise routine. He blew away my prison record for medicine ball sit-ups of 1790 in one hour by 120.

Graham Young – R.I.P.

A lot of cons will say what's he putting him in legends for, it's simply because Graham is the legend of all poisoners. I met him in Parkhurst in the 80s he was certainly not my friend and I wouldn't have trusted him with a pet rodent. He was first put away at the age of 14 and was sent to Broadmoor for poisoning his family, one member actually died.

Years later when he was released he poisoned once more. This time it was workmates and two of them died so off he went to jail for the rest of his life and in this case life means life as he died in Parkhurst in 1990. His life in prison was almost spent entirely in isolation as he kept trying to poison people all of the time. He actually attempted it in Parkhurst by putting some substance in the cons water boiler. He got both his arms broken for this attempt – he was a very dangerous man.

I believe he shouldn't have been released from Broadmoor. The doctors kept him pretty much sedated with heavy tranquillisers over the years of his incarceration. I did, however, feel compassion for Britain's number one poisoner. Obviously when he got his arms broken he deserved it but he was a very sick guy who couldn't help himself, oh yes a definite legend in his own twisted mind, one that I wouldn't invite home for Sunday lunch!

4

Officers Club

Lunch Box Blues
Parkhurst 1979

Years ago, in Parkhurst Prison, I surprised a works screw with a little present I put in his lunch box. I had a crap in my pot; it was a lovely sized turd. I wrapped it in polythene and tied a piece of red ribbon around it and a little note saying, 'Yours Truly, from the chaps.' Fucking maggot he was! Thought he was Hitler!

"I climbed Everest, I did, oh yeah!!
Gartree Prison 1989

This big fat cunt of a screw – X-rugby player X-boxer X-jungle guerrilla warfare X-S.A.S. X-Everest climber, you get the picture, full of shit! Got the walk! Got the talk! But got fuck all. He thought he would set Charlie Bronson off!

Would you believe he forgot to unlock my door. 'Forgot'. Opened the other 80 doors but forgot mine. Lucky he never lost his oxygen when he climbed Everest, eh? When he came back to open my door after I was nearly kicking it down he too went down like a bag of shit. Cowered up like a dog he did and he said, "No more, no more!" I then proceeded to kick the fat cunt down the stairs! Sadly two of his pals got involved so I had no choice but to attack them as well, at least they fought back like men. Ain't it always the way, slags start it off then others have to end it for them. Some screws are just born cowards – and liars.

Legends

Julian Broadhead
Probation Officer

This guy wrote Joe Cocker's autobiography and a great book on Sheffield, England, gang warfare. He writes under the name of JP Bean and this guy was my probation officer, but I class him as a personal friend. To me he's a legend and another chapter in my crazy world. He visited me for a number of years now and seen me happy, sad, low, high and he's also sat behind the infamous cage door of Monster Mansion to have a visit with me.

He hated a lot of the strokes pulled on me obviously though he was limited to what he could do for me to make my life more humane but what he'd done for me on more than one occasion I'll never forget. He's a loyal and honourable man, a legendary probation officer. Most probation officers give me the creeps, they're mice, they're afraid to make a stand and they're just a small piece of the system. However, with guys like Julian about it makes a big difference.

Lorraine Carroll
'Wonder Woman'

She's fit, she's strong, she's fast and can keep up with most guys in the gym and she's one of the best lady screws I've ever met. Lorraine worked at Winson Green, don't know if she's still there or what, I met her on the max secure unit and I got on great with her from the off.

She stands no shit from nobody and she tells you how it is – the truth, the facts. But under all her toughness there's a big heart and she's really a caring person who's got time for genuine cons. She helped me in many ways with good advice, gave me trust and she even seemed to know when I had a bad head.

I let her down the last time I was in the Green, as I jumped on the doctor to kidnap him. Wonder Woman wasn't on duty that day

Officers Club

but next day she come down to the block to see me...she was fuming, gave me a right telling off she did. But that's how life is.

Even though I let her down after all the work she put in to helping me I don't think she thought any the less of me. Prison life is, at times, boring and empty and it needs livening up a bit! Anyway Wonder Woman is the tops for me. I totally respect her and like her as a human being – keep up your training Lorraine, from your No 1 con, Charlie.

Mick Connell

This guy's a Parkhurst medic screw; I've known him for a long time. Some years back he lost his dear wife through cancer, it obviously cut him up bad. I left and returned some years later and there he was with his famous smile. He'd put his heart and soul into training and run marathons, worked out in the gym and stayed strong. He's a fighter and in my eyes he's a legend, his world was lost but he climbed back up to another one. Someone has to lock my door. Some do their job and it's just a job, others abuse their position, there are toe-rags in all walks of life. Mick and screws in his league are Gentleman.

Jim Dawkins
'Ex- Hardboiled Screw'

I met Jim in the maximum secure unit in Belmarsh prison in '93. He's ex-army – tough as old boots. One day he came into work smashed up with some teeth missing. It was on a

Jim in his MUFTI outfit

Legends

day my cousin, Loraine, visited me. She told him he looked like me, Jim replied, "Cor, I don't look that bad do I?" He's good stuff a true legend, always a good story to tell. Well nothing lasts forever in jail, the van arrived and it was time for me to leave for another prison. This was at a time when all my moves were made with me naked and in a body belt. I'd just wear a towel around my waist and they'd lock me in and off we went, as often as not the towel would be a waste of time, as it would drop off.

Seven screws and me would be in a cat 'A' van, some vans had cat 'A' cages in the back and others had seats. This time when Jim took me he sat next to me as one of the escort on the way to Bristol. After an hour I was feeling a bit peckish so I told Jim to look in the bag to see what the kitchen had packed up for me – it was boiled eggs. So Jim cracked a few and stuffed one in my mouth then he

Jim handing memorabilia over to Andy Jones at Crime Through Time Museum

Jim proving that ex-prison officers do have a sense of humour

152

Officers Club

gave me a swig of pop and then another egg, as the body belt's a restraint apparatus it locks on and your wrists are secured in cuffs in each hip area of the body belt. So in other words you're unable to move your arms. I'm the only con that's been in more body belts than anyone else.

Jim got himself a little carried away with them eggs and he kept on shoving them in and since my mouth was so full I couldn't really say a lot. Eventually I had to cough and a whole load of egg shot out. I said, jokingly, to Jim that he'd nearly succeeded in doing what the prison service had been trying to do to me for years – kill me.

I then told Jim to get my radio out of the box and see if he could get it working, this radio I'd had for years and years and when he was having problems pulling the aerial out of the Roberts Rambler I told him to pull it harder – he did. The whole aerial shot out of the radio and Jim looked at me sheepishly! I told him to shove it back in, as he looked a little faint.

This journey was one of the maddest ever and during the course of the journey we pulled up alongside a bus full of old people, probably going to some seaside location for a day trip. Anyway as far as I was aware the tint in the window of the van I was in was of sufficient enough strength to stop them being able to see in. I stood

Charlie and Ex-Hardboiled HM Prison Belmarsh 1996

Legends

up and waived at them but I knew they couldn't see me but fucking hell I swear I saw some of them ladies blinking. Later, when we got off, I looked at the window and it must've been my dark glasses that made it look tinted!!!!!! If any of them old dears are reading this and they can think back to seeing some geezer flashing at them from inside a van then I apologise.

Once we arrived at Bristol Prison we got out of the van and I was escorted to the block and I went straight into the strongbox and I never spoke to the Bristol screws. I shook the Hardboiled screw's hand and the door slammed up. I kept silent for 28 days, I never left the box and then I was moved on. I returned to Belmarsh some

HM Prison Belmarsh 1996

time later and Jim was still there and still as mad as ever.

Since then Jim's become an Ex-Hardboiled Screw, as he's jacked his job in due to the way he'd seen things going on. He still writes to me and was recently turned down, in spite of having no criminal record, for visiting me. The Prison Service refused his application although the police passed him!!!! They gave a load of bollocks as the reason, blah, blah. Jim came to court to give evidence on my behalf at the Phil Danielson siege trial at Luton Crown Court on St Valentine's Day in February 2000. The judge refused me permission to call him!!!!!!! Jim was prepared to spill the beans on the way the prison service had treat me and he later on was featured in a national Sunday newspaper and a daily paper spilling the beans on the Prison Service. Jim's since helped with appearing in the video documentary about me (details at the end of this book) and he has a story to tell. Jim – it's people like you that give me strength – Stay Strong.

Tanya Dent
'Sex on Legs'

I met Tanya in Belmarsh seg unit, she's one of the best lady prison officers I've ever met – she's totally fearless and full of life. I got on with her from day one cos our natures are much alike. Tanya's since left the Prison Service and gone into a new job helping youngsters, last I heard.

Tanya was on duty the day Fatso governor Carroll done adjudication on the day of Princess Diana's funeral! He was the only governor in England sitting on nickings that day; all the other jails put it off for that one day. The fat rat comes to my cell door as I was listening to the service on my radio so I gave him some verbal abuse. Tanya made it clear to him it was out of order doing this on this particular day, that's why I respect her cos she spoke up for me, as she knew I was spot on.

Most screws just play along with it all and never say a word cos: One) They're afraid to. Two) They don't wanna get in the bad books. Three) They're too brainwashed. But Tanya's a pure tiger, she fights for what's right and will stick by a con if he's right. That to me is good morals. She's a legend alright cos she's honest and calls a spade a spade.

I done her a set of cartons, which she framed and hung up in her home – she's proud of them and shows them to everybody. She was always very kind to me, gave me respect and always had a smile. Once a big con got a bit lippy through the door to her, a lot of cons were frightened of this geezer, but Tanya just opened his cell door and went in, on her own, and put him in his place! That's how she is - 100% solid. Fair but firm.

I've some fond memories of Tanya, as she made me laugh a lot. I only once ever got upset with her cos she smokes and she blew smoke in my cell door, but she never did it again cos she knows

Legends

how it affects me. Tanya knew she was safe in my presence, that's why she treat me so well and trusted me.

Legends are like that. They believe in people they trust. But to cross a legend you could be in serious trouble.

Tanya also had a legendary laugh. (Mad) Like a manic relapse, which I love. Most mad people have wonderful laughter, anyway Tanya made it into my book of Legends – and she's here to stay.

Bob Duncan
'The Computer Wizard'

Bob Duncan's a screw in Winson Green; I've known him for some years. He's just a typical screw. Don't give a crap, does his job, gets paid, it's a job. But Bob's got a brain, he taught himself to use a computer, he spent all his lunch breaks on a computer. He spent his days off in front of a computer. A lot of hard work – but it's paid off and he's now a wizard at it. He can take a computer to bits and put it back together – with his eyes closed!

I've got a lot of respect for this Wizard, as to look at him he just looks like a guy who wants to knock back 10 pints and fight the world. He probably did do that in his younger days but to become a computer wizard for me is some achievement and for that I make him a legend.

He wanted to get me on to some sort of computer course; he was even prepared to work with me himself. But I was 'high risk' and it was a no go, nobody would trust me but Bob would've given it a go and I don't forget that sort of trust placed in me. But that's how prison is. Some want to tread on your face and some want to help a guy out of a hole – nuff respect to the Computer Wizard.

Dr Ghosh

This little lady no longer works in the Prison Service; she works with ladies now – can't blame her after working so long with prisoners, something like 20 years she put in to it. I was once on a rooftop siege at Broadmoor and Dr Ghosh was called in, she shouted up to me, "Charlie, stop it and come down." Who could deny such a lovely lady her request so I obliged and came down.

Her job is to look into people's heads and see what makes them tick, she's a top psychiatrist, and she certainly helped me to

Officers Club

unwind. I remember when I was at Belmarsh in the early 90s and Dr Ghosh was called in to act as a consultant to oversee the screws were handling me right cos she'd worked with me at Broadmoor and since then she responded when I asked Steve Richards to see her for info for my autobiography, *Silent Scream*, and like any legend she helped. Dr Ghosh – I miss you.

John Howis
'The Ultimate Training Partner'

I've worked out with the toughest, hardest men in the system. Even outside I've worked with the best!! And there's none better than John Howis. I met the guy in Belmarsh seg unit; he's a screw, and a total fitness fanatic in every sense of the word. A man I admire.

He would come out on to the yard with me and work out with the medicine ball for my one-hour's exercise. I'd do 1,000 sit ups as he threw the 18 pound ball at me. Then he'd do 1,000 as I slung the ball at him!!! We worked on, me doing 100, sometimes 200, then he'd do the same – right up to 1,000. Pain, sweat! Even at times blood, as quite often the ball would slip through your hands and smash into your face! John 'never' stops, even when he goes to the prison gym he switches off from everything and everyone – and works alone.

It's a great shame he hasn't got his own gym outside, as I'd put money on it that it'd be the No 1 gym for all serious hardcore trainers. He would be the ultimate guy to work with youngsters who are heading for problems. He could work out all their aggression and direct them into a better way of life. Maybe even train up a future world champion in the boxing game.

He'd certainly give them some self-respect and liven them up a bit. He pushed me to the limit and made my life a better one. I

Legends

rate John Howis as one of the all time great trainers. No shit – he gets it done, max respect.

Chris Hunter

I despise prison doctors - I even hate psychiatrists more! They're all so false. Out of my prison I can count on one hand how many decent doctors I've met. Chris Hunter is one of these few, many are called but few are chosen. He was my shrink in Ashworth in the 80's. A great man who worked hard on cases that most had long given up on. Chris had a different approach; his way was to sit down and listen, then talk. He was the doctor who saved me; I do believe I would be long dead if it wasn't for this man.

Broadmoor and Rampton were killing me with drugs - I hated them. They were using the 'Liquid Cosh' to control me – these drugs were destroying me. Chris took me off all medication. I was later told that no patient had changed so much for the better than I did. Chris Hunter's a legend in his own profession – he took chances. Nine out of 10 times it paid off. I arrived labelled a "No Hoper", an "Incurable" and a "Dangerous violent man."

I had actually just left behind five years of HELL! Chris gave me a break, a new lease of life and it paid off. It was to be six months before I was involved in any incident. Unfortunately the incident would have me slung back into the cages but Chris proved if you treat a man well then he responds well.

Dave King

This guy's a 53-year-old prison officer, a man to be reckoned with superb fitness, healthy and full of life. He came into the prison service late in life, after 20+ years of training in gyms and competing in all sorts of fitness feats. I met him in Belmarsh max secure unit and strangely enough we look alike plus our philosophy on life and death is identical. Mr King's a gentleman with his baldhead and well-trimmed goatee beard. He travelled to work everyday on a bicycle, which was a round trip of 40 miles. He was picked by the governor to work with me whilst I was at the unit. We trained together out on the yard, he taught me many exercises I never knew and he built me up and made me a stronger person. Everyday he was working he made it his business to come and see

158

Officers Club

me and say these words, "Good to be alive, Charlie." A great man and a true friend. He held the key to my locked door but he opened up my mind.

Big Tony Lebatt

Tony's a screw I met in Belmarsh; I first met him about eight years ago in the max secure unit. He was one of the screws who was picked to be with me most of the time and he was there the day my dying father visited me, as dad walked away all knew he would die in weeks – even dad knew it too. So it was the last time I was to ever see him. Big Tony treat my dad like a lord, he even had him laughing.

The last visit, ever, from my dad

That's why I can put this man in my book of Legends; he pulled me through a bad time and it's a time that will not be forgotten by me. In time it was Tony that was part of the escort that took me to another jail in my never-ending tour of English jails. In the van I was belted up in the 'body belt' and accompanied by six screws and all the way from Belmarsh to Lincoln jail was a laugh, that's how Tony is. When I got back to Belmarsh a year or two later I found out he'd smashed his leg up bad. He still needed more operations but he came in, limping, to see me and he was still laughing – that's what makes a legend, be lucky.

Taffy 'Joker' Lewis

This screw I met at Belmarsh Prison not a single day passed by without Taffy making me laugh, a born comedian, a hard Welshman but a decent man. A lot of the cons would be walking

159

Legends

about miserable but as soon as Taffy's shift come on he would liven them up. A lot of screws are miserable gets, you'd think it was them serving the time but Taffy takes life for what it is. He's a laugh a minute but he's also a solid guy.

Andy Love

Andy was just in the wrong place at the wrong time. I've written about him in my autobiography, *Silent Scream,* so I'm not going to say a lot about him other than he was the librarian at HM Prison Woodhill, I took him hostage in '93 for eight hours. I picked him up, chucked him over my shoulder and ran with him to a cell – when I let him go I shook his hand. I got 4 years for that but I bear Andy no ill feeling. He must be a legend to survive eight hours in a cell with me, I wish him well.

John Marriott
R.I.P

The only other man I class as a governor with balls. He was slung out of Parkhurst over an escape. I got some fair treament from this governor. He once gave me a pickaxe, a shovel and wheelbarrow. When I was on my best behaviour; I'd asked him if I could make a fishpond. He at first laughed, as he thought I was joking, "No," I told him, "I'm serious." A couple of days later he called me up and said, "Yes."

I began my fishpond, I'd only had a few months left to serve and I thought if I created something to leave behind then it would be like a monument – a pond with fish is a sign of peace. A con with a troubled mind could find some comfort in a pond; just to sit down and watch fish swimming could be a relaxing thing. Let's face the facts it's better than watching walls and fences, oh and have you heard

Officers Club

about them fucking concrete sheep garden ornaments they've got inside Woodhill Prison, tell me who's mad – them or me?

I began my pond, my monument of peace. For three days I worked hard on that pond then, BANG! It all fell in like a bad omen. I was involved in an incident that resulted in four holes in my back. I was rushed to St Mary's hospital on the Island and saved. The pond was never completed but I'm told the hole is still there…empty! Maybe it's waiting for my return, maybe it's not meant to be, whatever John Marriot is a legend for allowing me a pickaxe, me Charles Bronson with a pickaxe – that was unheard of!

He was a governor just like Joe Whitty, he took chances and we, the cons, respected him for it. Obviously he wasn't always popular with a lot of the screws in fact I bet there were a lot of smiling faces when they moved him out of Parkhurst. John was made the scapegoat but he had the cons' respect. I bet there won't ever be another governor in Parkhurst Prison to be as humane as he was. Sadly John is no longer with us, a dinosaur from long ago with old values.

Governor Masserick

I picked this chap up on the exercise yard up in Frankland maximum secure prison in 1990 and carried him into the wing office for a little chat about my parole. Mr Masserick was the Deputy Governor at that time and after this incident he was soon promoted. Good luck to him. Any governor taken hostage by Charles Bronson (me) is a cert for a nice bit of promotion or a lump sum pay off.

He acted like a man and behaved himself and has no shame. (Unlike Governor Adrian Wallace who I took hostage – he was a cry baby, a little mouse and a coward, I got seven years for him. He wasn't worth seven seconds of my life. He's a coward who attacked me when I was held down by a whole load of clowns.)

Governor Masserick is a complete legend; I respect and wish him well. But I would say – you should go on a diet as you was rather heavy to run about with over my shoulders!

Mr Murgatroyd

He's a physical training officer at Belmarsh Prison and a right nice

Legends

guy. He goes back a long way and has worked with anyone who's anyone and I'd say one of the nicest PTI's (Physical Training Instructor) I've ever met. Always helpful and always a fair man, you can't ask for no more than that. Now in his late 50s and still a fit man. A younger screw upset me over something he'd promised to do, I got right upset over it and Mr Murgatroyd sorted it out and bollocked the screw. He said, "When you give your word, keep it. If you can't then explain why but don't wind Charlie up, don't say something you don't mean." That's how he works – straight. No pussy footing about be honest. I know many cons that speak highly of this man so you keep it up Mr Murgatroyd till you retire.

Murphy

This screw I met in Winson Green (See they ain't all bad at Winson Green.) then later in Walton jail. Murphy was just in the job for a pay packet. He's the type of screw who gets no pleasure out of banging cons up. To him it's just a job but he's more than just a 'screw'.

He's worked hard on writing a play! It's all about prison and I believe in time it'll be a big thing – maybe a film or TV series. Who else better to write a play about prisons than a screw? The screws see it all, hear it all and have it all to handle. Job experience of this kind could and would help any such play. People are fascinated by stories from prisons and I honestly believe Murphy will become legendary over his play script. Like anything else it takes time, I told him not to give up on it – hope he hasn't?

When the right time comes he could be made for life, as one big pay off leads to two! That's how Coronation Street started and all the other big dramas. The Bill was originally written by an ex-copper till he wouldn't conform to the arty farty brigade at the BBC and they manipulated him off the show. So right now Murphy isn't a full pedigree legend but I've slipped him in early cos that's how sure I am of him and his abilities in helping him become a playwright.

"GO FOR IT MURPHY". As I told you from day one, there's more to life than banging up doors for the next 25 years. With a sense of humour as mad as yours I know you're on to a winner, so keep the pen going. A good play can make you rich over night – go for gold.

Officers Club

Big Bob Richards
'The Chair Man'

Big Bob Richards was a screw in Brixton in the 80s when I was there on the special unit. He was a always a fair man, if you were entitled to something then he'd make it his business to see you got it. I next met him in the block in Belmarsh some years later. Whilst in the block, if I was out, I'd walk past the office and see Bob sitting in the chair and it became a joke. I'd say, "You'll end up getting stuck in that chair." So I done a cartoon of him stuck in the chair, so it became legendary – the 'Chair Man' was created.

Bob's a good man and many years ago, like myself, he was one of the original skinheads. Those were the days when a good punch up was what it was all about unlike the goons of today putting drugs into their veins. The skins were a smart mob with a style long since gone.

Sandy Shaw

Sandy taught me how to use a computer in Belmarsh Prison; she's one of the nicest people I've ever met inside of prison. I'd say she was a legend for all her patience and determination she applied to me.

A lot of teachers won't even come near me (Sorry Phil (Phil Danielson) didn't mean you.), as I'm a serial hostage taker. But Sandy knew I'd never harm her in any way – mentally or physically, as I'd never harm a woman or a child. I'd rather top myself before I ever done that.

That could be the answer to how I could be handled inside of prison, one woman could boss me about all day long, but 60 screws in MUFTI gear would have to carry me out before I behaved myself if they wound me up, which they're good at doing.

Sandy put a lot of trust in me and I repaid her with politeness and kindness. I say to all cons in Belmarsh, if you end up on Sandy's computer class please treat her with respect and you'll learn so much from her. Yes, Sandy, you made it into this legendary book; you're now a legend! Don't know what you're doing right now but stay strong. That's a lot to live up to but you've earned it – thanks for all you've taught me.

Legends

Judge Temple

This judge gave me three years for a GBH charge. Any other judge would've given me 10 years. It was 1985; I'd just cut up Mervyn Horley, in Ashworth Special Hospital. When Judge Temple gave me three years I almost fainted. He had to go into my legends; there had never been a judge in the history of my court appearances ever to treat me so well. I think he could see through all the mist. Obviously he never condoned my violence but he could see why I cut Horley up. Those three years should've taught me, as this man gave me a chance, but I never realised it at the time. If you ever read this, your honour, it will probably amaze you I chose to put you down as a legend but that's what you are – a judge in a million. I never forget a real man of respect; you're a good man.

Big Tommo

Tommo is a screw in Woodhill Prison, built like a brick shithouse. He looks an awesome character but take it from me he's a gentleman, one first class decent screw. When things hot up at Woodhill and they have to put on the riot gear many screws see it as a way of flexing their muscles to show how hard they are, their whole presence changes. The walk, the stance they even give the eyeball technique, the chewing gum, the old shoulders seem to get bigger, they're just a bunch of faceless nobodies pretending to be somebody but guys like Tommo don't need to act it or give it the large cos he can do the bizz he don't need a dozen men behind him. He actually looks embarrassed at times of pressure cos Tommo is the same all the time.

Guys like Tommo don't belong in these places, he sticks out. Being a screw isn't an easy job, I'd say it was the worst type of job to do simply as it's dealing with human life and many screws do try to do a fair job but some can't clean the likes of Tommo's shoes. Putting riot gear on and opening a con's cell door 10 handed don't make you a hard bastard if anything it makes you gutless. You may well kick 10 bells of shite out of us but on your own you're gutless. You should take a leaf out of Tommo's book and be a real man. Tommo chucked it in with regards working on the zombie units and I'm pleased to say he's working as a normal screw. Good on him – collect your pension mate and tell them to stuff it.

Officers Club

Governor Outram

For a prison governor to get a mention in legends is a rare thing, as most of them I see as my enemy. I trust them about as much as they trust me but there are the exceptional ones and this one is a legend for sure. A brave man, a man I respect, I knew Governor Ourtram up in Leeds (Armley) jails 25 years ago when he was just a young screw and he became governor of Belmarsh Prison and he's a fair man who believes in giving a con a fair chance. He stuck his neck out for me when no other governor did or would. He worked hard for me against all odds, he got me some gym, he got me some trust and he earned not just my respect but also the whole of Belmarsh jail's trust. It's a great pity that there aren't a lot more men like him in the system. He's seen it all, had it all and done it all. He was once a hard man and I mean fucking hard. I've had some tough times in his old block up in Leeds but he was always a fair man. It takes bottle to go up against the majority, and he did it with me – yes he's a legend alright. It's crazy how the world is!!! Years ago I would've tore the guys head off, now I'd buy him a pint and that's how legends come about. Respect, Mr Outram.

Stuart Palmer

I first met this screw in '93 at Woodhill Prison (Through my spy hole in my cell door.) He was one of the negotiators in one of my hostage sieges! I never knew him and never met him again till '98. But when I did I shook his hand, as he's a gentleman a decent man with a heart of gold. If all screws were like this guy I would never be in prison today. He's what I call a fair man and it's men like him that are a credit to the Prison Service – total respect.

Bill Peacock

This guy was a Broadmoor screw! I say 'was' because he was sacked! Bill's a man's man, an ex-squaddie and a bloke who likes a pint - straight from the army into Broadmoor. But he wasn't cut out for it. He once told me: "This is a mug's job." He hated locking us up, he also hated a lot of the other screws and he often had verbal rows with them.

Then one day he let loose and kicked a screw in the bollocks.

Legends

The screw he kicked was a rat – he went running to grass Bill up! Poor old Bill got the sack. Well if Bill Peacock should ever read this I'll tell you the truth. A lot of screws were gutted over it and so were a lot of loons. The rat you kicked I personally never ever spoke to him and I can tell you that a lot of the other screws didn't either. I believe he later retired. You're a good man, Bill, a man I respected, a man I've never forgot – take care mate. PS – You made my day that day, what a rat he was.

Robert Taylor

This guy's gonna be famous after this. Although not a legend amongst solicitors he's a legend cos he took it on the chin and didn't press charges. As I grabbed him hostage in Bullingdon prison in '96 I grabbed his pen and put it to his ear and told him I'd push it into his brain if he upset me. It's a long story but basically he wasn't my appointed brief and it took me by surprise seeing this geezer in the room instead of my usual lawyer.

This is the stuff legends are made from and I've immortalised him with a moment of madness and to top it all...he refused to press charges or make a statement against me. That's a real legend for you – Respect.

Joe Whitty

Some cons will be saying "Why the fuck are you putting another prison governor in your book of Legends?" Well it's simple – Joe Whitty is a legend. I'll always give a legend a mention in my book, Joe's a chapter of my life, he's a governor with balls, a man I respect and admire. I met him at Long Larten Prison, he gave me something at that time which hadn't been given to me by any governor (although since I can name a few more that have), which was respect and trust.

Officers Club

Sadly I let Joe down and I caused him some serious problems. I totally lost my mind and turned violent I smashed up a wing and hurt some guys. I was restrained in the body belt and shipped out fast. I was going through a difficult phase in my life at that time it was difficult to come to terms with who I was. I later went mad in another jail, I was losing control; I was heading back to the mad house. Joe Whitty came to see me in his own time and at his own expense. He talked to me and helped me see sense; he was a human being, a man of pride. I hear he's still governing, if so give this guy some respect.

5

Civvy Street

Gerry Adams – MP
President of Sinn Fein

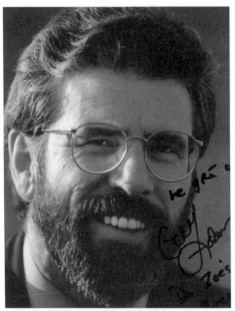

My attitude towards Gerry changed the moment I found out that it was Mo Mowlem, the former Northern Ireland Secretary, who authorised the bugging of Gerry's car. She could've caused World War 3 by what she allowed to take place. I mean look at the commotion about a few leaked emails from Tony Blair's office and they forget to say about the car bugging scam, so they're a two faced mob.

Gerry's gonna end up a legend out of all of this and could end up Lord Provost of all Ireland. I haven't singled Gerry out just to get publicity cos I'm already winning in the popularity poll between Jack Straw and me. Gerry's fought for what he believed in and there's nobody can say he hasn't fought, he's fought the system for being suppressed, he's fought the system over censorship, he's fought the system of torture, he's fought the system full of corruption, he's fought lies, and he's come out a winner, give the guy a chance.

I've been doing the same for years and years and it's people like

Civvy Street

Gerry that give me the drive to go on.

Okay I ain't got the manpower Gerry's got but it's building up out there and with enough persuasion I can get things moving just like Gerry's been able to do. When there's peace in Ireland and all them what was killing each other are sitting in the same parliament building getting paid for making peace they'll wonder what took them so long to get it on – Gerry, you're a born leader. **Website: www.irlnet.com/sinnfein**

Timothy Bavin

Timothy was the Bishop of Portsmouth and back in the 80s he was visiting Albany jail on the Isle of Wight. As usual I was in isolation and on a six man unlock! I was considered so unpredictable I

wasn't even allowed to go to church, as sometimes I would go of my own accord.

The Bishop met a lot of cons up on the wing and some of them said to him, "Why don't you go down to the seg unit to meet Charlie?" Being the great man he is he asked the governor if he could see me, which was a very brave thing for him to want to do, as I'm Britain's number one serial hostage taker, if you haven't already guessed.

So the governor and security staff brought the Bishop down into the depths of the prison isolation unit and my door unlocked.

There standing before me was a Bishop and the first thing that hit me was his 'Ruby Ring' it was a massive stone, bright red. I said to him, "That's worth a few bob," as I nodded towards his hand.

What a lovely man he was, pleasant, kind and such a warm

169

personality. It actually did pass my mind to grab him but that was only because I was living a very empty existence and I really only wanted some companionship. But I knew I couldn't be so cruel so I fought the urge off.

I believe he's now a member of the House of Lords but for me Timothy Bavin's a true legend for entering the belly of the beast and blessing me, not many people get to be blessed by a Bishop while banged up in prison. It was a great moral boost for me when at a time I was slipping deeper and deeper into a black hole. Thank you timothy! Although it was nearly two decades ago I remember it like yesterday – God Bless you Father.

'B' is for Bertha

There ain't a better friend a man could want than his medicine ball. Bertha's been with me for more years than I care to remember and she's the tops, never let me down yet. I remember when I was free, yeah it was a long time ago, Bertha and me stayed on a caravan site for a few weeks and I was with Jan Lamb. Jan had a leather skirt and I loved to see her in it, but Bertha was getting a bit lonely cos Jan kept hiding her in all sorts of places so I got Jan's skirt, tore it up and made a little coat for her. Jan asked me where her favourite skirt was, "Bertha's got it on," I replied. You should've seen Jan's face when I opened the cupboard door and showed her Bertha!!!!!!!

I held the prison medicine ball sit up record, for a short while, 1,790 in one hour. Bertha's been around, would you believe someone kidnapped her from Jan Lamb's garden shed. They left

Civvy Street

Me, Bertha & my Dad (Belmarsh 1994)

a ransom note and at first Jan thought they wanted £500 for Bertha's safe return but when she looked closer the ransom was for £50,000!!!!!!!!!!!! Fucking hell, there ain't that much money in the world.

Dave Courtney came in on this one and within days the word had spread and Dave had recovered Bertha.

All I've gotta say to Dave is a big THANK YOU cos Bertha and me we've been through a lot together. Bertha's in a safe place now - till we meet again, Bertha.

Henry Boxer Gallery

Anyone interested in my artwork can get ready for an exhibition that'll be shown at the Boxer Gallery for 'Outsider' artists like myself. Proceeds from my artwork goes into *Bronson's Children*, my new fund for humanitarian needs. Steve Richards, my manager for all civilian affairs, is working hand in hand with the Boxer Gallery and hopefully you'll get to see some of my art. The gallery's worth taking a look at cos it features all sorts of weird and wonderful pieces – right up my street. See the gallery at 98 Stuart Court, Richmond Hill, Surrey, England or visit their **Website: www.outsiderart.co.uk**

Jeanne Calment

I read an article about this old lady back in 1995 while looking for something to read when I was banged up in the block. If she isn't a legend then what is she? Jeanne's a free legend and what a great legend at 120 years old! And look at that cigarette in her hand.

171

Legends

I read that Jeanne used to live next door to Vincent Van Gogh and she remembered the night he chopped his ear off, so she's seen it all. As soon as I read it I said to myself, "She's gotta go inside this book cos she can teach us all a thing or two," God Bless you Jeanne on behalf of all of us living legends we all look up to you as the Queen of Legends.

Fidel Castro

CASTRO AND me ARe BROTHERS
KINDA ResPect THe GUY..
He BeLieves iN ALL He Does
A MAN UNTiL He Die
"ResPecT"

CUBA   LUTON

Yeah, I'd love to meet the geezer

I think this guy's brilliant, don't he look like me, or what? I mean the way he fucked them yanks off over his country, Cuba. He stands for strength and in my book that makes him a legend. A

tiny country like Cuba put the shits up President JF Kennedy, thought they were gonna have to bring out the nuclear bomb for such a small country cos Russia stepped in.

Now look at Cuba, a good place to holiday from what I hear and they've even supposed to have banned that paedophile Gary Glitter from the place – hope so and I know my old pal, Fidel, will have seen to keeping the place clean of scum like Glitter.

172

Civvy Street

I mean we've got Bacardi and Cuban cigars because of Cuba and now we've got a place that's gonna shake the world when it fills up with tourists. Drop Fidel a line and tell him how much you like him cos he's a soul brother and like me he's been fighting a dirty big system all his life, he's never gonna give up and when he's dead they'll make a film about this guy – so why wait to carve his name on a stone. Write to him at: Palacio Del Gobierno, Habana, Cuba – tell him your old china, Charlie, gave you the address.

Uncle Jack Cronin
R.I.P.

My uncle Jack for me was the boss man. He lived twelve floors up in a block of flats in Luton I loved him to bits and he loved me too. I lived with the boss for a short spell after my first 14 years away. I was lost to the world outside; I had nothing and knew very little. I had no real motive in my life only crime and violence. Jack helped  me one hell of a lot and he gave me back my true being, he made me believe in myself. We had some sure times together – times that'll remain inside my heart till it stops beating.

We'd walk the short distance up to the Moakes pub, in Luton, Marsh Farm and stand at the bar together, Jack on his whisky and me on my vodka. He was a proud man, a legend that was known in Luton for his honourable ways. Jack was actually born in East London but in the war years the family moved out of the East London blitz and come to Luton.

I got nicked over an armed robbery on a jeweller's shop, on that sentence I lost track I was in the block at Wandsworth jail and I was told Jack had died. They, the prison, refused my request to attend his funeral, saying I was just too unpredictable and violent, that hurt me but Jack remains in my heart as a legend, a man I looked upto. I was in Broadmoor with Ronnie Kray when his dear old mum,

Legends

Violet, died. Jack Cronin attended her funeral to show his and my respect to a great lady, which about sums up this legend, a man of honour, I miss him very dearly and always will. R.I.P. God Bless you, Jack.

Michael Fagan

This guy, in 1982, breached the Queen's security at Buckingham palace and he decided he was gonna see the Queen after he'd had a fall out with his wife and job problems. So there he was, in the early hours of the morning, he climbed over the railings around the palace, instinctively made his way into the palace and into the Queen's bedroom, barefooted, sat down on the end of her bed, picked up an ashtray, broke it and threatened to slit his wrists.

Since Liz is my landlady with the golden chair I've got cause to have concern over this incident. I mean it must've been a nightmare waking up to see someone as ugly as Fagan sitting there, he looked like Freddy Kruger. But Her Majesty kept her calm and managed to get Fagan to give himself up to the police. I mean what if Phil had of walked in, what would he have thought of Liz, "Oh yeah, Liz, what you up to?" But as it happens Phil sleeps in a separate bedroom.

Fagan got nutted off under the Mental Health Act and as far as I know he's now free, he would've been called the Six Million Dollar Loon if he'd walked off with Liz's jewellery but since it's all kept under lock and key he settled for a quick chat.

I've put Fagan here cos he's more guy to be pitied and he didn't harm the Queen, maybe a bit of a mad prank, you know like the guy who threatens to jump off the bridge.

Mohamed Al Fayed
'The British Gentleman'

I've gone off my normal path cos this geezer's the greatest guy to

174

Civvy Street

come forward and speak what he thinks and don't forget he lost a son – Dodi. He's always claimed that the British Government wanted Diana out of the way and that Prince Philip is a Nazi, we're talking about a sane man here who's had his phones bugged by the Government and has had to fight the system for British Citizenship, which they've refused him, he's even had one of his Royal Warrants taken away from him, the good old Queen Mother, though, has stuck by him by still ordering her china from Harrods store in London.

Al Fayed's a legend cos he told the truth when he said that Dodi had bought an engagement ring for Diana, with her blessing, yet Trevor Rees-Jones said the ring was a myth?! How come then that a jeweller in France, Claude Roulet, has a written receipt for that engagement ring for £60,000 and video footage shown in a national UK Sunday newspaper showed Dodi was in the shop on a particular date and that the jeweller confirmed he met both Dodi and Diana so she could choose a ring.

Reece-Jones slags off the ring as a myth, yet he allowed Dodi and Diana to get in the car and didn't even question the fact that they weren't wearing seat belts even though the car was gonna be in a high speed getaway from the paparazzi? Reece-Jones is full of shit and he knows it, fair do he's suffered and I don't wanna take that away from the guy but he wasn't a classy bodyguard and he didn't do his job properly.

How come Jones can't remember fuck all, has he tried therapy, how come at the moment before impact he can remember nothing from that? Not surprising is it then that I've found out from some tasty characters that if this Fiat Uno was in the tunnel in front of the chauffeur driven Mercedes that Diana and Dodi were in and it was a Secret Service carry on then it would've been fitted with a stop light on/of switch – now how's that for the truth. I mean Jones admits he had to look at a Bus Stop map of an area they were lost in to see where the fuck they were when Dodi and Diana went out shopping – on foot. Come on, the mother of the next King of England goes shopping and her bodyguard lets her go walkies and they get lost? Any good bodyguard would've had his radio and mobile phone to get help.

If that Uno was in the tunnel ahead of the Mercedes then it braked sharp while the stop lights were switched off, hence the white paint on the Mercedes from an Uno. The Merc hit the Uno

Legends

and veered to the side and that was that, along with a bright light of a good few thousand-candle powers blinded the driver of the Merc to make it really go off course. What about when Lawrence of Arabia died when his motorbike crashed – wasn't that down to the Secret Service, so if what Al Fayed says is to be believed about this plot to kill Diana then what I've found out can only add to his beliefs. I mean can you imagine if Diana was pregnant like they say she was, can you imagine the tie in to the Middle East and the way things would've changed.

Listen Al Fayed's no mug, men like him don't say things for publicity, they don't need to, why do you think the Government will not allow him to become a British citizen?

And that plonker James Hewitt was bragging about how he went into a bender and went to the very same tunnel where Diana was killed in and drove the same model Merc, after drinking a couple of bottles of wine, and drove at 120mph with four lady friends. He went through that tunnel and he says it proves the crash was rigged and the road was straight – no bends in it. Hewitt was concerned that the crash was rigged, was he? Then why didn't he keep his fat mouth shut instead of bragging about what he and Diana got up to, or was he paid to spill the beans so as to discredit Diana?

All I know is that Al Fayed's a good man, he helps countless charities, he even helps a baby hospice I've done drawings for and he lets the homeless borrow suits from Harrods to help them with job interviews. Al Fayed knows what it's like to lose your dignity and by helping the homeless he's worthy of a knighthood at least but the plonkers wouldn't give him one would they cos they're shit

scared of him. What about the chauffeur of the Merc, Henri-Paul, one blood test says he was okay and the other, some while later showed he was over the top?

Al Fayed tried to get the shite that Jones had ghost written for him for his book banned from going into a newspaper, he knew it was shite and that's the whole point, we all wanted to know about what happened at the moment or the moment before the impact, but how come he just can't remember – too easy ain't it.

Sir Mohamed Al Fayed

Mohamed hasn't been listened to when

Civvy Street

he says Jones didn't follow set down security procedures – too right he didn't. I make Mr Fayed a legend cos of what he's fought for and what he's said and cos he's a true British Gentleman. Okay they don't like what he stands for but they've got themselves to blame for taking 'cash for questions'. Proving how corrupt the whole system is. If the system had of come out of it cleanly then maybe what Al Fayed says about the murder of Diana and Dodi might not have been as solid – me, I believe him.

David Ford
'The Bond Man'

This man might as well be called Johnny Innocent cos he is INNOCENT. The police fitted him up. Sir Paul Condon, former boss of the Metropolitan Police Force, has failed to appear at court and defied two court subpoenas served on him!!!!!!!!!!!!!!! I'd love to tell it all but Dave's got a MASSIVE case going against the police at the moment. I've a question for Straw ov London (Jack Straw), "How come there's one law for the police and one law for the public???"

This case proves it. Dave had to put up with the police perverting the course of justice, committing perjury and stealing items from him, yes the Metropolitan Police are accused here of been thieving lying bastards. Dave got two years inside for handling stolen paintings? But you see those paintings were never stolen and they now hang in someone else's home when they should be in Dave's. But that's not the main part of this!

The police raided Dave's home and took bearer bonds worth several hundred thousand pounds away. And do you know what the police did; they booked half down to him and pocketed the rest of them. A police officer, Duncan Mark Hanrahan spills the beans on fellow police officer Nigel Grayston of the Regional Crime Squad. Hanrahan says in a statement that he was told directly from Grayston that he and a load of other officers were gonna cash the

Legends

remaining bonds that weren't logged to Dave on the property sheet. Since then Dave' started his own legal proceedings and up to now no less than 32, yes that's 32, London based lawyers have chucked the case as fast as they'd drop a hot potato, all fucking cabbage brains frightened of the law.

One hero was recommended to take the job on and that one person is the only person who's employed in the legal profession in the UK who's not frightened to tackle this sort of case, all the other solicitors who dropped the case are knob heads and in fact I might name them in Vol. 2 of Legends, that'd be a right laugh, eh? The guy on the case now is my lawyer, T. Go get 'em!

So up to now Dave's been fitted up by the Metropolitan Police, had art and bearer bonds stolen from him by the Metropolitan Police and I say to Straw ov London, "What are you gonna do about it?" Give the man his bonds and artwork back and do a Queen's Pardon. Cos if you don't get it sorted then it's gonna be splattered all over and names named and that's not blackmail, that's a promise! The judge what gave Dave time should be horse whipped, Condon should be horse whipped, the 32 lawyers who dropped the case should be horse whipped and the police who nicked his stuff should be shot with Sutcliffe's shit.

Ian Freeman
'The Machine'

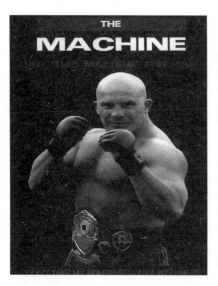

Ian, 33, from County Durham, England is known as one of the toughest men on the streets, in the ring he's known as one of the toughest men in the country. He easily beat the world champ in a Vale Tudo bout. They wear thin padded gloves and can do anything except, fishhook, gouging and kicking in the balls or biting, other than that anything goes! This makes him one of the toughest men in the world. I'd put him amongst the top five in the world for being a hard case.

Civvy Street

Ian's fighting career began around 13 years ago, he started as a boxer and he was quick to realise he had an ability to knock people out. Working in Sunderland as a doorman from an early age he had several hundred street fights - winning them by any means necessary. His fierce reputation as a fighting machine was soon established creating a reputation that would precede him.

Ian began his martial arts training in Ju Jitsu and he's now the Intercontinental Vale Tudo Champ. Vale Tudo being Portuguese for 'Anything Goes'. He got that far in the professional ranks in only 8 months and is now poised to conquer the world by fighting his way all the way to the top. To win the British rules championship he destroyed his first of three opponents in just 9 seconds!

This guy hits like a ten ton truck and can kick like a mule and as well as that he can fight like a lion. Ian's gonna go places and I reckon he'll outdo Vinnie Jones if he can get into films.

Living by a simple 'fuck' or 'be fucked' motto his name commands respect from those that've crossed him. He says, "Don't take my politeness as a weakness – so don't take the piss." It was only recently that Ian took up my Solitary Fitness training regime to help hone his already toughened physique; he tells me it's helped him – I'm happy to sponsor this sort of Iron Ambassador. I know Ian's got a book, his autobiography, coming out early next year, all about his fight to get to the top and I understand that if a film's made about my life behind bars then Ian's co-ordinating the fight scenes and he'll be doing some of the stunts.

He was invited to Charlie Kray's funeral and stayed with Dave Courtney while in London so it looks like Ian's made it into the big name circuit – Ian, whatever you do, do it well old son. **Website: www.totalmartialarts.co.uk**

Legends

Andy Jones

Jim Dawkins, wife of Needles, Needles, T, Andy Jones

Andy's got the biggest private collection of crime memorabilia in the world and part of that includes items relating to me, your old china, the watch I got from the Krays is in the display Andy's got on me. Andy, like me, is a bit of a celebrity cos when he opened his museum he had a lot of trouble from the local councillors. What does it come to when a museum in London gets £17m lottery funding for a display about the Holocaust and Andy's museum gets fuck all? Andy's got a massive Holocaust display that knocks spots off the museum in London what got the funding. So what's going on?????????

All the chaps are featured in the place and they all know Andy personally, it's a place I can't wait to see. Andy visits me regularly and every time we meet he tells me something new about the museum and what he's got planned. For a guy who was a former punk and a member of a band he's come a long way and what he's done is nothing short of legendary. Who would have the balls to put on the displays he's got on show, no one! He takes no shit from the planning officers and he's won a few court battles against them and he was even accused of being a gypsy, no disrespect to gypsies, gypsies are nice people and if that's what they meant then fine.

Andy, mate, we all love what you're doing – keep the shop window on display and don't worry about those bastards in the planning office – I hear one's retiring! Crime Through Time Museum, Newent, Gloucestershire, England. Tel: 01531 - 821888 **Website: www.crimethroughtime.com**

Civvy Street

Tahir Khan
'Simply T best'

T in Kosovo with some of the orphans he helped

This guy is the dog's bollocks when it comes to legal representatives and half as much piled on top of that again. He's only recently come into my camp and since then he's rattled a few cages within the Home Office, so much so that he even had his car bugged by them nice people in MI5$\frac{1}{2}$ or similar sorts.

The establishment are a little concerned over how he handles things cos even governor Yeomans at Woodhill Prison refused him access to seven inmates that T wanted to call as witnesses in my appeal – naughty, naughty, governor! Then there was a bust up in Woodhill when T arrived and the screws told him he couldn't take any money through with him on the orders of gov Yeomans!!!

T still took the money past the first checkpoint but then the second lot of wallies wouldn't let T in if he took the money, and do you know why he wanted the money? He wanted to buy me a drink from a vending machine, that's all but that rat Yeomans wouldn't allow him.

T then got in after chucking his money in a bin; bet the screws were fighting each other to get to it! T gets into the visits room and then he makes his move, I mean talk about me doing things! T told the screws we weren't coming out of the room till I got my chocolate and pop from the vending machine and if they wanted to bring in the MUFTI squad then that was okay with him, Governor Keeler (with a big 'G' cos he's got some brains, as opposed to Yeomans) came on the job and to save a lot of bother he pulled out his own money and bought the chocolate and pop from the vending machine. Now what other man could get me on a visit and get the gov to buy me the drinks and chocs, only T could've done that.

The story doesn't end there with T cos what a lot of people don't know is that he was threatened by a gang of idiots when he went to northern Albania/Kosovo to give money he'd collected to the children. What he did was uncalled for and he deserves a knighthood at the very least. He collected money and paid his own airfare over there and distributed $10 per child and $20 per family till the money ran out. Some unsavoury characters tried to rob T, but he wasn't daft, as he'd put the money down his Y-fronts.

The bandits come up to him and demanded the money he had on him, all T had in his pocket was $500 and he refused to hand it over but he was outnumbered and rather than risk any heavy trouble he handed the $500 over - wish I'd been there!!!! Okay they got $500 but they didn't get the $5,000 down T's Y-fronts.

So when I stood up in Luton Crown Court, after I'd been given my life sentence in the Phil Danielson kidnapping trial, and said to the judge that I was appointing Mr T as my new legal representative everyone thought I'd gone mad. Steve Richards put him on my case and all what I've gotta say about T is that I'd rather have him in my corner than the prosecution's corner.

This man's truly untainted by the seedy legal profession – no backhanders from barristers for him, no bungs from the prosecution to get him off the case or a favour in asking him to give them an easy ride – he's an 'Untouchable' and he's the best there is. There've only ever been one or two really outstanding legal reps over the years. Barrington Black from Yorkshire and a guy from the north of England, he's dead now though. Since Barrington Black's now a judge that only leaves T out of the whole of the UK who I'd let touch my cases.

Something new has come out of all of this, yeah there's always a silver lining in my concrete coffin. T's helping set up a fund for me called *Bronson's Children* (The Humanitarian Relief Fund). What it will do is to help people, cos I'm the Daddy it's called *Bronson's Children*, and anyone that needs real help will get it, fuck these charities that use 89% for administration and only 11% goes to the cause.

I mean I bet you don't see them directors of *Barnardos* or *Oxfam* and the likes running around in old banger cars – they get a good

Civvy Street

screw out of all the money coming in.

We want just about all of the money coming in to go to the people in need and who better to check that it does than T. So start getting them old £50 notes out and send them to my publisher's address for Bronson's Children or a big fat cheque will do.

Did you hear about *Children in Need* turning down money from the proceeds of a CD just cos the likes of Joe Pyle and Tony Lambrianou had helped out – fucking hypocrites. Any money from you will do, we don't give a fuck if it's from the Great Train Robbery cos people in need want your help now. Many thanks to Tracey Pearce, Bronsonmania Fan Club member, for being the first one to contribute £100 when she bought a pair of my cufflinks I put up for sale. That's £100 to help the 'real' needy.

(Left) Dave Courtney   T - A man for all seasons

Every Koestler Award prize money I've ever had went to a charity and all the proceeds I would've been entitled to from book deals involving Mirage Publishing and Steve Richards goes into that side of things. I don't pocket any money; all my drawings and cartoons have raised £000's for charities over the years. My aim is to become involved as much as possible in this side of things and to help whenever I can so when I'm free that's gonna be my life, I'm gonna travel around the world and the UK raising money for

Legends

Bronson's Children and I want T to be at my side when I'm out to do this with me.

Whitemoor Prison haven't, up to date, allowed me any art materials, thank gov Perry of Whitemoor and Peter Atherton, Head of the CSC Units, Prison Service HQ for this. I think they feel they want to deprive the needy of my artwork cos they all know what my arts done for charitable causes over the years.

Kate Kray

I'd decided to put Kate in this book long ago, long before she became an established writer. Kate, for those of you who don't know, was married to Ronnie Kray, you can tell why Ronnie fancied her by looking at the photo, she's a still a good looker now and that's what makes a legend – looks and brains. She's come a long way since co-writing *Pretty Boy*, my good pal Roy Shaw's life story. Kate's on to her fifth book now and when she visited me in Woodhill Prison I was stunned with her charm and the respect she showed me, after all she'd met a few characters while Ron was alive and since then, so I guess any fear factor was gone before she even got through the prison doors and her charm never left me for days afterwards.

She's had a tough ride and cos of her connection to Ron it hasn't been easy for her but she's managed to reach up and touch the rainbow out of it all.

The first person to admit that Ronnie was mad is Kate, she's got no airs and graces when it comes to that side of life but she's also a mean tiger, with a wicked sense of humour and loves spending time on boats, so I hear. Kate – keep smiling, keep them pearly whites in good shape.

Civvy Street

John Leaworthy
'The Chaplin'

I know what you're gonna think, "I thought Charlie didn't like sky pilots?" You're exactly right, I don't but there's always the exception to the rule and to show what an open minded guy I am here's a guy I met in Full Sutton jail; he was the prison chaplain and he showed me a lot of respect, I liked the guy. I once (or twice) had a smash-up and somebody told him that I'd smashed my flask and radio. John bought me a new one. I never forgot that.

He later got kicked out of the jail as he'd got a bit close to one of the women chaplains. So it tells you all that he's only human and being a chaplain he wasn't doing anything wrong – it's allowed but you know what prisons are like. Anyway this man didn't deserve such treatment.

I gave him this painting as a token of respect and anybody who knows me knows I'm a very touchy guy when it comes to giving my painting away. (They have to be special people.) John Leaworthy's special! Whatever you're doing now, John, my best wishes mate.

Jacqui Lilliott

I actually took this photo myself in the Grovesnor Hotel, in Park Lane, London. It's a long story but if you check out Mark Lilliot's write up in the 'Prison Directory' chapter it'll explain more. I didn't have the support team behind me when I was free and I lost the plot so very much and if it were now I know I'd be handcuffed (mentally) to a good team I've got waiting out there to give me the strength I need. People like Joe Pyle Snr., Andy Jones of Crime Through Time Museum, Steve Richards, James Nicholson, Tony Lambrianou, Reece Huxford, Jim Dawkins (Ex-Hardboiled screw), John Lodge and a whole boatload of other people that it would

Legends

take another book just to name them, but they all know who they are. Watch out for *Legends Vol.2.*

These two legends, though, are very much locked in my heart. They gave me so much in my short spell of freedom...more than they ever realise. Even though it never lasted and I soon ended up back inside jail. But I owe these two so much for their kindness towards me – never will be forgotten.

Jacqui and her husband Mark

Lord 'Frank' Longford

Me, your old china, and Lord Longford (Belmarsh 1996)

Civvy Street

Lord Longford is 95 years old, he still writes books, he goes jogging, he works in the house of lords and he travels thousands of miles in a week just to see people in prison, he's been my friend since 1989 and he's visited me in many jails throughout the country and he wrote a chapter on me in his book, *Prisoner or Patient*, he's also been on TV speaking up for me when everyone's condemned me, I've learned to love Lord Longford, as I believe in him. He's a legend alright and don't nobody doubt it, he's lived a marvellous life and even at his age he's just had another book out called *Lord Longford's Prison Diary (1995-99)*. In that book he gives a good account of how he met me and the things what've happened over that time.

The Rt Hon the Earl of Longford KG PC

5th January 2000

Thank you ever so much for your much appreciated letter and the lovely Peace Wish. We have all got separate gifts. You have won prizes for your art which are far beyond my compass. I have struggled along in public life. Who knows which is chosen the better part.

I have always felt that there was a instinctive friendship between us. I only repeat my promise that if it is humanely possible I will appear on your behalf wherever it may be.

From The Right Hon the Earl of Longford KG PC

He's one of my favourite visitors as he forever makes me laugh and we forever go on laughing, only once were we sad and that was when I wasn't allowed out of the cage for a visit, as I was considered too dangerous so Frank had to sit outside my cage door as I watched his eyes fill up. I could tell that it upset him to see me

Legends

in a cage like an animal in a zoo; it really upset him. That's why I love the man as he showed me compassion and kindness – go and ask him if he loves me and he'll tell you, "Charlie's my friend."

Bob Mapplebeck
'The Pastor'

Bob was a pastor who used to come into Full Sutton max secure jail; he used to bring in films and hold talks. Big Albert Baker introduced me to him and Bob's been my pal ever since. He later used to visit me on the Hull unit and whilst I was in the cage at Wakefield.

A truly remarkable man, a one off. He drinks tea till it comes out of his ears. Bob's just a lovely man who cares about guys. He's made me laugh at times when I've felt low and he put a lot of good vibes my way. I know it might look like I'm going against what I've

led you all to believe about me hating 'sky pilots' but first when looking at a man I take him on face value and there was noting pretentious about Bob and that was the first thing that made me see he wasn't just on a mission to save my soul.

He's one man I can't forget, as I've never met such a sincere man. He can see right into a person and he knows who's who. There's only one Bob Mapplebeck and with a name like that I'm not surprised – love you Bob.

Moneypenny

Now this little lady's gonna astound you cos here's a story I heard about her. One day she was visiting Rome and was out shopping when this guy comes up to her and asks her for an autograph, at first Moneypenny was a little coy as this guy was old and wearing a cassock, carrying a cross, speaking with a Polish accent and had

Civvy Street

a bit of his finger missing, looked like he'd been shot or som'et but an old wound. Moneypenny takes her camera out and asks a passer-by to take a few snaps of her and the old geezer and then goes for a cuppa at a café while she's waiting for the film to be developed at a nearby chemist's shop.

Moneypenny returns to pick her snaps up and the chemist shop's full of people eyeing up the photos what the chemist's showing them. They're saying, "Yeah, that's Moneypenny alright but who's that old geezer with her?" So there you have it a true legend if ever there was one.

Moneypenny deserves a medal the size of a bin lid for what she's done for all them underworld figures, especially Dave Courtney. No crimebizz show would be complete without her special skills. The people that she don't know aren't worth talking about, she's worked with the best and no one can tell her how to suck eggs, although many've tried. Wherever there's a do on then you can be sure Moneypenny's played some part in it and now it's time for her to make it big so she's branched out into the crimebizz world and is also acting as publicist to anybody of any worth and that means anyone cos she loves people and being around them.

Apart from being Dave Courtney's right hand woman she's also working for the MOJO (Miscarriage of Justice Organisation)

organisation, which is headed by Paddy Hill so anyone wants to find out anything about this then email Moneypenny. The M25 Three have also had help from her and that's just the start. MOJO are looking for funding from rich geezers and Moneypenny says if they don't pay up she'll be paying them a visit with a few of her friends, she's a hard case is our Moneypenny, when I say hard I mean harder than nails cos she's

stood the test of time, worked with the best. If she says she knows the Pope then take it from me she knows the Pope.

Legends

Anyone looking for a publicist or an agent then she's the lady for you. If you're looking to get a story in the newspapers then she's the lady for you, she's heard it all before and she's probably even got a T-shirt with your story written on it along with the 1,000's of others she's got locked away in her head. This lady is the best in crimebizz – we all love ya, Moneypenny.
Email: annmoneypenny@talk21.com

Pauline New
'Cellmate of the Month'

Pauline was my first cellmate of the month on my website: bronsonmania.com and she's to be a regular feature over the

Pauline New - An asset to my website

future months and maybe even years. My hope is to get a calendar of pin-up girls all posing with a Charlie Bronson theme, so any ladies out there wanna get famous then send them snapshots in but I reckon you've got a job on your hands to match

Civvy Street

up to Pauline's high standards.

Pauline's definitely an asset to the website and in some of the shots she's wearing one of my white shirts – sprayed on to her with water. Yeah, I'm still a man with a man's feelings but as for love...well it's early days yet – don't go spoiling me too early.

James Nicholson
'Le Prince'

James 'Le Prince' Nicholson is a very good friend of mine; he's worked for nearly 40 years on national newspapers – murders, bombings, sieges and the rest. He's got a few tales to tell from his first hand experience. He's usually described as a legend and his fellow journalists know him as the Prince of Darkness. One reason for this is his style of dress and another is because he's covered some of the nation's worst crimes.

He's usually dressed in black and in the dark winter months he usually wears a black 'Count Dracula' style cape, he drinks black Guinness, wears black tinted specs and has a black sense of jovial humour. He's the doyen of crime reporters and now based as a freelance at the Old bailey. He's the only crime reporter still working who covered the Moors Murders, the end of the Great Train Robbery Trials, the trials of the Kray twins, the Richardsons and other infamous gangland trials of the late 60s. All of the other great crime reporters have either retired or passed on to the darker side.

Legends

He's the only reporter around who covered the last hangings and one of his claims to infamy is that he was a friend of the last two hangmen, Albert Pierrepoint and Harry Allen. He's earned respect from police and villains alike and most of his friends down the years have been top detectives but he's also made friends of the nations top underworld figures. He's earned their respect cos both sides know he don't take sides and couldn't be disloyal to either of their quarters. Le Prince says, "Some of the underworld figures around today are just nice guys to be with." Of the Krays he says, "I drank with their father and became a fiend of Violet, their mother, I met both Reggie and Ronnie and now, sadly, there's only Reggie left."

Some of the other notorious friends he's got included Kenny Noye and the late Valerio Viccei. Le Prince could write a bigger and better encyclopaedia on underworld characters than anyone in the world. He's been my friend for years and he could've written a book on many characters but he says, "Why should I, they seem to all be doing so well themselves." I think he understands what I've gone through and what I'm still going through.

Eira Peterson
'The Duchess'

A boy's best friend is his mum; you'd better believe it in this case. Mum's been my strength throughout all of this, she's travelled miles all over the country visiting me and when she once come to visit me at Broadmoor she was told she couldn't see me. They didn't reckon on my Mum being as tough as she is, "I'm seeing my son and I'm not moving until I've seen him," she says at the gatehouse. Anyway by time Dr Lucas got to see her she was fuming. Lucas asked who was the person that was making such a fuss. In the end he said to my Mum, "It's you, you're the one that's

Civvy Street

mad, I can see where he gets it from now." What a lunatic he was, anyway Mum got in to see me even though I was in a right state cos

I'd just had a kicking and I was drugged up to the eyeballs – not a sight for anyone's mum let alone mine.

I asked for a photograph be taken of me and my Mum cos the last one I had done with her was 18 years ago – the Prison Service refused! Now can you see what I'm gong through with this lot? My brother's coming across from Australia to see me, he's been very, very ill recently and that's

Big Brother, John

the reason he's coming to see me and you know what, they're making him fill in forms to visit me! Come on, nobody as ill as he was needs this treatment. What about having a photo with him, will they allow it, they've got no heart this lot.

Peter Atherton's the man at the Prison Service Headquarters; he's the man with all the power over me. My lawyer's asked for a meeting with him over my treatment. Let's hope he sees sense and allows me that photo with my dear Mum. Mum, I love you more than anything in the whole world – God Bless you.

Smoking Joe Peterson – R.I.P.
'The Legend of all Legends'

This is a photo of my Dad, a great boxer in his day; a champion and he'd even sparred with the great Randolph Turpin. A few weeks before Dad died my younger brother, Mark, arranged to bring him to see me at Belmarsh. I was being held on the maximum secure unit. The screws made the visit the most humane visit I have ever had, as they all knew this would be the last time I'd see my Dad alive.

Charlie's Dad in 1945

It was the hardest thing in my life to

193

Legends

watch him walk away, although I'd just hugged him and told him I loved him I had to watch my old man walk out of my life forever.

But how must he have felt? He knew he was dying, he knew it was all over, he was A BRAVE MAN, A VERY PROUD MAN!

Belmarsh at that time was one of the most secure in Europe. Everywhere you look there are cameras and electronic doors, it's designed solely to house high-risk prisoners.

I watched my brother, Mark; go through the electronic door with Dad, when it closed shut my Dad did something that left me with the greatest memory of him the legend he was. He turned around and smiled, then stuck both fists up in the fighter pose. That about sums it all up, that's what makes a legend. You live a legend and die a legend.

Words are never enough when you've suffered such a loss but many of my supporters have helped me through all of this.

A month later he passed on. Only a legend would think of doing something like that. Inside the most secure unit in the prison system, a dying man thought of that so as to leave me with a positive image. Just for me...God Bless Him. A legend to the end.

Grigory Efimovitch Rasputin – R.I.P.
'The Mad Monk'

Well come on, you didn't think I was gonna miss this guy out did you? He was the top sky pilot in Russia, but a mad one so that makes him a legend. Rasputin would've been welcome into my cell any day of the week. This guy might as well have been the Tsar of Russia cos he had so much influence over old Nicholas 11 and his wife, the Tsarina, Alexandra. Rasputin weaved his charms and wheedled his way into the Russian Royal Family but a whole boatload of jealous people wanted him out of the way.

Some say that Rasputin was a German agent cos at that time the Russians were fighting a war against the Germans! So Rasputin

Civvy Street

was supposed to be passing info to the other side. Like me Rasputin was considered to be a loon of the highest order but if that was the case then why was they trying to kill him, like the Prison Service are trying to kill me? Oh yeah you'd better believe it! I've had my food tampered with, piss in the tea, threatened to be injected with petrol whilst in Broadmoor and had glass put in my food, bet you didn't know that. And at Whitemoor of late I had a screw stand outside of my door saying he was gonna put poison in my food, two cons are witnesses to what he said.

They tried to poison Rasputin by putting arsenic in a cake, they tried to shoot him, they tried to club him to death and they tried to drown him – he survived it all. The Russian aristocracy eventually murdered him in 1916. I feel we had a lot in common old Rasputin and me – brothers in arms.

Loraine Salvage
Angel of all Angels

If you look closely enough you'll see just how much of an angel she is, maybe only I can see it but I see a halo above her head and an aura around us both. My angel sees me through no matter how much pain or emptiness lies ahead, my beautiful soul sister reaches out to me. In the coldest darkest nights she comes to me and wraps me up in a blanket of loveliness. Some may well say, "Charlie's flipped it." Some may even say, "It's an unnatural closeness to have to a sister."

Well I say again look at this photo and see my angel's aura and halo.

Loraine once visited me some years ago behind the infamous walls of Broadmoor it was at a terrible low point in my life a lot of confusion, a lot of pain and a lot of no hope in my sights. I'd just tried to kill a man by strangulation so I was heavily sedated and closely watched – life was a haze of gloom a depressed world to be

Legends

Loraine holding one of the 7 Koestler Awards I've won

in. Loraine sat at the table and held my hand and looked into my pain and a hot flow of love travelled through my hand, which only days before had tried to kill a man, into her body an experience that's never left me and probably never will. A warm tender feeling of being wanted, and then my angel only has to touch me to humanise me and to clear my tortured mind. She left me that day with the words, "You're the best brother in the whole world." I've never strangled anybody since, sure I've cut a few up and broken a few legs but I've never strangled anyone. I put it down to the drugs and the surroundings and the fact that my angel saved me – thank you so much and God Bless you.

The Saviour

In the 80s I was caged up in Broadmoor, I was probably at the lowest point in my life. A friend asked this young lady to write to me (unknown to me her letter arrived at a bad time) along with this photo!

I was two weeks into a hunger strike; I was ill, weak, tired and depressed. I was basically killing myself. I read her letter. A thousand times. I stared at the photo a million times.

She was my saviour, a real living legend. Look at her eyes; if they're not saviour's eyes then

196

Civvy Street

I'm a blind man. I've not actually been in touch with her for about 15 years, after all we were only pen friends but she remains a legendary figure in my life. She probably played a big part in saving my life and she never even realised it! No doubt The Saviour's now married and maybe even a mother but she will always be a legend to me – thank you my saviour -- Mad Mickey Peterson.

The Swellbellys

You know who your friends are when the shit hits the fan and I can tell you now that the Swellbellys

are there for me whatever hits the fan! They're an Edinburgh hardcore/punk band with a political vibe and they've just released their 4th compilation CD, which features me, your old china, Charlie Bronson!! I mean there I am on that CD with the guys, you've heard nothing till you've heard this. The guys have outdone themselves this time. I designed the sleeve for the CD and I feel it's gonna get up there with the best of them.

I want to tell you about the Swellbellys and after that if you don't take your hat off to 'em you've gotta be seriously considered abattoir material. Needles, the lead singer, had written to me while I was in Woodhill and I passed the details on to Steve Richards.

Darren, Steve, DD Donnelly & Needles = Swellbellys

197

Legends

After a few telephone calls the Swellbellys agreed to travel to Gloucestershire to be filmed in the grounds of the Crime Through Time Museum.

The lads had a gig on the Saturday night and finished it in the early hours of Sunday morning, 2am, then travelled all the way from Dalkeith, in Scotland, six hours to get to Gloucester. They was walking around Newent at eight o'clock in the morning when Steve pulls into Newent, High Street.

In the back of his car he's got James Crosbie from Glasgow and as Steve realises the guys walking along are the Swellbellys, cos not every geezer in Newent's got things through their noses, multi coloured hair and tattoos all over them, Steve says to James, a guy with a broad Glaswegian accent, "James, I'll pull up alongside these lads, ask them if they know where the museum is?" Not surprisingly the Swellbellys looked a bit stunned when a Glaswegian dialect shouted at them, "Hey, Jimmy, de'ken where the museum is?"

These guys performed their song, which they'd written especially for me, from the morning right through to the afternoon they did their stuff. They went and had a cuppa, cos none of them are alcoholics, and they drove straight back to Dalkeith. By time the got back it must've been nearly midnight! That's the effort these guys put in for me, cos it was for me they gave their lot. If you wanna see what it all turned out like then watch them on the video documentary – *Sincerely Yours*.

They've got their 5th album out soon called *Never Give Up* and on that is a song I've written for the lads called *Suck out the Pain*, it's a ballad and a far flung thing from what they normally do, it's gonna blow your socks off for sure. The lead singer, Needles, has been all over on a mission to help me, travels regularly from Scotland to the south of England to meet people on my behalf, great guy and all of the Swellbellys are true legends, true Bravehearts, typical Scottish fighting power.

Don't be frightened of the way they look, they'd do more to look after you then some of them evil fuckers in the Home Office wearing suits would do. Listen, anyone wanna take these lads to the rainbow and back can forget it, they don't wanna conform to the way music's been cut 'n' diced by the sharpshooters in the commercial recording game – they're true hardcore and up for playing anywhere. They don't do drugs, they don't take hostages,

Civvy Street

they don't throw blood over you, they don't puke over you, they just give you a good time.

Website: www.theswellbellys.com

Here's some of the words from *Caged*:

Twenty-two years in the hole
Solitary confinement nowhere to go
His life, his fuckin' pain
Forced injection in his skin
Cold steel razor sharp
Left to rot in a cage of crap
Sanity caged with spite
Insanity is his might

Kicked, beaten, black and blue
A size ten boot from a screw
Ten on one in a cage of shit
No recreation and no visits
Loss of mind and sanity
They take away a man's humanity
Let's listen to his fears
Not try to break his dignity

The CD can be bought directly from Mirage Publishing (Details in rear of book)

Legends

Chas Watson
'The Tattoo Man'

Chas paid me the ultimate tribute; he had a tattoo put on his thigh. He'd read my autobiography, Silent Scream, and wrote to me asking if I'd design him a tattoo and Hey Presto! What you see is my own design. Chas wrote to me to say he was very proud to have

a Bronco original piece of artwork and that makes Chas a legend for being the first person in the world to have me tattooed on to his body. The drawing was done cos I had a dirty big beard and the reason for that big long beard was cos the system wouldn't allow me to have a blade in my hand and when they used to sit me on a chair and tell

me to sit on my hands whilst they shaved me I swore down I wasn't gonna shave till the year 2,000 after I was cut to ribbons by them barbarians. And that was a few years ago so you can imagine how long and bushy my beard had got.

I wrote to Chas saying the fur comes off the boat in 2000 and his missus reads the letter, she only goes and thinks I've made a model boat and wrapped it up in fur and that I'm gonna take the fur off the boat in the year 2000, talk about a laugh. Anyway the year 2000 came and I shaved it off so I created this drawing in readiness and sent it to Chas to see if it would do for the tattoo design he asked for. Lucky for him I did shave my beard off in 2000 otherwise he'd have had to have it filled in with a beard! Chas – they don't make 'em like you anymore, old son.

Ray Williams

We go back to the late 60s and have been pals ever since. I remember once he chinned some loon outside a bookie's shop and

Civvy Street

of all the guys to call as a witness in his defence he called me. Well as soon as I stood up in the witness box I guess all knew from then on we'd always be pals. Ray's like a brother; you can't be pals for over 30 years and not feel like family. Ray pulled out of the fast lane and went straight and hadn't been in trouble for 20+ years. I believe it was his lovely wife, Irene that saved Ray.

Ray's a special pal of mine rock solid and I consider him a priceless mate. I owe this man so much for all he's done for me over the years. He's now got his own business in Elsmere Port and he's as staunch as they make 'em up that way. A true friend to the end, he's stood the test of time unlike some who've been like stones around my neck. Ray my old friend, get my pint standing on that bar counter for when I'm out cos that's defo gonna happen.

Steve Wraith
'The North Connection'

As a 15-year-old schoolboy Steve Wraith read a book about the Krays called *Profession of Violence* by John Pearson. Steve, as part of his examination coursework, studied it – he passed with flying colours. Steve was excited at this and he decided to share his good news not just with his family but also with Ronnie, Reggie and Charlie Kray.

After writing to them he struck up a pen-pal friendship with the twins and finally he got to meet both twins within a week in April

201

Legends

1991.

The friendship grew and finally Steve was accepted into the inner sanctums of the Kray circle of friends and that included me, Charlie Bronson. He now counts the likes of Freddie Foreman, Tony Lambrianou, the Richardsons, Joe Pyle, Dave Courtney and a million other faces as his friends.

Would you believe this guy was one of the youngest editor's of a football fanzine magazine. He's currently in the promotions business – nightclub promotions that is. And being the clever guy he is he's also branched out into personal security and right know he's working on a Tyneside Pubs 'n' clubs guide which is going into a book: *Viv – The Final Chapter (Vol.3)*. People like Steve are hard to find, I mean a lot of people would be frightened in case they lost their job or something by allowing me to put them in my book of Legends, not Steve though – he's a legend alright. Oh, yeah! He's been putting together a book on the Krays and I think he was calling it, *The Krays - The North East Connection*. This would be a blinding book cos it would be from the inside, go on, give it a go,Steve.

6

Wasters & Mugs

Robin Ackroyd

He's a low life rat and I'll not forget what games he played with me and neither will a lot of other people. He got a pile of photos from my dear old mum and he promised to return them. He's ignored letter after letter about it, he swore blind he'd return her photo album, her one and only photo album! Then to top it all he told a pack of lies in a Sunday People newspaper article. Don't take my word for it; ask my lawyer, T, he'll confirm what that low down rat said to him when T asked why he'd done it. His reply, "Sensationalism."

The lies I refer to appeared in the Sunday People in which I'm supposed to have stated, 'I'm a walking timebomb and the system has lit the fuse. I now feel I could kill someone, what have I got to lose?'

I can confirm that no such piece was given to the Sunday People or to Robin Ackroyd and in the time span that such a piece was written from the Friday when I was sentenced at Luton Crown Court to the time it appeared it was physically impossible for Ackroyd to have interviewed me, my records will show and prove this. There's no record and no possibility that I could've called anyone on the telephone from the time I was sentenced at Luton Crown Court to the time the item was printed, indeed I had no communication with anyone over that weekend.

Prison records will confirm this as will my solicitor. The last person I spoke to in that court, As I was being led away, was Steve Richards, that was it and then come the Sunday a whole bundle of lies appears by Ackroyd and some geezer named Cyril Dixon. Because of that I've got to put up with a whole parcel of shit. I've been told that the Prison Service are keeping me in solitary for two

Legends

years since that article appeared cos they're terrified I might kill someone, how do I know, cos there are some nice people inside Prison Service Headquarters that tell my friends what's really going on.

Some people have said that I would've been kept in solitary regardless of that article, I say that's bull cos if that were the case then how come I'd been a well behaved little boy for 14 months at Woodhill since taking Phil Danielson hostage at Hull jail and it got me nowhere, how come then, uh?

Such lies can only add to the length of time I'll spend in solitary confinement, do you really think that the Prison Service Headquarters will consider lessening their already stringent conditions in which I'm held after they've read such crap? There were even more lies spun in the article as it went on and Ackroyd's just ignored everybody hoping that it'll go away.

Ackroyd then sent me an agreement under special cover from a firm of lawyers in Portsmouth, Addison Madden –Solicitor asking me to sign an agreement for a website, I didn't sign anything cos he's a pratt. But you know what he still went ahead even though I hadn't given him permission and used photographs stolen from me and my mum and was saying things I'd never instructed him to say! So Steve Richards had it stopped cos we were setting up the official website of bronsonmania.com.

The firm of lawyers, Addison Madden then bottle out when Steve approached them to ask what was going on. And he wrote to them saying:

Your claim that Mr Robin Ackroyd has not instructed you on the matter of a website is a little baffling in that I have the original agreement (copy enc) that clearly shows the name of 'Addison Madden' – top of page.

I also enclose copy letter from one of your assistant solicitors, Julia Mutlow, again the address of Addison Maddison appear top of page, can you please advise?

Also enclosed is copy letter from Mr Ackroyd sent via Julia Mutlow, clearly stated at top of page, again can you advise?

I feel that some rules have been breached in that clients' mail sent to prisoners can be sent via 'Rule 39a', which I'm sure you're aware of. Certainly it would seem that Ms Mutlow has used this rule to defeat the prison censors at HMP Woodhil. Since I am not aware of any dealings Addison Madden have with Mr Bronson it would seem

Wasters & Mugs

that your claim to having no such instructions from Mr Ackroyd would seem fair, however I am keen to investigate whether the 'Rule 39a' is being abused particularly as Charlie has many letters under such a rule from his bona fide solicitors.

I cannot see how you can allow the use of such a rule to be used under the umbrella of Addison Madden when in fact it would appear that Ms Mutlow is acting for Mr Ackroyd in an unofficial capacity yet using the cover of her job to do so in a seemingly legal way, can you comment, please.

That of course would explain the letter denying that Addison Madden act for Mr Ackroyd, but I must admit until that is clarified after you've read this letter I must still for the purposes of legal service consider you to be acting for Mr Ackroyd, all what I've explained above would indicate you do act for his interests.

So there you have it, I've been mugged off enough and I'm not taking anymore of it. The fact is Ackroyd lied and then went on to do more than he was entitled to cos he thinks I'm banged up he can walk all over me, I could forgive the lies if he'd just come clean and said, "Look Charlie I wanted to make a packet out of you and so I sold this dodgy story to the newspapers, give me a break I need the cash, oh and here's your photographs and your mum's album back." But did he say that, of course not. He's deprived you of some nice photos, naughty, naughty, naughty!

Angela Archuleta

She was supposed to be helping in the Sincerely Yours video documentary. Came over from the USA to visit friends in England and Ireland. She'd been visiting prisoners over the years and was always threatening to get their work published and she was working on a book we were putting together, she'd been making this promise and that promise and saying how she was publicising my conditions over in the USA yet when Steve pushed her on who she'd been talking to she couldn't name anyone and she'd been sitting on our work for years, not even written a chapter or anything. She'd been to visit me once and made so many promises but in the end it turned out she'd wanted to fill her own life up with people like me.

Steve was travelling around the London/Sussex areas, he'd done 3,500 miles in 10 days interviewing and filming people in connection with me. Angela had made arrangements to be at a particular hotel in London, which Steve telephoned...to cut a long story short Archuleta made all of the excuses in the world, she couldn't travel on a tube eight miles out of London to meet Steve, then she said the phone in her hotel wasn't working, but made no effort to go to another phone, then she comes down with an attack of the hives, yet a few days later she's off to Ireland travelling around the place like there's no tomorrow.

She gives a whole bucket load of excuses and even tries to get Steve into trouble with Dave Courtney and then says he told her Joe Pyle was a 'villain' and 'never forget that.' Steve lives, eats and breathes these guys and wouldn't use such a word as 'villain'.

She then has a load of my paperwork and written manuscripts I'd been sending her over the years so I ask her for them back and she then goes and makes a fucking song and dance over them and decides to pull Dave Courtney into the frame by telling Dave what a rat Steve is and so on, if he's such a rat then why did he send her $50 for the postage and all the work was mine, he even sent her stuff back. In the end I had to get my prison to send her letters back as she was whinging on about this interview and giving me earache over it and then she writes to Steve, here's some extracts from her letter, after reading it you can make your own mind up as to whether she should be in this chapter:

'...stop playing your little twisted games. ...you obviously know very little of what is important to prisoners but I have passed your comments on to Dave.

(As it happens Dave's one of the nicest people in the world so her veiled threats were ignored, but had Steve not of known Dave Courtney he might have wondered what the consequences were going to be.)

All of your self important little protests with regard my letters does not alter the fact you did not send the money until I asked for it yet again. Was it perhaps because you had to get the money of (her poor grammar) *Charlie first because you were afraid to part with any of your own even though you stand to make a great deal of money out of him? You are only interested in people who can make money for you aren't you Steve?* (More poor grammar) *I did not ask for the money because I needed it but as a principle as you were* (more poor grammar) *both making demands on me even though I*

206

never hesitated todive (more poor grammar).

...incidentally I have taped al of our telephone conversations in order that you would never again be able to accuse me of being a liar. (She should be able to prove then that Steve was calling Joe Pyle a 'villain', eh?) I will be more than happy to supply Charlie or anyone else with these taped conversations should you call me a liar again. (Bet she can't produce one of them for what she claims was said?)

You are so full of your own self importance (more poor grammar) it is almost laughable – what in your childhood gave you this need of self importance? (More poor grammar) (Seeing people like the Krays running around winning respect gave Steve this need.)

As for you telling me what I can or do not do with regard to Dave Courtney is laughable. Who do you think you are to tell me what friends I can contact (??????????????, she's lost it) Dave is an old friend of mine and if he didn't want to help me I assure you he wouldn't so don't even go there as it is none of your business you pathetic little man. Incidentally I realize you are smart enough to presume I will show him all your correspondence which is why you wrote those favourable comments (Why then doesn't she send Dave the tapes to prove otherwise?) about him but bear in mind he is also very smart! We are also aware you are trying to infiltrate into their world to further your own means but again people like Dave are not fools and at least you keeping (more and more poor grammar) us all amused so I suppose you have some value!

I contacted a friend of mine who is an editor (pity she didn't do this to help me with the manuscript I sent her years ago) of a magazine in London and she informs me you are a 'Desk Top' operator who does not even have an office but work out of your home. You have very little credibility in the publishing world (no wonder the newspapers keep ignoring Steve when he gives them the truth about my conditions, what she means is he ain't greasing the right palms) and she advised me if I was thinking of doing anything with you not to invest any time or money. (No one asked her for money, in fact Steve sent her $52) You are not even on the web site (News to me?) and poor old Charlie thinks he is on what you call "An Atlantic rowing mission" – poor sod!

You mention in your letter I should pass your comments on to Paul Ravilious (see they're all connected this lot) but as you full well know I have no communication with him so I must disappoint you in that

207

Legends

direction. I will say this for Paul though he was a good friend to Charlie (she's a good judge of character, ain't she?) over the years and at least he has passed Charlie's things on to a reputable writer (yeah, Ackroyd and look how reputable he was he nicked my photographs, set up a dodgy website, told lies in a newspaper article about me and other things, he knows what things!) who will be more successful with Charlie's work than you could ever be. (Proving what I said about Ratvilious passing all the stuff on to Ackroyd what was meant for Steve.)

I passed your book on to a couple of well known writers in this area and they both agreed with me that your writing style was poor – you command (more poor grammar) of the English language for a so called professional man is also very poor. (Not bad for a dyslexic left-hander forced to write with his right hand as a child who now writes in a puritanical style learned from the Americans!!!) ...I suggest you stop writing letters that are full of your own self importance (more poor grammar) and accusing me of trying to make trouble. You are not an honorable man as you say as despite everything...

I have a wonderful family and live in a place people like you could only dream about. I ski, ride, hunt, fish, and play my music. Why in God's name would I be jealous of a little worm like you or wish to make trouble. The truth is Steve Richards all I have done is try to defend myself against your barbs and threats. (Full of poor grammar.)

I suggest you come down off your little soap box, stop telling me who I can and cannot write to or what I can or cannot do. I will advise you my family here is a very important one with great influence and you may check that out any time you like. It is one of the most influential families in the county, my husband having two uncles who are judges and one who is editor of the local newspaper. I am asking you for the last time do not write to me again or I may take action of my which I assure you will not be beneficial to your professional career. Your reputation is already tarnished amongst many over there so I suggest you do as little as possible to tarnish it further than you already have.

Angela Archuleta

Wasters & Mugs

Make of that what you will and since Steve had no objections to the letter going in it shows the type of people I've been up against. Okay, Angela was once a friend but she let the team down and for that she gets herself so angry at missing the chance to really help me. I've got so many people who want to help me but see when the cards are down they all run.

Peter Atherton
Director of High Security Prisons

Hasn't responded to a long letter from T, in which T asks to have a meeting with Atherton. Atherton is responsible for my conditions. While at Whitemoor, August 2000, I'm still on a riot unlock. The same shields that have been in a cell a few doors down, a cell where the guy is having a shit up (dirty protest by spreading his shit all over himself and the cells), are the same shields poked two inches from my face – dirty bastards want me to catch something! Atherton's the guy responsible for me not being allowed to have a photograph taken with my Mum. Write to him at: Prison Service Headquarters, Cleland House, Page St, London, SW1P 4LN. How would he like it if he had the same shields poked in his face?

Paul Boeting
Prisons Minister

Build more prisons, lock 'em away and throw away the key. What are they gonna do when the prison population hits 100,000, cos it's gonna happen. Build more privately run prisons, make more tagging orders, more combination orders, more deferred sentences, more suspended sentences, more probation orders, more curfews, more and more and more! What's the use of it all if the system can't cater for one guy like me????????????????????? They've broken more rules than a box of broken china plates when it comes to me, sack the lot, fill the place up with baboons, cos they'd do the same job if not better.

Legends

Senior Officer Cawthorne
Woodhill Prison

I was sent a large piece of artists card, about three foot by two foot, he refused me to have it. It was sent to me so I could do a drawing on it for auction for Zoë's Place Baby Hospice in Liverpool. Steve Richards sent him an art set and told him he might as well do the drawing. The plonker sent the art set back, didn't even try to do it. The babies were deprived of extra funds thanks to this man.

Joyce Connor

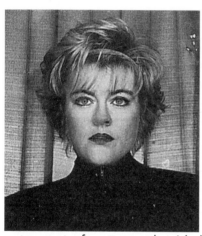

Joyce started writing to me when she heard and read about me in a magazine. She was serving five years for drug running at the time. Born in Scotland but moved to Canada as a child. She strung me along alright. We wrote to each other for years and had an understanding; she became my princess. When she was released my good friend, Dave Courtney, arranged to pick her up from prison in a hired Roller. She spun some sort of patter and said she wasn't allowed to be picked up from prison so Dave arranged to pick her up from Northampton railway station at 6pm.

I'd sorted her a party. Joe Pyle had laid on the booze and grub, as some friends of his who ran the Million Hares club helped out, Dave put on the car and his time to make sure Joyce was looked after.

Joyce was supposed to be at a telephone for the following day, we'd arranged for me to call her. I've explained a bit about this earlier on so I don't want to bore you. Top and bottom is she used me and she's a loser. She's not the person I thought she was. She even sent me a photograph of a Canadian pen friend serving time in Canada for robbery. Asked me if I could find him a job through my connections when he gets out and visits her! He'll be slipping

210

Wasters & Mugs

her one or two lengths unless she hasn't already had a length or two slipped her way already.

Anyway I've got Pauline New, my first website 'Cellmate of the Month', coming to visit me soon. I've got dozens of ladies who write to me to keep me occupied and I love the attention from them. Joyce, grow up, good luck with your Canadian Robber, two timing slag!

James Felix

This guy's a clown but I just had to give this pratt a mention. Felix is a black guy, a kick boxer but he let the Luton chaps down big style, many chaps have volunteered to pay him a visit, but I don't think it need come to that. Felix was in the motor the day the old bill jumped out with tools. He was charged with me for conspiracy to rob a bank. I got him off, he spent six months on remand and at the trial I worked my butt off to get him home.

Seven years later and he hasn't sent me one card or even a stamp. That about sums up the criminals of today compared to the ones of yesterday – no morals and no code of conduct. I don't regret helping him walk out, I'm just gutted I never shot the rat, but you know as I look back on it I would've been on his low level so I'm pleased I didn't and since I've given all of that up now to concentrate on helping others it wouldn't be right me doing that, would it?

Edward Fitzgerald, Q.C.

This man told me to plead guilty to the lot, he was brought in to help me and as far as I'm concerned he might as well have been camped in the same place as the prosecution. I sacked him and went on to win two out of my four charges in the Phil Danielson hostage-taking trial. I defended two of the charges to the hilt and I've got a good chance of winning my appeal against my life sentence. One week later Fitzgerald was defending that evil bitch Myra Hindley in the House of Lords, no wonder he wanted an easy ride from me - go to my website and hang Hindley.

Legends

John Golds
Prison Service Headquarters

Told me in January 1999 I was gonna stay at Hull Prison special unit for a number of years, told me to my face. Two weeks later I'm told the place is closing and I'm to pack my stuff in a box cos I'm being put back into solitary confinement!!! He admitted this in court.

Roy Grantham

It was the early 1970s at Parkhurst Prison where this geezer got lemon with Ron Kray. It cost him half his boat race. He had more stitches in it than a prison mailbag and he was left with some nice Mars bars (scars) for his trouble. Ronnie was always a good judge of character (As Grantham got out of jail and turned supergrass.) but the eerie thing is he must have had some morals, as his conscience just couldn't handle it!!! He hung himself in a police cell up in Liverpool. The thought of more bird was just too much for the slag or the fear of bumping into Ronnie again!

Howard League for Penal Reform

Said they didn't deal with individual cases, plonkers!

Inside Time
The National Newspaper for Prisoners

What a load of plonkers who run this, frightened of their own shadows and lost their bottle. They ran a competition in 1999 and it went very successful thank you very much. It gave prisoners an opportunity to submit items for my Open Arts Competition, the winner went into my book Silent Scream and there were loads of other winners that received free books and certificates. This year we asked them if they'd run it again and all what they replied was that there'd been trouble regarding my books being banned from prisons but they said fuck all about the competition and they weren't even interested in seeing the video documentary where I'm being beaten up. I thought this sort of newspaper was there to help communicate news to prisoners - bollocks is what I say. Too

212

Wasters & Mugs

frightened of the big knobs and having to please their masters is more like it. I say to them, stuff your newspaper up your arse and lick the boots of your masters, be slaves cos I'm never gonna bow down to the system.

Alright so my books might be banned at Woodhill prison but my publishers have supplied loads of prisons around the UK and the world and only had trouble with Woodhill and The Wolds Prison run by Group 4½ and the Wolds was eventually sorted. But that didn't need to stop Inside Time reviewing the vid or running the competition, I mean look at the crap they review anyway?

Fred Lowe
Con Killer

Me at Hull in 1999 with Con Killer Lowe

This guy was a misunderstood man, he killed for valid reasons, he told staff what he'd do and he did it a number of times. I could live with that but what I couldn't live with was his refusal to come to court and give evidence on my behalf at my hostage taking trial. He refused to leave his cosy little cell at Durham Prison, with his telly in the corner and his grub. He seen it all at Hull, as he was banged up in his cell as it happened. But do you know where the fat

Legends

bastard was when it was kicking off, he was in the kitchen making a sandwich and only after he'd done that did he go back to his cell, all for himself, fat lazy cunt!

Ray Gilbert was at Hull at the time and he was eventually re-housed to Durham but he still got himself under secure escort to a prison nearby in case he was needed at my trial. He wasn't afraid to leave his cosy little cell and he put up with a few days of crap to help me out. Lowe is just too far gone to realise what loyalty is and he's never gonna be released anyway so he prefers his comforts to helping his fellow man.

Paul Lucas

Paul Lucas! Strange, same surname as the Broadmoor Gestapo doctor who turned me into a zombie. This toe-rag set me up on a bank job! It turned out he got nicked over some gun deals so he done a deal with the pigs to get me blown away. I arrived outside the bank and armed cops were there in wait for me but I survived, such is life.

MIND
The Mental Health Charity

They was asked to help me by Steve Richards, replied saying it wasn't their position to help, referred him to the Prison Reform Trust!

Moments of Madness

He was a slag! A traitor! A liar! A friend of mine for years. Both of us in and out of jails. I caught him; I punched him up good style! Every punch hurt me as much as him but it had to be done! I then dragged him to the balcony, 14 floors up! I hung him over, I held on to his feet. He was getting heavy, years flooded my brain! Shall I let go! Can I, should I?

Fuck it...I pulled him up! I'm a softie at heart but he shall remain nameless... Why? Cos next time I'd have to let go...once a rat always a rat! And that rat has done more ratting. It's pleasure with me! I like to sort it myself; I couldn't get enjoyment from paying others to do it. I've never seen the sense in that. I like to be there...doing it...hearing it...smelling it. That's me! Oh well...we

Wasters & Mugs

all have our strange ways, one thing's for sure and that's when my charity gets off the ground I'll have to become more responsible so don't worry if I start helping people instead of bashing them up.

NACRO
National Associating for the Care and Resettlement of Offenders

Plonkers, they was asked to help me by Steve Richards, didn't even reply!!!!!!!!!

Martin Oldham

My ex-lawyer advised me to plead guilty for the Phil Danielson hostage taking charges, the one where I won two of my four charges at Luton Crown Court in my Valentine's Day Trial. He said I didn't stand a chance of winning and then when I'm up he fucked off to France on holiday so I ended up defending myself after I sacked my QC who was just as bad and he told me to plead guilty otherwise he said he wouldn't be able to defend me!!! I sacked him on the spot and one week later there he is defending that evil piece of stench, Hindley. No wonder they wanted me to cop for it. I'm gonna win my appeal cos that's the way it is, you'll see.

Oldham told Steve Richards that he was putting in the paperwork for the Scrubs assault on me from 1994; he promised that it would be done by November 1999 – it didn't happen. Now my lawyer, T, has to clear up after him.

Legends

Norman Parker

This man wrote Parkhurst Tales – what a load of shit, bollocks. I've gotta give this pratt a mention, like who is he, what's he ever done – I'll tell you...sweet fuck all! A bit like McVicar – riding on the backs of those that suffer, trying to be a smart arse psychologist. Parker comes across in the books like he's the fucking daddy; he's more like the mammy – a dreamer. He put himself over in the books like he fought the system, like he was born to lead the chaps. I'd follow him alright, with a big axe. Parkhurst tales, that's all it is – tales, stories. He's even got most of it wrong. He writes about the twins (Krays) like he's a good pal, like he was on the special unit with them when a guy called Grantham got a bottle in his head. Norman you better stick to writing kiddies bedtime stories or get a job in Mothercare as a top bouncer cos that's all you are mate - a joke.

Prison Media Service
Sue Daniels

The House of Lords has given a ruling that a prisoner who is fighting injustice can nominate any member of the media to report on their claims of injustice and receive a media visit in prison from them. How come in my case then, after I sent them letters requesting Steve Richards, my lawyer sent letters and Steve Richards sent letters, that he hasn't been granted permission to see me. They've broken them rules, there are no rules for me see. Steve has seen other prisoners under this ruling and he knows the law about it, so he hasn't filled out the wrong forms or written to the wrong people or asked the wrong person. They've got no excuses. Sue Daniels replied in one solitary letter to Steve that she wasn't aware that I had a claim for a miscarriage of justice!!!!!!!!!!! We requested this in February of 2000 and still nothing from them, definitely a case of them sorting me out good style.

Prison Reform Trust

Plonkers, no help at all.

Wasters & Mugs

Sir David Ramsbotham
Prisons Inspector

This guy needs to take viagara cos he's impotent. All his reports do fuck all. He condemned Woodhill Prison, nothing changed for me at all. He said there wasn't much there or going on to help mentally stimulate prisoners, blah, blah. So what happens, I'm still unlocked by the riot squad with shields poked into my face. His reports are only of use to help people get clean laundry and an extra helping of carrots on their plate.

Paul Ravilious
'Traitor'

This plonker let me down good style, "Till the end Charlie," that's what he said to me, so why did he write me a sorry letter and have his phone cut off and hide away from everyone – cos he says he couldn't take the pressure, well when he was getting paid from them newspapers behind my back and saying he was just doing it for the sake of doing it he was pulling his plonker.

What about when he was writing to that cunt Michael Sams the killer of Julie Dart and the kidnapper of Stephanie Slater. Sams sent him a painting, he didn't tell me he was communicating with this piece of rubbish, why, cos he was selling them paintings on that's why. He didn't want me to know how slimy he was.

Then when Steve Richards sent him one of the first Silent Scream books what does he go and do, he goes and sucks up to Ackroyd by sending him it and Ackroyd rubbishes the book saying its "crap". If its so crap then why he has he copied stuff word for word? Then I gets a whole van load of stuff sent to him and Steve paid the carriers for the transporting of it what does he tell Steve, "Sorry,

Legends

Steve, there wasn't really any items of interest in the stuff." He gave Steve a little carrier bag of stuff to work from – all worthless stuff. So Steve had to go around and see a lot of people for the info on me, worked his balls off he did.

Then what does he go and do, he gives Ackroyd the whole load of stuff that was intended for Steve – that makes him a traitor for going against us all. He had the cheek to want back in some there months later after he'd done all of that. Steve even had a PO Box number near to where he lives sorted for all my fan mail to go to and this address was printed in my first ever book, Birdman Opens his Mind, so we had hundreds of people writing to the wrong address thanks to mindless Ratvilious. Incidentally he sold the Sams painting to Andy Jones at Crime Through Time Museum, so we know it's true.

Peter Roberts

This man is the most insensitive plonker you could imagine. He breached a trust - he was a family friend. He works for the North Ceredigion Post as a consultant Editor. He heard some news that my brother in Australia was ill and he went on to sell the story to a national newspaper. He betrayed my family for money and the point is I wasn't even told the news, so when Steve Richards heard it he had to phone the prison I was in to make sure if I'd heard it that it wasn't as bad as it was made out. My family had held this dire news from me, so you can imagine if I'd read it in the newspapers before I'd even been told about it? The press are a good thing to have around but such insensitivity shows a total lust for money – greedy bastard!

Straw ov London
Jack Straw

He was sent a pair of gloves to stop him dirtying his hands on me. He might as well of been sent surgeons gloves to keep my blood off him as well. He wants to bang people up if they've got a psychological problem. Spike Milligan had better get his kit ready then, Lord Bath's supposed to be eccentric so surely I can expect him in the cell next to me as well as Freddie Star, the list is endless. When you look at how much money they've pulled out of the mental health sector I can see their game, bang 'em all up, shoot the bastards if they try to escape, blame their madness and section them off under the Mental Health Act. He wants to look at his own family before he starts thinking about throwing away the key on us lot.

<u>An open letter to Jack Straw, from me:</u>

Serious acts of inhumanity are taking place against me. In the 14 months I spent at Woodhill I had no proper bed and I now have back problems. I had no natural air in my cell and my 'window', if you can call it that, does not open. I had no toilet seat. I am denied progress, although my reports were excellent. My solicitor, T, is denied access to interview witnesses for my appeal, witnesses that are inmates of Woodhill Prison.

My solicitor travels for four hours to see me and he's treated like a dog. I have had five people who wanted to visit me at Woodhill and all were denied to come and see me. None have records and all were passed by the police but all denied by Woodhill governors. Every inmate in the Woodhill unit was allowed to have photos taken with there visitors, except for me. I've not had photo taken with my mother since 1960. It's been explained to Prison Service Headquarters and they still deny me this right.

I have an appeal coming up and it's now obvious that I'm being pushed to the limits so as to get a reaction from me and that reaction would count against me and get the Prison Service off the hook for how I've been treated. My lawyer is applying for legal aid so as to investigate the treatment I've suffered over the last 20 years at the hands of the Prison Service, are you going to stand in the way of that or will you help me?

Governor Yeomans is a very sad man, I mean a case for early retirement cos he's going to have some problems over the next few years as he can't handle men properly. It goes on, Mr Straw, the reports on the place prove it, it's a hate factory and I am now getting very ill mentally.

I'm treat like a dog and I am being denied all my rights. I ask you personally to come here and see for yourself and see the barbaric way I'm being treated. I gave good behaviour for nearly 15 months and all I got in return was torture. They even put a paedophile a few cells up from me and they know I hate paedophiles, as I'm sure you also do?

Legends

I look forward to hearing from you,

Charles Bronson

Cameron Styles
Directorate of High Security Prisons

His reply to one of my fans was a bit hilarious, to say the least:

In general the Prison Service is obliged to protect the public by holding people committed to them by the courts. It cannot make value judgements about their guilt or innocence. The Prison Service is committed to providing constructive regimes which address offending behaviour, improve educational and work skills and promote law abiding behaviour in custody and after release.

Yours sincerely,

Cameron Styles
Directorate of High Security Prisons

I think the geezer's referring to prison officers when he writes such crap taken from what's up on every prison wall on notice boards around the country. They've done fuck all for me in my time. Twice I was released from category 'A' status straight on to the streets with no help or fuck all, no pre-release courses, no behavioural help, no half days out on shopping trips, no home leaves – nothing!

Woodhill Prison

It might as well be in an SS Nazi Prisoner of War Camp for what good it is. When it was first built it was built as a prison that would help disruptive prisoners like me, a prison governor helped in its layout, he later resigned in disgust at the state of the place. They might as well wear Nazi uniforms in the place and walk around doing the goose step march shouting, "Sieg Heil, Sieg Heil." The place needs pulled down and a car park built in its place. Why not turn it into a crematorium, cos the cells are hot enough. I had to breath through a steel vent; sleep on a bed of concrete a few inches off the floor.

220

Wasters & Mugs

On 4-7-2000 at Woodhill CSC unit at approx 7.30pm Schultz (Next door neighbour.) asked me if I've got a stamp for his legal letter. I put it inside a paper and sent it to him with the night screw, who was a female, she took it and said he can't have it. I said, "What a load of shit, a poxy stamp." He needed it to post a legal letter in the morning. In the morning the stamp was on the table outside my door with my breakfast. I said, "The stamp's for Shultz." They never spoke, all six of 'em. I presumed Shultz got it, till later — he never!

This was one of many kicks in the face to upset me. So I got upset, I felt sick. I felt depressed. My breathing wasn't right, I was sweating, I was getting upset. Confused, disturbed! It felt like the walls were squeezing me. I had feelings like this some years ago. 'Claustrophobic bouts of madness'. Now it was worse and I had no window, no air, I felt bad.

My door unlocked at dinnertime. (Feeding time, six screws or more.) Push a cardboard table outside the door; your food gets put on the table in a plastic tray! 15 months I'd lived like this in this airless cell. 15 months being fed like a dog.

I crashed out on to the landing and said, "I've had enough, get me a doctor." I wanted an injection, cos that's all I know from my past; I was very bad in the head. "Put me to sleep, fucking kill me!" They ran off the wing and left me. I just lost my senses. 15 months in these conditions had finally snapped my sanity!

This is supposed to be a progressive unit so why was I denied progress? Even a window with air would've been a start, a bed, a toilet seat, a notice board to put photos on, why was I denied all of this?

I began to smash the place up, what little there was to smash up, more in pain and anger. For approximately five hours nobody spoke to me! Although there's an office, which had screws in it all the time it's got bars on the window and unbreakable Kevlar sheets up, at all times there was a screw or screws in it but nothing was said to me.

At about five minutes before they rushed in a female screw come to a door, she shouted through the glass. I shouted back, "How do we end it?" I continued, "I want it peacefully," all the cons heard me say this. Keith Pringle, Tony Steel, Schultz. Next a male voice boomed, "BRONSON GIVE YOURSELF UP, I GIVE YOU A DIRECT ORDER TO COME OUT." How could I come out, I had no keys to

Legends

open the door to get out? Then all four doors to the unit crash in. Dozens of MUFTI! It was like an SAS operation! They proceeded to come at me from all four doors.

I picked up a metal tube! Then for the first time a governor shouted at me through the bars in the office, "BRONSON...SIT DOWN! SIT DOWN!" The MUFTI kept coming...so I ran at them and smashed the bar at the first shield! They then piled on me! I was kicked, punched and secured in a body belt! My right eye just went on me, totally blurry! By this time there was no less than 50 screws in the wing – 50!

I was taken to the strong box and left naked in the belt. A doctor looked through the flap; he asked me if I'm okay. I said, "I can't see out of my right eye." He left me, no treatment! Some time later I was put in a van, still in the belt, and moved to Whitemoor seg special cell. On arrival I saw a doctor, I told him my eye's injured! He gives me a tetanus jab and eye cream and a patch. My body had cuts and bruising, not externally serious, most of the damage is internal. They like to punch up a body not the face!

My lawyer, T, was booked in to see me on Friday 7th July at Whitemoor but they changed it and told him he couldn't see me till 13th July, cos they know the bruises will be gone by then, cleared up. That's my only criticism that T didn't force the issue and demand to see me or to have got a writ from the High Court to see me. I'm not criticising T directly here cos he knows the score but the Prison Service have a way of manipulating people into thinking it's all okay, they made out I had already had some visits booked and T had to go abroad so it was a bit confusing all round, but at least he knows for the next time and he was angry at the prison for this underhanded method, he'll not forget it.

At least I awoke in the morning with air on my face – I had a window and a bed with a real mattress, a proper bed!

But what I want to know is why was a paedophile like Victor Miller put a few cells away from me at Woodhill? They orchestrated it and it needs looking into. Sending in dozens of MUFTI to sort me out doesn't really achieve anything. I was informed that a lot of MUFTI were brought in from other jails. When Woodhill staff are trained to do it, so this seems a blatant set up over the last 15 months to destroy Charlie Bronson.

This sort of action only fires me up, I wanted to walk off peacefully but I was denied this gesture. Also the damage I done

222

Wasters & Mugs

was in the first hour, the remainder was calm.

I asked T to get a hold of the video tape so he can see exactly what occurred as it could well be me taking Woodhill to court over their unprofessional conduct. It'll prove to all what an evil place Woodhill is. But I will bet that videotape will disappear or they'll say there wasn't a tape in the machine – I rest my case.

Oh, one final thing, Victor Miller's door was kicked in and buckled; he raped a 12-year-old newspaper boy and then killed him! He's been deselected – that means he's been given better conditions cos they say he's had too much stress with me kicking his door in, which incidentally the Prison Service have me up on internal discipline charges for damaging his cell door. I've since had Miller added to 'Vote for a hanging' booth on my website along with half a dozen other dirty rotten load of evil motherfuckers.

Wormwood Scrubs Prison

I was beaten up here in 1994; full details in *Silent Scream*, no man can know what it's like to go through this. My father had just died; I was refused to go to the funeral and to cut a long story short I was done good style. Pull the place down is what I say.

Governor Yeomans
Woodhill Prison

Denied my solicitor, T, access to seven inmates at Woodhil Prison, T needed to interview them for my appeal against my life sentence. Governor Yeomans has perverted the course of justice, a criminal offence, he hasn't been arrested? Told my lawyer he'd have to be sent a visiting order from each of the prisoners?! Do you know how long it takes to get passed to see an inmate if you apply to see him if he's category 'A' status – at least three months! A lawyer is allowed the same access to prisoners as God and he has 'lawyers' privileges', Yeomans has breached those rules and he knows it.

He even went so far as to stop my lawyer taking money in so as to buy me drinks from a vending machine. This man should be dismissed, and that's not just from me but also from barristers. Don't worry Yeomans this will be raised at my appeal, you can put your job on that!

7

Irish Cream

King Albert

I first met Albert in the block at Wandsworth jail in the 80s; he was a big Irish man serving life. We were later to meet up in many jails along the way. He was a fearless man, nobody or nothing ever got in his way. He trained hard in the prison gyms and he showed respect to everyone that deserved it.

There are many stories I could tell about the King but I've picked one that will show what the system's all about. Albert grabbed a screw and took him hostage in Parkhurst, he demanded a helicopter, and it looked all set to go off and that his demands would be met...till fellow cons jumped him!

That incident never poisoned the King against cons; he just shrugged it off and said there's good and bad in all men. Albert's free now after serving 20 years and I've heard along the grapevine he's doing well for himself. That pleases me – God Bless King Albert.

Vince Donnelly

I first met Vince 20 years ago, anyone who done bird in the maximum secure jails over the last 20+ years must know of him or know him. Vince is a pure Irish rebel. When he was arrested he shot himself in the chest rather than come to jail but he survived – lost a lung. He served a good 20 years and got repatriated. Like all Irish he loved to drink so he spent his time brewing up the hooch. I went to several of his cell parties, he'd take out his harmonica and give it a blast, *Danny Boy* was my favourite. Once in Full Sutton jail he lost his head and served up three screws, held

Irish Cream

one with a knife to his throat. That's what you get when you upset a legend; see.

Gerry Hutch
'The Monk'

Nearly as clever as the late Martin Cahill the Monk's been a thorn in the side of officials for some years. For a man to receive a tax bill for nearly £400,000 for just one-year shows he's made it. The Monks' totally against drugs, he's into property in a big way and it was from £25,000 compensation he received from the Dept of Justice that he was able to buy property in 1988 and of course he could legitimately explain how he'd come about the money.

Accusations were flying about that it was the Monk who'd some part in the murder of Martin Cahill but the General's men were satisfied he had nothing to do with the murder. It seemed that the Monk just wanted an easy life and settled down in a leafy suburb, sending his children to private school.

One of the greatest crimes committed in Ireland took place at the Brinks-Allied Security Depot in North Dublin on 24th January 1995 and one of the men put in the frame for this £2.8m robbery was the Monk. But, sadly, the Monk had taken no part in this raid and he told the press, 'The Brinks was a brilliant job. The best of luck to whoever done it.'

The Monk's been attributed with taking part in various record breaking blags and one of them happened in January 1987 a Securicor van carrying £1.5m was robbed near to Coolock, North Dublin. If the Monk did take part in this raid it wouldn't be used on drugs and in fact the Gardai admired him as being 'a clean player'. Just like the General did he prefers little limelight and so I say, good luck to the Monk.

Fitzy the Leprechaun

This little chap has gotta be the smallest con in the UK, all his clothes are ordered from a boys shop, he's only 4 foot 10½ inches tall. I last seen him in Whitemoor Prison seg unit, he was doing 28 days punishment. I've also bumped into the little bleeder in Frankland and Wakefield prisons. This guy's a tenacious terrier, fearless with the heart of a lion and he backs away from no

Legends

man. For a man so small to have so much going for him size with him doesn't count for anything. Hey, he burnt a church down and got life – a little cherub like him deserves a mention.

Noel Gibson

I met Noel for the first time in Parkhurst and in many jails since. He got life in the early 70's; he's one of the staunchest and proudest Irishman I've ever met. He's spent many years flying around the dungeons and is a unique and intelligent man. He's taught himself to speak several languages and play the guitar, never smokes or drinks, forever into sport and is a gentleman in every sense of the word. In all of the years I've known him I've only ever heard other guys speak the same about him. Nothing is too much for Noel. He's often sat in my cell and given me advice I've needed.

Josephine Hayden

Josephine is 53 years old and was a member of the Republican women's organisation, Cumann na mBan. She was the only woman Irish Republican prisoner in the 26 counties and was incarcerated with 12 ordinary women prisoners in the women's 'C' Block of Limerick.

Josephine's been denied Political Status, had two heart attacks and one near fatal heart attack, developed one kidney infection, forced to walk up three flights of stairs daily, inadequate proper medical attention, denied visits with her family and repeatedly refused to be relocated.

When Josephine suffered her first heart attack it took the authorities over an hour to reach her cell and transport her to Limerick Regional Hospital. Prison authorities blatantly defied the advice of the cardiologist at Limerick Regional Hospital and moved her back to her cell.

One month later, Josephine suffered a second heart attack; and was forced to climb several flights of stairs to use the bathroom facilities. She had also contracted a kidney infection due to the unsanitary facilities in 'C' wing and she was denied both exercise and fresh air - being kept in a cage like I was.

It's difficult to believe that in a country so dedicated to the idea

Irish Cream

of motherhood, this mother of two young children could be subjected to such barbaric treatment. She was denied visits with her children in Dublin, and at times it was nearly impossible for them to make the trip to Limerick. She'd not seen them in over a year and the Irish government denied her the most basic of her rights as a mother.

The plumbing in the 'C' wing of the prison had completely shut down, which only worsened her health.

The future of the very image of 'Mother Ireland' is in trouble cos those who claim to be the most concerned for women's rights allowed an Irish mother to be denied the right to care for her children.

Paddy Hackett

The Irishman I have so much respect for. They came no prouder than this man; he got 20 years in the early 80s. One of his bombs blew his arm and leg clean off! All through his sentence he refused to wear prison clothes so he just wore a blanket, as he didn't class himself as a prisoner therefore refused to wear such clothing.

I once watched Paddy in the gym at Parkhurst; he used to put his stumped arm through the hole in the weights and worked out. This is why I feel so proud of him and his fight to survive. I would say I admired this man's survival instinct more than any man I've ever known. Paddy once hit a screw over the head with his false leg at the Scrubs (HM Prison Wormwood Scrubs). He was a legend from the start. Last I heard he got released from Parkhurst and is now a free man.

P J Judge – R.I.P.
'The Executioner'

Peter Joseph Judge was one of the most feared men in Ireland, yet he was one of the nicest gentlemen anyone would ever wish to meet but you'd never want to turn you back on that smile! He couldn't really be described as 'Irish Cream' but more as 'curdled cream'. Born in Dublin in 1955 he soon became a criminal at the age of 12; he became a joyrider, one of the first in Ireland.

At the age of 13 he was popping bullet holes into a family's home when he was dissatisfied with a hair 'do' that involved

Legends

having his hair dyed, he thought he was having the piss took out of him when other kids stared taking the piss out of him.

Another incident involved him trying to reverse his car over a Gardai, pleasant little fucker wasn't he? South Dublin, the more well to do area, was his key target for nicking cars from but he soon outgrew such playful crimes. He never admitted to anything and with his soft-spoken ways he would pass for a normal person but he was soon recognised as being a psycho.

Judge became a blagger and was successful but his violent side soon came out and he was to get a long stretch, 20 years, for robberies, he even tried to kill the police, but his gun jammed.

Judge was designed for modern crime; he was an assassin and a cold-blooded killer. He turned his empire into a drugs distribution racket and was a drugs baron. He'd got rid of his stammer and turned bisexual (fair swap, if you're that way inclined) and tidied his act up but he'd a liking for beating both his female and male lovers up...savagely, even chasing them into police stations demanding they come home with him. He was a sadist and turned into a Gazza type character often breaking his girlfriend's fingers.

He used all sorts of ploys in his drugs empire to store money gained from drug dealing – nobody would rip the Executioner off! Money was coming out of his ears but he was still paranoid about being ripped off.

William 'Jock' Corbally had grown up with Judge and in 1990 Judge gave the two sons of Corbally £800 worth of cannabis to sell for him – they ripped him off. The whole thing got out of control and it ended up with Judge being attacked by Jock and this led to one of Jock's son's, Graham, going missing but he turned up unharmed.

Two murders were put down to the Executioner; murders that were said to be gruesome, even Judge's own friends were terrified of him. Judge was ripped off over a delivery of cannabis and one of his henchmen, Godfrey, bumped him for a large sum. Godfrey was gonna pay the price. Judge was now starting to go into turbo boost, he went after a drug dealer on his patch and kneecapped him – no one would make a statement. Godfrey was then picked up from his home by two henchmen working for Judge, he got two shots in the crust – again nobody would talk.

Judge had now been elevated into super thug status and he was

Irish Cream

starting to flex his muscles and people were starting to pay respect to him, cos sometimes that's the only way.

More murders were put down to Judge, even if he didn't do it he loved to take the credit for it to help his reputation. Jock Corbally hadn't been forgotten though and he was lulled into a trap. Corbally was driven into a field and Judge and his friends met him. They beat him with iron bars and in the middle of nowhere he wasn't gonna get help, was he?

Corbally was beaten to a pulp but not enough to completely kill him, Judge wanted Corbally kept alive long enough so he continue the punishment, which he did by stabbing him about the body and then finished Jock off by smashing to pieces his pearly white teeth, which Judge was always jealous of. A lime filled hole was where Corbally was dumped and just before the body was put into the hole Judge couldn't resist the temptation to slash Jock's throat!

Like anything though it all come to an end. In a cold December month in 1995 Judge was leaving a pub in the early hours of the morning, he was stalked and two bullets were blasted into his crust as he sat in his car. Some fingers point at the IRA for taking him out for the heroin he supplied to local kids, some say it was cos he took out Jock Corbally. Whatever the reason it was one of the better things to happen to Judge for what he'd inflicted on a whole community.

Roisin McAliskey

Roisin McAliskey is the daughter of Irish activist Bernadette Devlin McAliskey, Roisin was accused of attempted murder, stemming from an IRA mortar attack on a British army barracks. Despite overwhelming evidence placing her at home in Ireland during the period in question and despite being pregnant, she was arrested, subjected to heavy interrogation and then forced to suffer deplorable conditions in prison in England.

Roisin faced extremely poor health throughout her pregnancy and was denied proper pre-natal care until three days before she gave birth while under armed guard. Roisin had a baby girl. After months of international outcry, Roisin, who'd never been formally charged with a crime, was finally given bail by a High Court judge, enabling her to be transferred to a special mother and baby unit in

Legends

a psychiatric hospital.

After lobbying by international groups, it was announced that the extradition to Germany sought for her would not go ahead on health grounds. The Home Secretary, Jack Straw, said any move to extradite her would be unjust and oppressive in light of her deteriorating condition. So maybe the guy has a heart after all, but since I'm suffering jut as much, nah I don't think he has! Roisin had suffered a mental breakdown following her six-day interrogation by the RUC in Belfast's Castlereagh holding centre and the following transfer to Holloway prison.

Roisin had been moved to the high security Belmarsh Prison, which isn't a bad prison, at one stage before being returned to Holloway again. Roisin had been treated as a maximum-security prisoner throughout and was strip-searched around seventy times during her pregnancy.

In April '98 Roisin McAliskey returned home to Ireland to Coalisland for an emotional reunion with her family after 16 months detention in British custody. Bernadette McAliskey said her daughter was recovering well from her ordeal and her granddaughter, baby Loinnir, 4 years old, was in great health.

Her boyfriend, Sean McCotter, accompanied her and the baby home from London, where he'd been living since the birth of his daughter. Roisin, Sean and the baby are living together in the family home at Co Tyrone where Roisin was initially arrested by the RUC in November 1996. This sort of treatment to a pregnant woman shows the lack of compassion in the British judiciary.

Dingus McGhee

This is one terrorist I truly admire; he's not a bomber but a real soldier...trained to kill. All the villains respect Dingus. He was on a dirty protest (where his faeces (shit) is covered on his cell walls and he smears it over himself.) for a year. Dingus blew a few heads off and got 30 years for it. He escaped out of Whitemoor unit, he's a rebel until the day he dies, he can't ever be beaten but I want him to know that we all respect him. A man who goes out to fight for his beliefs and makes man his target is a survivor. A year on a shit up, that's what you call endurance, I bet it must have hummed in the Belmarsh unit. Cor blimey I'm glad I didn't have to smell it.

Irish Cream

George Mitchell
'The Penguin'

From Balleyfermot, north Dublin and another one of the General's gang. He received his nickname from a newspaper in 1995 and it's stuck ever since. Believe it or not but the Penguin used to also work as a lorry driver delivering biscuits around Ireland!! The Penguin was said to be one of the top ten gang bosses in Dublin in the 80s.

The Penguin though succumbed to the drugs trade and started supplying cannabis and ecstasy in 1991 after he was released from prison. His fortune's supposed to be in excess of £10m and his links go as far as South America.

Mickey Boyle, a long time associate of the Penguin, was now a registered police informer and in 1995 he was regularly spilling the beans on the Penguin's criminal plans. One of the Penguin's English connections, Peter Daly, had his name given to the police by Boyle and they were told that Daly was having problems with another London firm, the Brindle family. The Penguin had been asked by Daly to help sort his problems out.

The Brindles and the Daly families were at war since two 'associates' of the Brindles threatened Peter Daly's brother, John, who owned the Queen Elizabeth pub in Walworth, London's East end. The feud continued over the years pulling nearly everyone who was somebody in the London underworld into it. Operation 'Partake' was launched on both side of the Irish Sea so as to foil the Brindle murder plot. In the end it was to be Christopher Brindle that was earmarked for a 'hit' by the very man who was a police informer – Boyle!

At Boyle's trial, for the wounding of Christopher Brindle, he blamed it all on the Penguin and down to the fact that he only wanted to injure Brindle and had hoped that police, hiding in a nearby furniture wagon, would have intervened sooner before jumping out and shooting him. The whole thing stunk to high heavens, obviously the police wanted Boyle to kill Brindle and then they wanted to shoot Boyle dead for what he'd done, it would have suited the police. Both Boyle and brindle survived a number of bullet holes. Boyle later received three life sentences.

The Penguin though made a sharp exit and was clean away, he went to live in Holland, shifted his heavy money out of Ireland but

Legends

his luck was to run out when he was caught handling stolen computer parts, he was given three years in 1998 for the £¹/₂m haul – not bad going for a Teflon Don.

Fearless Paddy

All 5ft nothing and 10 stone, but he had the heart of a lion. Paddy got 21 life sentences in the 70's over the Birmingham pub bombings. I met Paddy in Parkhurst two years after he and five other Irish men were convicted of the bombing. They became known as the 'Birmingham Six'. The Birmingham six in fact were all innocent men. It took 16 years for the truth to come out. For 16 years they suffered and lost their liberty.

When I met Paddy it didn't take me long to realise just how innocent he really was. He showed me mountains of paperwork and told me things that opened my eyes to the truth of it all. I always felt in my heart that Paddy was an innocent man.

Later, I met three of his co-defendants and again I felt that they were all victims of a police stitch-up. Six Irishmen in the wrong place at the wrong time. For me Paddy was the hero, he never gave up the fight. He spent years in the blocks (solitary). He bombarded MPs with tons of letters and he went on hunger strikes, he would NEVER give up hope. It was Paddy who kept the fight going, for this fight he's a Legend.

I don't believe the Birmingham six would be free today if it weren't for Paddy. The great thing with Paddy was he'd time for everybody, even after all he'd suffered – a true fighter to the end. You must try to picture a man with 21 life sentences on his card outside his cell door. I've seen men cry with 21 days! How can anyone understand how these six Irishmen felt, and of course their families? Obviously it's of no consolation to the bereavement of the victims' families and the many that were injured in the pubs.

BUT...the police fitted these six men up. Fearless Paddy could not be held responsible for something he didn't do. Too many fits ups have gone on and fuck all's been done against the coppers that lied to get them nicked – bent coppers!

Lucky Paddy

They brought Jimmy into Winson Green Prison when I was there in

Irish Cream

'93. They'd charged him with gun running because he was Irish. They had him down as a terrorist so they put him on high-risk category 'A'. It was a real nightmare for Jimmy as he'd never been in jail before in his life. I spent three weeks with him before they moved me on but in those three weeks I educated him the best way I could. I gave him advice and made sure he knew the SP, I got him doing press ups, jogging in the yard and I made sure he had his reading material. I also told him what to expect if he got a guilty.

He'd been caught picking up a bagful of guns, with him being Irish it never looked good. He was maybe looking at 10 to 15 years' imprisonment. Six months later he wrote me a letter and low and behold he'd got three years, I couldn't believe it, I was made up for him. He must be the luckiest paddy I've ever met. One minute he's on high risk, treated like a terrorist looking at big bird, tons of porridge then he only gets three years – that's the luck of the Irish for you.

Roy Walsh

Roy was in an IRA team in the 70s, he let off some bombs outside the Old Bailey and Scotland Yard. I liked Roy even though we had a fall out. Respect is due to Roy, as he served 20 years like a good 'un and he served it hard – lots of moves and lots of solitary. I remember once in Wandsworth Prison dungeon something that made me sad; "I feel I'm a stranger to my own family," Roy told me. That was one of the saddest things any con's ever said to me plus he meant it. I know he's out now and I wish Roy all the best in the world. I'm not a lover of terrorists but I love my fellow man.

Stephen Walsh
'Rossi'

From his first crime of stealing a bicycle at the age of 16 in 1965 Rossi's went the full nine yards and became a Godfather of Irish crime. He was given the nickname of 'Rossi' cos he was so good at kicking a caser (football) and after having a trial for Arsenal he was named after the great Italian player Paolo Rossi. The English soccer fraternity knocked him back so he went on to play League of Ireland football. His aggressive and arrogant attitude lost him any chance of making it big - he couldn't beat himself.

Legends

Rossi was starting to become a bit of a Teflon don when he won a robbery trial and in another he received an eight-year sentence...suspended. He was arrested over 20 times by the Gardai under section 30 of the Offences Against the State Act for various crimes ranging from murder to robbery but as always there was insufficient evidence and he walked.

During Rossi's career he was to become a local Robin Hood figure and once when the local dockyard had containers of Mars bars go missing it was the kids in Rossi's area who were eating Mars bars for some time – he'd hoped to have found the containers full of TV sets! What he didn't know about the law could be forgotten, everyone approached him for advice and when they introduced a scheme where the police could be investigated if the public complained Rossi had the new system blitzed with complaints and at one point there were more police under investigation than criminals!

His list of scams is endless, even employing professional accident claimants to make claims against the gas company when they had to renew gas mains throughout Pearse House. He was a member of Martin Cahill's gang and even brought the General along as a celebrity guest to visit one of the junior football teams he sponsored.

Rossi's luck ran out though when he was tried for an arson attack on a pub. Judges, not a jury, tried him, as it was said he had too much influence over the community. After a lengthy three-week trial in which he ended up sacking his legal team after only four days he was found guilty and given a total of 15 years behind bars. He's due out in 2005 but in the meantime he's appealing, I hear he's even got a fax machine in his cell! I might change my nationality and go to an Irish jail.

Rossi deserves to have a chance in life and all the help he gave his community shouldn't be overlooked, okay he might have been a bit heavy at times but all the kids loved him and they're the best judge of a character – Rossi, give 'em hell mate.

8

The Manchester Mob

PAUL MASSEY

I met Paul in Full Sutton in the late 80s, a good Manchester guy with plenty of bottle. He does his bird well always in the gym, fit and strong. I've just recently heard he's got another 14 years after being out for a long spell and then while he was in for that they served him up another $3^{1}/_{2}$ years making it $17^{1}/_{2}$ years. It's always sad to hear of good guys returning to prison but what can you say, it always happens to the best. Paul will survive; hopefully he'll be lucky on his appeal as his sentence was a bit strong.

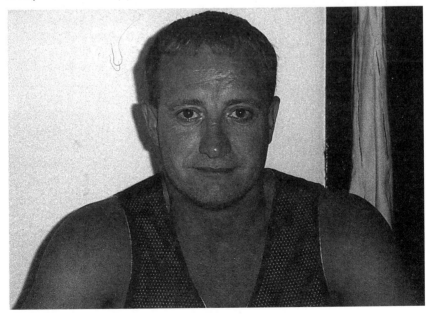

Paul - HM Prison Whitemoor 2000

Legends

Paul was portrayed in a documentary on godfathers of crime as a real heavy and that was while he's waiting for his appeal! His solicitor was contacted by Steve Richards to advise that the documentary should be stopped cos of the appeal and the solicitor did fuck all to stop it – I reckon the solicitor should take Paul's place – fucking clown.

Would you believe that Paul has won that many appeals that the law in Manchester have tried every dirty trick in the book to get him nicked. At one of his trials the police said they saw him doing a dodgy deal on buying some diesel, the law was digging a hole, pretending to be workmen. But when it was pointed out that they couldn't have seen Paul cos there was a fucking 6 foot wall between them and him they changed their story to say that they'd climbed a tractor to see over the wall – fucking clowns.

Paul has had a whole catalogue of wrongs done against him. He got 5 years when he was wrongly identified by a woman police officer and was verballed up. Some 23 months into that sentence he won his appeal and got fuck all for compensation and no police were charged with perjury or sacked!

His next stint was 6 years for £6,000 worth of forged notes, the judge said there would be 'No bargaining for time off' due to him serving 23 months on his previous sentence – clowns the lot of them. He got one year for fraud and the other 5 stretch for the forged notes.

In another incident he was charged with conspiracy to murder a guy called Brady Doyle at a surprise party in a nightclub full of people. The law wanted to get him done for this and he was remanded for a different matter but come the day of his trial no evidence was offered and all charges were dropped.

Then there was the time when he was set up with blackmail charges against a businessman and another one where he had five threats to kill people outside of a police station against him but as usual the charges were all dropped when it went to Crown Court.

Piccadilly nightclub was bad luck for Paul, as shots were fired and he was looking at three counts of conspiracy to murder and spent three days in custody before the charges were dropped. Anyone remember a mass fight at a boxing do in Manchester, Paul was on remand for six months. 26 witnesses failed to turn up for this case!

Paul was remanded for a couple of months on another set of

The Manchester Mob

fitted up charges for conspiracy to rob and as usual the charges were dropped. To say that Paul's had it hard would be an understatement and now he's doing 17¹/₂ years, can't say anything on that, as he's looking for an appeal and I hope he gets it.

Here's a bit from Steve Richards relating to an incident involving a prison officer from Whitemoor Prison, where Paul's banged up: I had a telephone call and here's a transcript of it, "I'm calling from the Home Office, security. Do you publish a magazine called 'Legends'?" The conversation went on and during it this man didn't make his position clear and he tried to put his position across as being directly from the Home Office, not from HM Prison Whitemoor, as it was indeed the place he was calling from. All of our telephones are tapped by MI5, how do I know...well that would be telling. We tape all of our telephone calls no matter what or how trivial the calls are. They tap even our Emails!

I managed to identify the caller as Mark Yendley so I immediately lodged a complaint by telephone to Whitemoor Prison. When it was put to the man that the Prison Service hadn't been very cooperative with us over certain matters in the past and that I'd been in touch with the Prison Service he said: "At Cleveland House?" I corrected him and said: "At Cleland House!" Yendley didn't make his point and put the phone down on me sharpish! We traced the call right back to Whitemoor Prison and back to Mark Yendley.

I can tell you why he put the phone down on me, it was because I told him I'd chase him to the ends of the earth and I'd pursue him over the underhanded way he called us and tried to find out something by devious means. So there you have it, even while Paul's behind bars he's pursued by devious means.

Paul now writes his tributes to the Manchester Crew:

Paul Flanerry, Ray O'Dare and others from Cheetham Hill are known as the **Hillbillies.** The Hillbillies come on the streets of Manchester in the late 70s known for an explosion of violence involving armed robberies and gang war between Cheetham Hill and Moss Side and for their brutality against screws outside of Strangeways Prison over the violence and brutality to black inmates. When brutality was returned to the screws it stopped brutality to the black inmates.

Legends

Cheetham Hill	Moss Side	Salford
Paul Flannery	Howard Swarray	Bobby Spears
Ray O'Dare	Jay Bennet	Pava Corkovic
Adertoros	Cleve Beagul	Steve Lydiate
Shearer	Ian McLeod	Damian Noonan
		Mullens
		Lee Anderson
		Lee Taber

Cleve Beagul

Respect to Cleve who I met in Strangeways in '95 when we crossed paths and nearly ended up fighting each other but from that day we became very close friends and still are today and I come to be the Godfather to his son.

Mark Boomer

Boomer, my co-accused, was lucky the police were caught on video planting the gun on him or he would've been serving life. Police were caught by their own video surveillance giving Mark a good hiding and they planted a gun on him in March '99. Four coppers kicked Mark about the head, as he was doing nothing to give them grief! An armed copper even pushed the surveillance camera to the side so they wouldn't be caught doing this.

Greater Manchester Police Force tried to cover it up and should be up for perverting the course of justice. Mark was charged with possessing a loaded gun, the one they planted on him! A .357 Magnum was planted in Mark's coat pocket. The copper tried to say that because Mark had been given lesser charges he should be content at that! They said he could be doing life.

The police suggested that disclosing the contents of the video to the court would risk future police operations. This police officer lied and he should be up on charges of fitting up and perverting the course of justice, who is he! The video was only discovered by accident and the police had no intention of ever showing it to a court because it caught them all in the act. Witness statements mentioned the video camera and it took Mark's solicitor, **Chris Davies**, to uncover it all. Chris said, "It was hardly surprising why

238

The Manchester Mob

the police didn't want us to see it and it took a month of legal wrangling to get it."

Judge **Timothy Mort** at Manchester Crown Court discredited

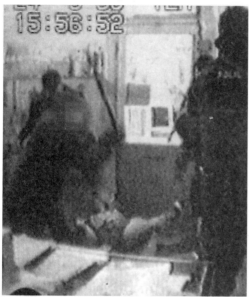

the police evidence and Mark only ended up with three years for conspiracy to rob. Mark is going to sue the police when he's free and in the meantime what's happened to the bent coppers of Greater Manchester Police Force? How many have been charged with serious assault, perverting the course of justice, suppressing the video evidence, harbouring a criminal/criminals and acting in an unlawful manner, none!

Mark being beaten by police (1999 on video)

Cheetham Gang

The Cheetham gang known as the **Hillbillies** come on the scene in the late 70s and are still strong today. Machetes and guns were regularly used in violence and gangs burst on the streets of Manchester from then on. The violence in Moss Side started to explode in the late 80s up to now with many people dead between the **Gooch Boys** and the **Doddington Firm** most of the people shot dead consist of young men. We've had a peace treaty between the Gooch Boys, the Doddington and the Hillbillies to stop violence and death to so many young people and to help so many families suffering the loss of their loved ones. I would like to send my respects to **Howard Swarray, Jay Bennett, Megga** and the rest of the Gooch Boys also respect to all the Doddington Boys so have peace and make money and rid the police off your backs. Respect to all the Salford lads at the moment many are in jail mainly for robberies or violence. Pava doing 23 years, **Lee Anderson, Lee Tabber, Tony Earman, Matty O'Neil** and **Mac**

Legends

plus many more in jail and out of jail.

Pava Corkovic

Who I met when he was about 15 years old since then Pava's served two years in prison for an attempted robbery, released and then sentenced to 10 years for robbery and ramming police off the road on their motor bikes and hijacking cars to escape. After serving his sentence he's since been arrested with Tony Earman, Lee Tabber, Lee Anderson, Matty O'Neil and **McFarland** for armed robbery and conspiracy to rob. Pava was sentenced to 23 years in prison, McFarland; 15 years, O'Neal and Earman; 14 years, Anderson; 13 years and Tabber; 12 years. All these people are still in prison today and I respect these people highly, Pava is innocent of all these charges.

Paul Flannery

Paul Flannery also survived his life when his car was surrounded by five men in Moss Side who all opened fire at him. Paul survived only having received one shot! Not long after that attack on Paul's life the police raided Paul's house with no verbal warning that it was the police. Paul believing it to be a hit on his life dived through the window to escape for his life and he landed on his back. When the police attacked him they dragged him up the road and bundled him in to the police van and manhandled him at the police station in Manchester and it was later when Paul was taken to hospital it was found that

The Manchester Mob

his back was broken!

After Paul had spent nearly a year in hospital and on his first day out **Tony Johnson** was shot dead and **Tony McKie** was also shot and survived the attack. Paul Flannery, **Derrick Noonan, Damian Noonan, Dessy Noonan** and **Michael Sharple** were all charged with murder and attempted murder. After McKie was shot and he was in hospital I visited him and he was asking me if I knew who'd shot him, as he didn't know, that's what he asked me yet he gave false evidence in court saying he'd seen Paul Flannery the Noonans and Sharples but his evidence wasn't believed and the jury found them not guilty – Respect to Paul and Jay.

Paul won £30,000 compensation at Manchester Crown Court in 2000 - when sick solicitors defending the case raised Paul's criminal past - when he proved that police lied. Paul was dragged over ground when he was arrested with a broken back!

The coppers just dragged him and photographic evidence proved that the police have once again lied. All of the officers involved should be prosecuted for perverting the course of justice and every case they've ever worked on should be re-opened as they are now all proven to be liars.

The police considered Paul to be a dangerous criminal, which then makes them dangerous and violent criminals for what they done to Paul. They raided his house, gave no shouts of who they were or nothing, Paul had to dive for cover, out of a first floor window straight onto a fence. He's paralysed from the chest down now!

Tactical Aid Group Police Officers did the damage to Paul. Who's to say if they had of carried him that his back might have been saved? Two eyewitnesses came forward and a custody sergeant said that Paul was dragged into a police station and left lying, naked, on the floor! None of the coppers were named; they should all be named and sacked.

Assistant Chief Constable **Med Hughes** said: *"We will consider the judges comments in relation to the handling of prisoners to ensure the highest quality of service is always provided by officers."* What though will he do about his lying violent police officers, answer that Mr Hughes? How can lying police officers expect to be respected by the public, every time they arrest someone how do we know we can trust them?

Legends

Stephen Lydiate

Recently found guilty of conspiracy to murder and kidnap and false imprisonment – he got 22 years in August 2000 at Preston Crown Court. Steve was sitting at a pub with his son when shoots were fired at him but he was wearing his bullet-proof vest, 14 shots were fired at him. Even though his vest saved him Steve has a bullet left in him. The court heard that four men were taken hostage in a reprisal attack said to have been ordered by Steve.

James Kent was taken hostage by four masked men, he was shot in both legs and had salt poured into the bullet holes. They said it was done because Steve wanted to find out who'd been shooting at him. Kent got free after a few days of being tortured.

The war went on and another man, **Tony Shenton** was also shot in the leg after he was kidnapped from his home. He said he was told that his wife had also been kidnapped and she was going to be sexually abused, he was later let go after 13 hours. Two more men were shot, one in front of his wife and kids before the police turned over what they called a hideout in Salford. Machine guns and all sorts of other guns were found.

The result of a three month court case led to **Michael Boyle** getting 15 years, **Jason Danson**; 10 years, **Paul Allerton** and **Asa Dwyer**; 8 years each.

Steve's a great guy and when you think that the trial went on for three months it shows it wasn't as straight forward as it was made out to be. There was no real proof of Steve being there or being involved but he was pulled in just because of his name and connections. He was shot at and still carries a bullet in him, he was with his son who could have been killed! What's happening about that? Steve's going to fight this set up and win it.

Some of the guys convicted, it was said, had to hide in an old people's home in Swinton…dressed in women's clothes, they had to shave their heads and wear wigs for a week while staying

The Manchester Mob

undercover. Guns were found there hidden in the loft and it was said that a gun was accidentally fired while some of them were held up there. What looks like a wild session of torture wasn't down to Steve and I know he'll appeal against this – Respect.

Gary McDonald

Who has spent many years locked up from the age of 10 from approved school to detention centres to borstal to prison. In '85 he was sent to prison for 10 years whilst serving that sentence him and his brother, **Matty**, escaped from Strangeways Prison. While on the run Gary committed more armed robberies and was sentenced to another 16 years on top of his 10-year sentence. Gary only just served all of his sentence in summer time 2000 – Good Luck, Gary, on your release, respect.

Damian Noonan

Also respect to the number one doorman, Damian Noonan, who kept the doors under control in Manchester because of his respect and has a very hard job on his hands because of gangs that carry guns in the Manchester clubs plus stopping people selling drugs at the clubs he controls, as Damian is against drugs and wants nothing to do with drugs. Damian could make so much money if he allowed it but won't get involved at any cost. He was shot because he wouldn't allow drugs to be sold in the clubs he runs but he survived because he wore a bullet-proof vest. The police harass him so much because he won't give them any information as most doormen are known for this plus Damian is well known for helping the community he lives in, Salford. People in Salford respect him highly – Respect to Daman.

Ray O'Dare

Ray O'Dare survived being shot twice, one in Salford and once in Moss Side, at the Moss Side carnival – Respect.

Also respect to the **Shearers** and the **Adertoro brothers** from Cheetham Hill who received eight years in prison and were not out long when they received 16 years and **Dave Adertoro** got 26 years for armed robberies but it's well known Dave's innocent.

Legends

The evidence that convicted him was he was in company with the robber that day. Dave was in the wrong place at the wrong time and it's cost him 26 years.

His brother **Tundy** who was wanted for the same robbery as Shearer and Dave was on the run till the armed police surrounded his car. Before he could surrender the police opened fire to kill him. Tundy returned fire to save his life with an AK47 and a chase took place from Lancaster to Rochdale in Manchester.

Because of the police many innocent people were shot and lucky for Tundy he was wearing a bullet-proof vest that saved his life, as he was shot many times himself also his co-accused was handcuffed up and legs tied and on video the police were seen firing shoots around him as he was under arrest. The same police are involved in beating **Mark Boomer** (See heading 'Mark Boomer) and planting a gun on him on video.

R.I.P.

Sadly missed are **Chris Swarray** and **Martin Bennet** who were shot dead in '99 and will be missed by many people and their families.

Also respect to **Ian McLeod**, **Paul Clements**, **Fly** and **Kevin Lewis** of the Doddington firm who were also shot dead and will be missed by their friends and family and lets hope the peace in Moss Side stands and no more people need to die or be locked up so keep the peace and respect from Salford.

Albert Scott

Albert has been working at PMS security since his release from his 10-year sentence. While Albert was in an open prison he escaped while waiting for his parole answer, we rushed him back to prison and told him to get his parole answer first, lucky for Albert he wasn't noticed missing and he got his parole. Another time before that Albert escaped and while we were all in this house the police surrounded it. I asked the police through the house window, "Who do you want?" They said, "Albert Scott." So there was about six of us in the house at that time and we all shook Albert's hand and said "See you soon." The police burst in and never even noticed Albert sat there waiting to be arrested!

The Manchester Mob

Bobby Spears

I met Bobby at a rave in Salford after my release in '88. Sadly for Bobby his brother shot his girlfriend dead and himself not long after my release. I know I was Bobby's strength at that time as I went through the same as Bobby when my brother and his girlfriend killed themselves many years before that. Bobby being a one to avoid jail and being very successful with his security and his own house, girlfriend and son Jordan so keep the good work up, Bobby, your old friend Paul – Respect.

Alan Wheat
'Mallet Head'

Known as Mallet Head because of the shape of his head. Mallet Head was on trial for attempted murder and while the jury were out to give their verdict they were sent home for the following day because they couldn't reach a verdict. Mallet Head was taken back to Liverpool jail for the night and while on the coach being taken back to prison he and the other cons beat up and tied the escort up and escaped. The following day in court the jury had come back and found Mallet Head not guilty! When he was finally arrested he was sentenced to four years for the escape. When released he took up security work in Spain and he's been very successful since – Respect, Paul.

Paul, my old china, that was brilliant. Listen, I know you're waiting for the appeal court decision on your own case later this summer after having had the evidence reheard at the Royal Courts of Appeal. It's not easy waiting for an answer...chin up.

How they could keep you waiting another month for the answer while they go sunning their balls off in some sunny place I don't know, cheeky bastards. As if a man's liberty meant nothing to them – God Bless, Charlie Bronson. Right it's back to my write-ups – enjoy or I'll send Pauline New around to sort you out.

Legends

The Manchester Mauler

Big Steve got a life sentence in the early 70s, he was only 19 years old but a big powerful lad and fearless, not long after he received the life sentence he was moved to Wakefield top security prison where he took a workshop screw hostage. Armed police were brought in, Stevie released the screw unharmed and he was later sent to Broadmoor. He's still locked up and has served over 25 years. Bear in mind he was a lad of 19 when he was sent down he's lost a lot so it must be time to let him go home now.

Dominic Noonan

I met Dominic in Wandsworth Prison block – he's one of the Noonan brothers, a well-known family. There's loads of stories to write about Dominic but I guess the best known one was in Leeds Prison in the 80s. Dominic climbed up on a roof to protest about prison brutality the screws went up after him and slung him off – they broke his leg!

Dominic spent years in the dungeons but he survived it and got out, sadly though he returned and is now serving 14 years. Dominic wants to write a book, if so then what a book it would be for the Manchester area, recently Dominic's changed his name to 'Dominic Lattlay-Fottfoy', he's done this all legal and above board. Dominic's writing a book and I hope he gets it off the ground, should be explosive! The legend will survive again.

Darren Ramsey

I met this guy up in Hull Prison in 1990; he was a cat 'A' remand prisoner and a Manchester lad nicked for armed robbery. They used to put us out on the exercise yard together. Darren used to help train me up, we got a gym mat and a 10 kilo medicine ball he would sling that ball at me for a solid hour as I done my sit ups.

One day Daz slung it and it slipped through my hands and I almost pushed my nose into the back of my skull! But I'd go through it all again just to see the look on his face! A great guy. A great friend. Darren later got a 'Not Guilty' and went home – only right too!

The Manchester Mob

Andy Vassell

I met Andy in Risley jail back in 1985, a Manchester legend, a well-respected man. Andy helped me through a crazy time in my life. The 80s were violent years for me. If I wasn't up on prison roofs then I was taking hostages or smashing in somebody's face.

Andy came into my life at a good time, as he was a cool guy, smart and intelligent. I learnt a lot from this man. He made me stop and think and count to 10. He ended up with nine years and he served six, he kept fit and strong and went out and won.

Men like Andy Vassell are a rare breed, a dying breed but they live on in my book of Legends for all to see. When I met Andy – Stevie Wonder had a No 1 hit with – *I just called to say I love you.* We used to sing that every day at the top of our voices and at times the whole wing used to join in. You be lucky Andy – I just called to say you're a legend.

Matty Wainwright

Matty's done the rounds, units, blocks, dungeons and they label him violent but it's no wonder. He's got more scars on him than Al Capone but cowards always did these scars slyly, always! He was threatened with a knife on the unit in Woodhill in '96 so he used self-defence and the con got hurt bad but what's Matty gotta do, let the con stab him? Matty done what any sane man would, smashed his way to survival. A good Manchester lad is Matty a man I respect and admire.

9

The Scottish Clans

JAMES CROSBIE 1937 –

James Crosbie - 2000

James Crosbie was born on January 15th 1937 into a respectable, working class Roman Catholic family, and was the middle son in a family of three brothers. James was never in serious trouble until 1954 when, at the age of 17, he appeared in front of the Sheriff Court on charges of stealing and was sentenced to two years probation.

In September 1954 he joined the RAF under the delusion that everyone in the RAF got to fly about in aeroplanes. He soon discovered his mistake and, as a regular airman, exercised his option to buy himself out. He was in minor breach of probation two or three times and in February 1955 he was sentenced to four years Borstal training for office breaking and stealing. James served two years in Polmont Borstal, Scotland, and when released he was immediately called up for National Service.

In 1957 he appeared at Aldershot magistrates' court for stealing an officers car and was sentenced to six months. When he was released from Wandsworth Prison in 1958 he failed to return to his unit and began living in London.

In 1958 James appeared at the county of London Sessions and was sentenced to three years Corrective Training (it didn't work!) on charges of receiving stolen property. A year after his release from Maidstone Prison he appeared at the Old Bailey charged along with Jack Witney (later sentenced to life imprisonment for the murder by shooting of three flying squad detectives in 1966) and two other men with Conspiracy to Rob, along with two further charges of Possessing Offensive Weapons. This time the sentence was $3^{1/2}$ years.

When he left prison this time James travelled to Ghana, West Africa, where he stayed with a relative who was the manager of a cocoa mill in Takoradi, a coastal town of that country. He finally returned to Glasgow in 1965 and later on in that year was sentenced to 18 months for attempting to break into a bank in Riddrie, Glasgow. He was released from Peterhead in April 1966 and married on November the 5th that same year. By now he'd started a small wrought-iron business and was doing very well till an offence of his past caught up with him and late in 1967 he was sentenced to 18 months.

When James was released in 1968 he returned to his wrought-iron shop and worked successfully for several years. During this time he took flying lessons and became a pilot, taking an extra courses at Southend airport where he trained on larger, twin-engine aircraft. In the meantime his business was growing and he'd bought a small factory and expanded into manufacturing furniture. In 1971, he expanded further, renting a large main street shop in Springburn Road, Glasgow retailing furniture, which he imported himself from Germany. By now his family, consisting of his wife Margaret and his son Gregory, born in July 69, had moved to a semi-detached house in the suburb of Bishopbriggs.

On May 23rd 1972 James and an accomplice carried out an armed raid on the Clydesdale bank, Hillington, and stole over £65,000, a record haul for a bank robbery in Scotland.

On April 30th 1974 James and another accomplice raided the Clydesdale bank at Whiteinch and stole £87,000, a new record for

Legends

a bank robbery in Scotland. About two months later James was arrested, charged with the Whiteinch robbery and remanded to Barlinnie Prison. Through a blunder by the police he was given bail and promptly disappeared before they could charge him with the robbery at Hillington. Two months later, on August 8th, James single-handedly held up a branch of the Royal Bank of Scotland in Edinburgh and stole £17,000 (still the biggest amount stolen by a lone bank-robber in Scotland).

20 YEARS IN JAIL FOR BANK ROBBER ON A BIKE

By ARNOT McWHINNIE

TRAINEE pilot James Crosbie CYCLED biggest-ever bank robbery with his £ rucksack.
Yesterday, the bank raider with a pass and big spending WALKED from the High jail sentence.

The high-flier

JAMES CROSBIE, who holds a pilot's licence, was the high-flier who came to earth with a bang.

Fittingly, his file number on the membership list of Glasgow Flying Club was 006 for, following in James Bond's footsteps, he loved planes, guns, women and fast cars.

He was a flamboyant character, variously described as a "lovable rogue", a "plausible villain", and a "fun-loving Walter Mitty". Everything he did, touched or sold, pointed to a larger-than-life personality crying out to impress.

Everything he did, he was out to impress . . from piloting a plane, to a life of crime

Two days later, when attempting to get out of Edinburgh, he was spotted by two Glasgow detectives and arrested as he walked out of a shop.

At the High Court in Edinburgh, Lord Robertson took note that James had failed to cooperate with the police in the matter of naming his accomplices or returning any of the stolen money. Telling James that, in his opinion, he was the most dangerous man in Scotland, Lord Robertson sentenced him to 20 years.

During the first year of his sentence James made two escape attempts by sawing through his window bars, but he never made it over the wall. He was kept on 'A' category for over three years before being allowed to attend education classes or out onto the outer yard to watch the prison football matches.

During his time in Peterhead James took up writing. In his first attempt at the annual Koestler Awards Scheme he won first prize in both the novel and playwriting categories he'd entered. He also attended education classes and passed about six 'O'-levels, three 'Highers', and gained two distinctions when passing the HNC Certificate in Business Studies.

The Scottish Clans

In all, James served a total of 12 years and eight months before being released from his 20-year sentence. On his release from prison he was accepted for the English Literature and Scottish Literature BA course at Glasgow University where he passed his first year in the top 10% of the class.

In 1988 James purchased a television set and a video recorder using false details to obtain credit. He was arrested for this and later sentenced to three years for fraud, which put an end to his university aspirations.

On finishing the three years James moved out to Spain where he lived until he was arrested at Dover in 1993 for smuggling 20 kilos of cannabis into the country. He was sentenced to 18 months at Maidstone Crown Court for this and served most of his sentence at Stamford Hill Prison on the Isle of Sheppey.

James returned to Spain on his release and continued operations there until in 1996 when he was caught at Birmingham airport carrying 50 kilos of cannabis. This time it was Warwick Crown Court and he was sentenced to 4$^{1}/_{2}$ years. He spent his sentence as constructively as he could, bringing his total of Koestler certificates up to nine (Which I've gotta beat cos I've got seven to date.) and passing an advanced level course on creative writing.

On his release from Haverigg Prison James returned to Glasgow where he got married for the second time to Marlene. He's currently living in Glasgow, working hard on his writing and has written the film script for my life story based on my autobiography, *Silent Scream,* which we hope to have turned into a film before I'm released, anyone interested? James has also written his own life story called *ITS CRIMINAL* and hopes to see it on the bookshelves by 2001. I've read it and up to now it's a blinding read, in fact nothing's come out of Scotland, in the true crime sector, as good as this book for a good few years. James has also written some thrillers: *ASHANTI GOLD* and *PAYDAY FOR SOME.* To show you how good James is at writing I've asked him to guest write some of the following write ups cos he's the man who knows all about Scottish legends, as he's done enough time and he's two ahead of me on the Koestler Awards. (But I aim to get 10 and then retire the champ!) See James in the video documentary *Sincerely Yours.* Give it hell, James!

Legends

Sawney Bean and his cannibalistic family - @ 1600

The first written reference about Sawney Bean and his incestuous, cannibalistic family appeared about the year 1700. Arguments have gone on as to whether the Sawney Bean family actually existed or the story was simply a myth or a legend that grew as time went on. However, several books on the subject are agreed that Sawney Bean was the son of a hedger and ditcher who lived in the county of East Lothian, eight miles east of Edinburgh. Sawney himself took up the same occupation but became disillusioned and ran away with a woman to live on the west coast of Scotland in the county of Galloway. The couple took up residence in a deep labyrinth of caves on the seashore directly beneath the well-known Bennane Head, three miles north of the small coastal town of Ballantrae.

It is said that Sawney and his wife lived in these caves for twenty five years without once visiting any city, town or village and during their time there they spawned a completely incestuous family of eight sons, six daughters, eighteen grandsons and fourteen granddaughters. Throughout their lives in the cave the family supported itself by robbing and murdering any stray travellers that ventured within reach of their cave. Once their victim had been killed the body was taken to the cave where it was butchered into manageable pieces then pickled, smoked and cured for the family's consumption. Often there was too much food and Sawney would order arms and legs and other parts of the carcases to be thrown into the sea. These limbs were often washed up on shore causing great fear and consternation among local people.

Spies were sent to scout the district but without exception they either disappeared forever or returned empty handed. Unable to find any obvious explanation for the body parts found on the shore, and in the complete absence of any other likely suspects, several innkeepers were accused of robbing and murdering their guests. As well as these fruitless efforts many an honest traveller was suspected and hanged, as well as dozens of unfortunate strangers who were executed in an effort to rid the countryside of the evil killers. And yet, in those days of religious fear and belief in the hereafter, it was noted that not one of the condemned persons made a deathbed confession. These innocent people were

252

arrested and tortured, blamed for the killings and put to death and for a while the local inhabitants would be satisfied that the murderer had been brought to justice. That is until more arms and legs were washed ashore and all their fears were rekindled.

The story goes that one night a man and his wife were riding past Bennane Head when Sawney's family attacked them. The man saw his wife dragged from her horse and butchered before his eyes. He was trying to fend off the ravening family when a group of horsemen returning from a nearby fair approached them and his attackers ran off into the night. For the first time a victim of the Sawney Bean family had escaped and lived to tell the tale.

When news of the woman's horrific murder and her husband's lucky escape was reported to the authorities it was decided to petition King James VI for assistance in apprehending the murderous pack. In reply the King despatched four hundred mounted men and a pack of bloodhounds to thoroughly search the surrounding area. The local authorities had organised searches before and had even passed the open entrance to the series of caves below Bennane Head but, because the entrance of the cave would obviously be covered by water at high tide, no one had thought to enter the caves. The bloodhounds, however, refused to pass the entrance and set up howling and barking and trying to pull their masters inside the cavern. Dragged in by the panting hounds the searchers were astonished to discover that the caves penetrated more than a mile into the cliffs and wound their way upwards in a series of smaller chambers all interconnected by narrow paths and tunnels. Eventually they entered the living area of Sawney's family to find a scene of almost indescribable horror. Suspended from ropes were human legs, arms, hands and feet of men, woman and children, all victims of the hellish Bean family. There was body parts pickled in barrels and smoked cured thighs hanging from the roof. As well as the human remains there was an enormous pile of clothing, gold and other valuables that the family had collected over the years.

Sawney Bean and his entire family were taken in chains to the Tollbooth in Edinburgh and from there to Leith where they were executed without benefit of a trial or any legal process. The male members of the family were dismembered, their hands and feet being severed, and left to bleed to death while their womenfolk, children included, were made to watch. After every male member

Legends

of the family had expired the entire female side were burned to death on three separate bonfires.

There are many people who believe in the Legend of Sawney Bean, and certainly he lived in East Lothian and moved from there to Galloway. It is also true that the caves below Bennane Head, just off the A77 north of Ballantrae, exist as described. And it is also true that very many people, mostly unknown travellers, disappeared forever from the Galloway area around 1600 – 1630.

There is evidence that The Legend of Sawney Bean is true, although maybe exaggerated a little. There has been books written and folksongs sung – *The Ballad of Sawney Bain* (an alternative spelling) - *Sawney Bean* by Robert Nye - *The Cannibalistic Family of Sawney Bean* by John Mackey - *On the Trail of Sawney Bean and His Cannibalistic Family* by R Deen - *The Legend of Sawney Bean* by Ronald Holmes to name only some.

Bible John ?

The City of Glasgow Police also have a question mark after the name 'Bible John'. For although they know he murdered three young women in the late 1960's after picking them up in Glasgow's famous Barrowland Ballroom, and even though they had an eye witness, they have never been able to identify the man they call Bible John.

The first murder took place on 23rd February 1968, when nurse Pat Docker went dancing at the Barrowland Ballroom. She was found beaten up and strangled with her own tights.

Efforts were made to trace her movements after she left the dance hall. Taxi drivers were questioned and 1,000 posters showing her picture and asking for help were distributed, all to no avail. No one came forward and no progress was made towards the solving of the brutal murder.

The next murder occurred on 17th August 1969. On the evening of Saturday the 16th. Jemima McDonald visited the Barrowland, where she was seen in the company of a tall, smartly dressed man with reddish-fair hair that was cut unfashionably short. Thirty hours later Jemima's body was found battered and with her tights pulled tightly around her neck. Police failed to make any progress in solving the murder.

With the third and (as far as we know) last victim, the police

The Scottish Clans

became confident that they would catch the killer: they now had an eyewitness who had spoken to the man.

On the night of Oct. 30th Helen Puttock went to Barrowland with her sister Jeannie. There she met and danced with a man who had introduced himself as John. At the end of the evening both girls and 'John' shared a taxi, dropping Jeannie off first before carrying on to Helen's home.

The next morning a man out walking his dog discovered Helen's naked body in a lane. She had been badly beaten about the head and strangled with her own tights.

A shocked Jeannie was able to give the police a description of the man who had escorted them home, mentioning also that he had a biblical turn of phrase; hence the sobriquet - Bible John.

A distinctive Identi-kit photo was produced and widely circulated, and for months, even years afterwards, anyone remotely resembling the picture was questioned and eliminated. Despite this, the police drew no closer to their quarry and Bible John remained anonymous. It was even suspected that a policeman or a serviceman could be responsible for the murders. The height, unfashionably short hair, neat appearance and good

articulation making this a distinct possibility.

Detective Superintendent Joe Beattie, the man in charge of the investigation, committed hundred of officers to the hunt and the case has never been closed. As late as February 1996 the body of a suspect, who had been buried for over sixteen years, was exhumed and his remains tested for DNA evidence, but still no positive results were forthcoming. The file will never be closed.

Bible John - An Identi-kit picture

James 'Jimmy' Boyle 1944

Jimmy Boyle is yet another product of the Gorbals, and was the second youngest in a family of four brothers. With his mother working at three different cleaning jobs in order to support her family, the young Boyle spent much of his time dodging school and roaming the tenement streets and back courts along with other kids in much the same family situation. Stealing and running about in a gang had always been the norm for children born into the ghetto of the Gorbals and Jimmy was no exception. Jimmy was admired by his peers for his daring-do activities, but it was when he turned twelve and graduated to Saint Bonaventure's Junior Secondary school that he moved up a league and began to build a reputation for himself as good fighter, as well as an accomplished shop-lifter and thief. By now he was the leader of 'The Scull' gang, a breakaway group from the 'Young Wild Cumbie'. However, despite his involvement in stealing and shop-breaking, it was not until 1957, at the age of thirteen, that Jimmy recorded his first criminal conviction, he was charged with Theft - stealing the money and contents of a bubble-gum machine.

Jimmy was held in Larchgrove remand home before being sentenced to two years probation. That same year he received a sentence of fourteen days for Breaking and Entering office premises. In 1958 it was shop-breaking and this time his sentence was twenty-eight days - his 'record' was growing.

Jimmy left school at the age of fifteen and later that year, 1959, he was arrested for stealing a safe from a garage. The police could find no evidence that would convict him. Later that same year, however, he was caught stealing a cash-box from a fairground stall and once again charged with theft. When he appeared in front of the Sheriff he was remanded for reports before being sentenced to an indefinite period of training at Saint John's, an Approved School that stood next door to the, by now, familiar Larchgrove Remand Home in the East of Glasgow. Jimmy failed to return from a 'home leave', preferring the lure of London to the discipline of Approved School.

One night in London, Jimmy and a pal came across an electrical-goods shop; its window was broken. They reached in to help themselves to two transistor radios and, as soon as they had their hands on the loot, two constables leapt out from their hiding place and done them. After a court appearance, Jimmy was ordered to be returned to Saint John's - released in 1960.

Jimmy worked at several jobs during the 60s, even a spell in the shipyards. He decided to try London once again, often travelling back to Glasgow for a quick visit. In 1961, during one of his flying visits, he was arrested for shop-breaking and remanded to Barlinnie prison (The Bar-L) for Borstal reports. Later, he was sentenced to Borstal Training and transferred to Polmont Borstal. His time in Polmont was uneventful, except he was found to be suffering from bronchial tuberculosis and had to undergo two operations in hospital. He was released from Polmont in 1962 after serving just fourteen months of his sentence.

In 1962 Jimmy became involved in his first violent crime when he was caught up in a running gang fight in Crown Street, Glasgow. During the melee several innocent passers by were stabbed and Jimmy ended up being charged with seven accounts of serious assault. Once again he was remanded to Bar-L, but in January 1963 he was bailed out on the assault cases.

Plaincothes police officer draws his baton to defend a razor attack in Glasgow.

Shortly after this Jimmy was set upon by a rival gang of brothers, who hacked at him with hatchets and other weapons, leaving him for dead in the street. But he made his way to hospital and received treatment. The next day his enemies were saying they had "done Boyle up" and that he was "finished". In order to scotch the rumours Jimmy got himself smartly dressed and with the help of his friends, went down to the pub where the brothers were drinking and boasting of how they had "tuned Boyle up good style". The brothers were stunned when their 'victim' appeared at the bar in apparent good health, nodding and grinning over at them, totally demolishing their morale and laying the lie of their boasting.

In 1963 Jimmy went back down to London where he began money lending, but one evening a policeman stopped him for questioning and Jimmy assaulted him. He was sentenced to six weeks in 'The Scrubs' and 'gate arrested' by the Glasgow police on the morning of his release. Flown under escort to Glasgow, he was put on trial for the seven assault charges he was already on bail for and sentenced to two years.

In Barlinnie he was suspected of stabbing another prisoner, but lack of evidence meant he wasn't charged. However, not to be

Legends

outdone, the authorities placed him on Rule 36 (a fancy name for solitary confinement), saying he was a subversive element. After six months of Rule 36 Jimmy was allowed back into the mainstream population in 'A' hall, an adult wing, where it was hoped that the older men would effect a calming influence on him. He completed his sentence without any serious trouble.

By now Jimmy's gang had moved into the 'protection' game, looking after the moneylenders as well as illegal Shebeen (unlicensed drink sellers) operators. Money was pouring in, and all the gang had to do was let their interest be known to make sure everybody behaved themselves. Jimmy settled down a little, sharing his life with his new girlfriend, Margaret.

One night eight detectives raided Jimmy's flat and arrested him on a murder charge. To his surprise Jimmy found himself accused of murdering and robbing a man called Lynch, the robbery part of the charge making it a capital crime where the death penalty could be imposed. He was sent for trial at the High court in Glasgow. But owing to Jimmy's stout denials of even *knowing* the murdered man, a good alibi, and a dearth of witnesses for the prosecution, the trial ended on the second day with Jimmy walking free from the courtroom.

Two weeks after his acquittal on the murder charge, Jimmy became involved in a fight with two men, one of whom lost an eye, the other receiving a severe cut to his hand. Then the police found out that Jimmy had been at a party where a man had been stabbed to death and he promptly found himself once more on remand in the Bar-L. The Procurator Fiscal decided to hold the murder charge in abeyance and decided to proceed with the lost eye and cut hand assault charge.

Jimmy appeared at the Sheriff Court for a jury trial and was found guilty of the assaults and sentenced to two years. A few months into this sentence he was taken back to the High Court and the murder charge proceeded with. Witnesses were hard to find, there being stories in the press about 'missing witnesses', leaving people fearful of what might happen to them. Then shortly before the trial, the chief prosecution witness had his house bombed.

The trial began and there was very little evidence against Jimmy, no prosecution witnesses available. The trial was only in its second day when the Procurator Fiscal offered to accept a 'not guilty' plea to the murder charge. Jimmy pleaded guilty to 'Pushing and

The Scottish Clans

Jostling' and was sentenced to three months.

In January 1966, just after Margaret gave birth to his son, Jimmy was transferred to Peterhead to do his sentence. At this time he was still only twenty-two years of age and already he had amassed a fearful reputation. It was probably because of this reputation that he found himself isolated under the iniquitous Rule 36 where he immediately went on a 'dirty' protest and soon found himself consigned to the 'silent cell'.

Jimmy was released from prison in January of 1967 and returned to the Gorbals, taking up once again with his old associates and offering 'protection' to the illegal moneylenders. At the same time, he opened up his own money lending book as well as operating illegal drinking Shebeens. Things were going well for him now, but one evening in July 1967, Jimmy went to the house of a man named 'Babs' Rooney who was behind in his payments. In the course of an argument, Jimmy slashed him across the chest leaving him bleeding severely, but when he left the house Rooney was still very much alive. The next morning Jimmy got news that Rooney was dead and the police were busy raiding houses looking for him.

Jimmy, knowing that the police would make every effort to convict him, lay low in Glasgow for a few weeks before moving down to London where the Kray twins, Reggie and Ronnie, arranged a flat for him. He stayed there for two months until armed police raided a pub in East London and caught him sitting having a drink. He was immediately flown back to Glasgow and charged with the murder of 'Babs' Rooney.

The trial began in November 1967, and this time, despite a witness having his house bombed, he was unanimously found guilty. Lord Cameron sentenced him to 'Life Imprisonment' with the recommendation that he serve no less than fifteen years.

Jimmy was no sooner in the prison when he had an altercation with a hall governor, punched him in the face and tried to smash him over the head with an inkwell case. He received a severe beating-up and was forced into a straightjacket before being thrown into a padded cell. Somehow or other Jimmy escaped from the straightjacket and proceeded to wreck what little there was in the cell, tearing off the heavy canvas covers and stripping the coir stuffing from the walls. He was held in the punishment cells until December 1967, during which time he received news that Margaret had given birth to a daughter. Shortly afterwards he was taken through to Edinburgh for his appeal to be heard. The three judges took about five minutes to throw out his appeal and when Jimmy was taken down he was escorted straight to Porterfield prison in Inverness and placed in the punishment cells.

In January 1968 Jimmy was indicted for the assault on the Bar-L governor and taken under armed escort to Glasgow High Court where he pled guilty and received a sentence of eighteen months and returned to Porterfield. He was only back a few days when he smashed up the governor's office and was immediately flung into the silent cell. Deciding to be as awkward as possible he began a dirty protest, smearing the walls of his cell and his body with excrement and warning the screws that he would attack them and any governor at every opportunity.

Four months after he arrived at Porterfield Jimmy was moved to Peterhead to make room for four rioters who had attacked the screws in the tailor shop there, badly stabbing one or two of them in the process. On his first day at Peterhead Jimmy punched a screw and was hustled straight down to the punishment block. There he was badly beaten, but he fought back, biting a screw in the neck in the process. As a result he found himself on three charges of assault. In retaliation, and in order to strengthen his own defence, Jimmy counter charged the screws with assaulting him.

In October 1968 Jimmy was tried at Aberdeen High Court on the three assault charges and was found guilty of two of them. He was sentenced to four years and returned directly to Porterfield punishment block where, for almost a year, he went through a series of minor assaults in his running battle with the screws. But in November 1969 he was refused permission to buy Christmas presents to send to his children and once again Jimmy attacked a governor, this time spitting on him and trying to force his desk on top of him. He was removed to a newly built punishment block and thrown into a cell. However, as the building was just newly built Jimmy discovered that the cement between the bricks was still relatively soft. He ripped the cover off a ventilator shaft and proceeded to dig out the cement. Within an hour he had broken through to the cell next door, greeting its surprised occupant with a crazy grin. In the course of the night, with the digging squad getting bigger every time they broke through a wall, the individual cells became a dormitory. They then began to prepare for the arrival of the morning shift of screws by building a brick barricade across the width of the cells, ready to defy any attempt to move them. The screws attacked with water hoses and fourteen-pound sledgehammers before finally subduing them with their long riot sticks and dragging them back to their original punishment cells.

Later Jimmy was charged with his attack on the governor and, along with the others, destroying prison property. He spent six months in solitary without once leaving his cell and in May 1970 was sentenced to a further six months for his attempted assault on the governor and destruction of prison property. From the court he was taken to Peterhead prison where he decided to settle down and try and get some sense into his existence. For over a year things quietened down, then a man named Bennet who was serving fifteen years, plus a life sentence for stabbing another prisoner in Peterhead, was stabbed three times while walking down a corridor. Although there was no evidence that Jimmy had anything to do with the stabbing, he found himself once again in the punishment block on Rule 36. He spent two months there before being allowed back into the prison mainstream.

Early in December 1971 Jimmy received word that his mother had died and he was taken down to Barlinnie under heavy escort so he could attend her funeral. He was kept handcuffed to two prison officers and armed police surrounded the graveyard keeping watch on him and the crowd throughout the entire ceremony. Immediately afterwards he was returned to Peterhead.

On the fourth of January 1972 there was a disturbance during the evening recreation when a prisoner went berserk and smashed the hall television sets and other furniture. The following day Jimmy was dragged out of his cell and taken to the punishment block where he was assaulted and almost drowned in a sink full of dirty water. He was severely beaten and when he came to he found

Legends

himself in the cages of the segregation unit at Porterfield, buckled into a straightjacket. The next three months passed in the cages then the prison department returned him to Peterhead.

Back in Peterhead the prisoner Bennet let it be known that he intended to "do" Jimmy and the result of this was a pitched battle in the exercise yard, which soon developed into a riot. The next day both Jimmy and Bennet, along with some others, were charged with rioting and assaulting prison officers. Confined to the cellblock, Jimmy found himself confronted one day by Bennet, who had a knife. During the fight Jimmy managed to take the knife from Bennet and stabbed him several times in the chest, puncturing his lung. Later that same day Jimmy was charged with the attempted murder of Bennet and a few weeks later he was returned to Porterfield.

In December 1972 Jimmy appeared at Aberdeen Sheriff court along with the others charged over the yard riot in Peterhead. However, after legal argument the Sheriff dismissed the charges and Jimmy was returned to Porterfield.

Just after Christmas that same month, during a period of association, a riot broke out in the cages area of Porterfield, when Jimmy and four other prisoners attacked the officers on duty. One of the screws lost an eye and others received stab wounds before the prisoners were beaten unconscious. A week later all the prisoners were charged with attempting to murder six prison officers. Now Jimmy had two High court appearances to look forward to: the attempted murder of Bennett and the attempted murder of the six screws at Inverness.

The Bennett case was tried at Aberdeen High Court in January 1973 and Jimmy was happy to be acquitted before being taken back to Inverness. It was just over a month after this trial that Jimmy was given his civilian clothes and driven southwards. Not having been told where or why he was going, he was surprised to find himself being driven to Barlinnie prison where he was admitted to the, often rumoured about, revolutionary 'Special Unit'. This new Unit was designed to give psychiatric support and help especially difficult prisoners to grow into more responsible beings, and to show them that was some light at the end of their long, individual dark tunnels. It took Jimmy some time to come to grips with the relaxed regime in the Unit and he found it difficult to settle. And always at the back of his mind was the knowledge that

The Scottish Clans

he would have to return to Porterfield, and the cages, to stand trial for the riot and attempted murder of the six screws.

After about three months Jimmy was taken back to Porterfield and under massive security precautions, including a police helicopter, the trial began. By the end of the trial the attempted murder charges had been dropped and the men involved were found guilty only of assault and attempting to escape. They were all sentenced to six years on top and after the trial Jimmy was taken back to the Special Unit.

Once he had settled properly into the open regime at the Unit, Jimmy turned his mind first to clay modelling and then on to sculpting in stone. Mr Richard De Marco, the director of an Edinburgh gallery, praised his work and within a few years of entering the unit Jimmy was invited to hold a public exhibition of his work. The exhibition was a great success and Jimmy found himself getting commissions, one of which was a giant Gulliver for a children's park.

In 1977 Jimmy had his autobiography published - *A Sense of Freedom* – it was an immediate success. Sarah Trevelyan, a psychiatrist, was impressed enough by the book to visit Jimmy in the Special Unit. Their relationship developed into love and in 1980 they were married at Balfron registry office.

Shortly after his wedding Jimmy was transferred to Saughton prison in Edinburgh to complete the final part of his sentence. He was given work in the education unit there and after about a year placed on the Training for Freedom scheme. This meant he lived in a hostel within the prison but went out to work every day, in his case community social work. He was released exactly on his fifteen year recommended time and lived in Edinburgh with his wife, Sarah. There, against strong opposition from local residents, Jimmy and Sarah opened a centre for the care of drug addicts and social inadequates: The Gateway Exchange.

* Footnote from Charlie:

I was in the block in Long Larten in 1990 when the prison was about to do a documentary on long term prisoners. It was to be a forum organised by inmates, they wanted me, Charlie Bronson, to appear on it so as to express my own personal beliefs on the subject of long-term isolation. I was picked to go on a group and Jimmy Boyle was invited to be on the same group. Jimmy had himself served time, quite a bit of time!

Jimmy's a legend to many both inside and outside of prison, he's written several books and started up the 'Streets Ahead' scheme in Scotland to help junkies and the like, did a great job. He's now a law abiding and hard working man. He's also probably best known for his sculptures and artwork he produced while in prison. The Krays always spoke highly

Legends

of Jimmy so it was a privilege to meet up with the guy. He spoke up very well for the cons and for a man who was once labelled 'The Most Vicious Man' in Scotland he's achieved a lot in his life.

Now, in the year 2000, Jimmy Boyle is a success story that can only be admired and is an inspiration to anyone who feels that there is nothing left in the world for them. Keep strong Jimmy, your pal – Charles Bronson.

Paul John Ferris 1963 –

The youngest son in a family of four sisters and one older brother, Paul Ferris was born and brought up in the notorious, crime laden, Blackhill district in the northeast of Glasgow. With a bank robber father who spent time in and out of prison for robbery and tax evasion, it reflects great credit on his mother that Paul kept himself out of any serious trouble as a young boy. However, although he did not fall foul of the police, the bullying he received as a schoolboy at St Philomena's primary school marred his early years. At only nine years of age Paul found himself having to suffer the attentions of a new generation of a notorious Blackhill crime family, the Welshes. Every day he, and other schoolboys, were bullied and had their money taken from them by the young Welsh family, eight brothers in all, who would quickly come to the aid of any of their siblings. But Paul refused to give in to the Welshes, taking his licks and bidding his time, telling himself that one day he would wreak revenge on the Welsh family. It was this lust for revenge, and the taking of it through lone razor and knife attacks on the bullies, that began the reputation that was to drive Paul into a life of gangsterism, violence and mutilation.

Paul left St Roch's secondary school at sixteen without having come to the attention of the police and began work in a brewery, but he became disillusioned and soon turned to crime. His first conviction was for a robbery in Airdrie, when he and a pal attacked a man depositing money in a night safe. One of the first things he did in the Longriggend Remand Unit was to slash another prisoner, sending an obvious message to the rest of the inmates. He left Longriggend with his name and reputation even bigger in the minds of the young Glasgow criminals.

Paul's next sentence was twelve months in the tough, Glenochil Young Offender's Institution. During his stay there he formed a gang, the 'Glenochil Wolves', and led attacks on the sex offenders that were there. It was later claimed that the 'Wolves' were directly to blame for the suicides of at least ten sex offenders between 1981 and 1984. Paul is quoted as saying that the figure gave him: "A lot of peace and satisfaction".

As a lifelong friend of Arthur Thompson Jnr, Paul was welcomed into the fold of the Thompson family. Arthur Snr, the most well known crime figure in Glasgow, recognised the potential in the young Paul and was keen to recruit him as an enforcer for his money lending and drug dealing businesses. Impressed by the power of Arthur Snr, Paul was pleased to become a member of what was the foremost crime family in Glasgow, where he was treated almost as a son. By the age of just nineteen he had become chief enforcer for Arthur Thompson, meting out punishments and exacting revenge on anyone who offended against 'The Godfather'.

In a world where cheating, conning, and conniving were the daily bread, Paul's talents were in constant demand and his stature in the underworld continued to grow. Anything he was asked to do, he would carry out with enthusiasm, whether it be stabbing, shooting, or blowing up someone's club or pub. One time, when Arthur Jnr paid £50,000 for two kilos of cocaine and received two house bricks instead, it was Paul who was sent in to recover the money and punish the offenders. And he was still only nineteen when he was ordered to punish a thug called William Gibson for informing on Arthur Jnr, who had recently been sentenced to eleven years for drug dealing. Paul saw Gibson, with his brother and some friends, in a car late one night and gave chase, catching up with them and shooting into the car, before wounding Gibson in the leg. Paul was later charged with four attempted murders but was acquitted by a jury at the High Court, who brought in a "Not Proven" verdict. (This is a verdict available to a Scottish jury, and it is reputed to really mean: "We know you did it, but we haven't proved it").

Despite working for the Thompson family, Paul and his two best friends, Joe (Bananas) Hanlon and Robert Glover carried on with some of their own criminal enterprises and, inevitably, he ended up back in prison. However, whenever he was in prison Paul

Legends

continued to cause trouble to the authorities. In the newly built Shotts prison in 1982, where he was serving a sentence, a prison officer was taken hostage and held for two days, while millions of pounds worth of damage was done to the showcase building. 1987 saw Paul back in Glenochil (adult prison), serving three years for firearms offences. Shortly after his arrival the prison erupted in violence, with assaults on staff, acts of sabotage that finally culminated with every wing in Glenochil exploding in a long, wrecking riot, almost closing the place down.

However the Thompson family had disillusioned Paul and he was beginning to feel used by them. For the last few years he had been at the forefront of any violence that was required, recovering bad debts and settling old scores. He was constantly in the front line and realised that little cash rewards were coming his way. The split was already widening when Paul was arrested in Rothesay, Scotland, on drug charges. He believed that Arthur Snr had informed on him because he was setting up his own drug and protection empire. In the end he was acquitted of the drugs charges but jailed for possession of a shotgun. But as far as Paul was concerned, Arthur Thompson, the man he had once revered, was now a hated enemy.

When he was released from prison after the shotgun charge, Paul went to stay in London for a while. There he made contact with men in the drugs scene, doing deals and moving drugs up to Scotland. Soon he and his two henchmen, Joe Hanlon and Rab Glover, were making serious inroads in to Arthur Thompson's business. A very serious rivalry was growing between Paul and the Thompson family, which was bound to end in violence.

The business of the Rothesay drugs charge still rankled with Paul and one day when he spotted Arthur crossing Provanmill Road he drove at him in his car, running him over then turning and coming back to do the same again. Arthur recovered from the 'accident', but now open war had been declared between Paul and the Thompson family.

By September 1991, Arthur Jnr was nearing the end of his eleven year sentence and was due his first home leave from Noranside, an open prison where long term men served out the last few months of their time. For months Arthur Jnr had been mouthing off and telling everyone that he was going out to "take over" the Glasgow drugs trade and run Ferris out of town. On the first night of his

The Scottish Clans

home leave, as he was walking towards his father's house in Provanmill Road, someone ran up to him and fired a bullet into his back. Arthur managed to stagger to his father's front door and gasp that he had been shot before collapsing. He was rushed to hospital but the doctors were unable to save him. The bullet had entered his body and destroyed vital organs, Arthur Jnr, the young pretender, was dead.

There were no witnesses to the shooting but it was widely believed that it was Paul Ferris, Joe (Bananas) Hanlon, Robert Glover, and a fourth man who was never identified, who carried out the murder. In any event, on the morning of young Arthur's funeral, both Hanlon and Glover were found shot dead through the head outside their local pub, The Cottage Bar, in Shettleston, Glasgow. No one has ever been charged with their murder, and although it is generally agreed that it was a revenge killing by Arthur Snr, no grasses and no witnesses meant no charges.

Paul was charged with the murder of Arthur Thompson Jnr and appeared at the High Court in Glasgow. After the longest murder trial in Scottish legal history, spanning fifty-four days, and three hundred witnesses, Paul was found Not Guilty of the murder. He walked free from the courtroom to be cheered by a large crowd who had been gathering outside the building all day.

Once the trial was over Paul returned to his old haunts, undetered by the mutterings and threats from the once powerful Arthur Thompson. He would walk openly along Provanmill Road, passing casually by the house called 'The Ponderosa' where the Thompson family lived. No one made any effort against him, even although there was a rumoured £30,000 hit on his head.

In 1993 Paul moved into the legal security business, starting up a company called Premier Securities. His company supplied doormen for clubs, as well as security staff for stores and building sites and Paul seemed to have found his niche. But Paul was still having some trouble in his life.

In 1994, in Manchester, Paul was caught with a small quantity of cocaine in his possession. During his trial he argued that he required the coke for his personal use to help with a serious skin complaint he suffered from. He produced medical evidence to back his story and the end of his trial he was found not guilty.

Everything seemed to cool down for a while, but the police, suspecting that Paul was engaged in serious crime, launched 'Operation Shillelagh', and were keeping him under close surveillance and on 23rd May, 1997, he was arrested coming out of the house of a known gangster, John Ackerman, in Islington, north London. He had a large cardboard box in his arms, and when the police inspected its contents the box was found to contain three Ingram MAC 10 sub machine guns, six magazines, silencers, explosives and electronically operated detonators. Paul denied all knowledge of the weapons, explaining that he thought the box contained printing plates and £250,000. Needless to say, the police found this hard to believe and he was charged with the illegal possessing of firearms and explosives.

During his trial at the Old Bailey in July 1998, Paul repeated his claims, but the jury took the same view as the police and found him guilty as charged. The judge, Henry Blacksell Q.C. gave him a severe lecture before finally sentencing him to fourteen years. But after Paul had gone downstairs to the cells it was pointed out to the judge that the maximum sentence he could pass on him was ten years. Accordingly, Paul was brought back before the judge and the fourteen years was reduced to ten, the legal limit that could be imposed. Later, when Paul appealed against the ten years on the grounds of severity of sentence, his ten years was reduced to seven. He was classified a category 'A' prisoner and transferred from Belmarsh to high security Frankland, in Durham. If he is not granted early parole, Paul will be due for release in January 2002.

James Griffiths 1935 – 1972

Griffiths began his life of crime at the very early age of six by stealing things from his house and selling them on at school, where he was also guilty of being a pickpocket. At the age of nine his mother, who said he was out of control, took him to Rochdale Juvenile Court. By the time he was ten years old she had committed him to an orphanage.

In 1948 when Griffiths was thirteen he appeared at Rochdale Juvenile Court charged with breaking and entering and he was sent to approved school. When he left the approved school he became

The Scottish Clans

obsessed with stealing cars and was eventually sent to Borstal. His Borstal sentence completed he joined the RAOC (Royal Army Ordinance Corp) as well as settling down to marriage and having a baby son.

1956 saw Griffiths break into his brother's house and steal goods and cash. From then on he served several sentences for burglary and theft, then in 1963 he was sentenced to four years at Parkhurst for 'Robbing and Wounding'.

While at Parkhurst he became one of the few men to escape and get off the island. After his escape he went to Scunthorpe and returned to committing crime. He was caught, sentenced to another four years and returned to Parkhurst. He was transferred to Blundeston, Suffolk, where he met Paddy Meehan, and on his release he travelled to Glasgow to meet his new friend. One of the jobs Griffiths pulled was to break into the ex Secretary of State Michael Noble's house, where he stole valuable antiques worth thousands of pounds. He was also continuously involved in the stealing of luxury cars and those he couldn't sell, he ran over a cliff into deep water in Loch Awe, Argyleshire.

It was because he was dealing in stolen cars that he went with Paddy Meehan to rob the Motor Taxation office in Stranraer. They hoped to obtain vehicle documents that would enable them to move on some of the cars he had stolen and hidden away. Once they arrived in Stranraer however, they decided not to break into the offices and returned to Glasgow empty handed.

Eight days after the abortive trip, Meehan was arrested for a murder that had occurred on the same night they had passed through the town Ayr on their way to and from Stranraer. Meehan gave up Griffiths' name so he could prove his alibi, but when the police went to see Griffiths he began shooting at them with a high powered telescopic rifle and a shotgun. Then Griffiths began firing at pedestrians from the window of his flat. He shot and wounded seven people as armed police raced to surround the building.

Griffiths managed to escape from the building and hijacked a car at gunpoint, but the car crashed at the Round Toll, on the corner of Possil Road. From the car he raced into a pub brandishing his rifle and demanding a bottle of brandy. An old newspaper vendor, Willie Hughes, made to pick up his glass and Griffiths shot him dead. Leaving the pub, Griffiths hijacked a lorry, ordering the driver to head away from the scene. A police sergeant spotted the

Legends

hijack and followed the lorry in a taxi to Springburn, about two miles away. Once in Springburn, the lorry turned into Kay Street, a short cul-de-sac, forcing Griffiths to abandon it and race into a tenement building.

He took refuge in an empty flat and began shooting at people from the window. The police soon had the building surrounded, but by this time Griffiths had shot several more innocent passers by. Finally Chief Superintendent Callum Finlay shot Griffiths through the letterbox of the flat, killing him instantly.

On the day he died Griffiths shot a total of fourteen innocent people before he was killed by gunfire himself. Many people believe that Griffiths died in exactly the way he wanted.

Paddy Meehan 1933 - 1994

In 1933, Paddy Meehan, born in the Gorbals district of Glasgow, earned his first conviction at the age of eight for stealing old timber from a derelict building. Later that same year he was caught pulling a branch from a tree and once again appeared before the Sheriff on a charge of 'Malicious Damage'. In 1934, when he was nine years old, young Paddy was caught riding a stolen bicycle and charged with theft. This being his third conviction, he was promptly sentenced to two years in approved school and for the next nine years he was in and out of one approved school after another. In 1944, at the age of seventeen, he was charged with Breaking and Entering a garage and stealing tools and was sentenced to ten months borstal training.

In 1945, shortly after he had been released from Borstal, Paddy got married, but very soon after his marriage he was indicted for breaking into a shop and stealing clothing coupons. This time he was sentenced to fifteen months imprisonment in Barlinnie.

Paddy blew his first safe in 1947, once again to obtain clothing coupons, and from then on this became his favoured method of 'earning'. He had a successful run of just over a year before he was captured. Then in 1948 he was sentenced to three years for safe blowing again and sent to Peterhead prison.

When he was released in 1950 Paddy kept a low profile and worked at his 'trade' with some degree of success until 1953, when he was caught breaking into an explosives store. This resulted in a two-year sentence and once again Paddy found himself in Peterhead. When he was released from this sentence Paddy returned to Peterhead and helped another prisoner, Teddy Martin of Glasgow, to escape. Once Martin was clear of the prison Paddy took him to a rented house in the town where they lay low. It was well known that Peterhead's isolation made it easy for the police to put up roadblocks and this was how most escapees, Johnny Ramensky in particular, were recaptured. With this in mind, Teddy's friends had already prepared a set of prisoner's clothing, and after a phone call to report that Teddy was out; this clothing was placed in an empty house in Glasgow. After an appropriate delay the Glasgow police received an anonymous phone call telling them that Teddy was hiding at a certain address, but when they raided the house all they found was the prisoner's clothing. Satisfied that Teddy Martin had reached the city, the police lifted the roadblocks, leaving the way clear for Paddy to drive Teddy home in style.

In 1955 Paddy blew open the safe in a bank in Oban and stole £12,000 in cash as well as a large amount of jewellery from safety deposit boxes. But that same year he was captured attempting to blow open the safe in a bank in Beauly, in the Highlands, and was sentenced to six years. During this sentence a group of prisoners piled onto a lorry that was unloading next to the football pitch and smashed through a gate out onto the road. Unfortunately the lorry went straight across the road and crashed into the ditch. Paddy leapt from the lorry and ran to the prison gate shouting that he had been kidnapped and demanding to be let in. He got away with it too!

After he completed the six-year sentence Paddy went to London and in 1961 he was caught once again blowing open a safe in a branch of the co-op. This time he was sent to the Old Bailey and given eight years preventative detention. It was when he was serving this sentence that he escaped from Nottingham prison and apparently disappeared. What Paddy had done, and he told me this himself when I shared time with him in the Peterhead punishment block, was travel to West Germany and from there he went up to the East German border and demanded asylum! The East Germans allowed him into the country but put him into a soft prison that was mainly for holding people like journalists and political prisoners. The East German officials did not really believe that he had escaped from prison in England, or that he actually wanted asylum in East Germany when every second person there was trying to escape. They suspected that Paddy might have some other reason for appearing among them.

He was held in the prison for seventeen months before they finally decided he was telling the truth. What finally convinced his interrogator that he was telling the truth was the fact that Paddy, more often than not, refused to go on exercise if the weather wasn't nice. The other prisoners in the place, all first timers, were always tearing at their doors when the guard shouted "Frei stunde" (free hour) while Paddy would just lie in his bed and ask what the weather was like. Only an 'old con' would behave like that. So finally Paddy was offered asylum and a job to go with it. It so happened that he was fluent in German (this was what had made him decide to head there in the first place), so the captain in charge of Paddy offered him a job in the town library transcribing books. But the captain also warned him that if he got into any trouble in East Germany he would go to a real prison for a very long time, and that East German prisons were very much tougher than anything in the UK. Paddy was asked to decide - stay in the Eastern sector, or go home. He choose to go home, and they dropped him off at Checkpoint Charlie into the arms of the British security services who flew him back to England.

When he got back to Britain Paddy demanded that his seventeen months in the East German prison should count as part of his eight-year sentence. He even claimed that he had saved the prison department money by letting the East Germans pay for his keep! They fell for that one too!

At first Paddy was sent to Wandsworth prison, but within a few months he was transferred to Blundeston in Suffolk. It was while there that he met James Griffiths, the man that was to play such a catastrophic part in his life.   Later on Paddy was transferred to Parkhurst and he was released from there in 1968, heading straight back to Glasgow.   Later on in 1968 James Griffiths, the man he had met in Blundeston, turned up at his house and they began associating together.   At this time Grifiths was stealing luxury cars, and those he couldn't sell he would drive off a cliff into the deep waters of Loch Awe, Argyleshire.   It was Paddy who suggested that they break into the Motor Taxation Office in the town of Stranraer where they could steal unused logbooks, which would enable them to sell the stolen cars more easily.   They set off one evening to drive to Stranraer, their route taking them through the seaside town of Ayr.   However, once they reached Stranraer, Paddy, for one reason or another, decided not to carry on with the break-in and they returned to Glasgow, once again passing through the town of Ayr.   What they did not know was that that same night two Glasgow criminals were also in Ayr, intent on carrying out a 'tie-up' robbery at the bungalow home of a Mr and Mrs Ross.   Mr Ross was the proprietor of a Glasgow bingo hall and it was rumoured among the Glasgow criminals that he kept his money at home.

Late that night the two robbers forced their way into the bungalow and attacked the elderly couple, beating up both of them until Mr Ross told them where he kept his money.   After giving them this information the couple were tied up and forced into a small cupboard and left there while the villains helped themselves.   After getting the money both robbers then settled down to wait until morning, when it would be safer to for one of them to go and pick up their car.

At six-o'clock in the morning one of the men began to walk towards the centre of town where the car had been inconspicuously parked.   Not far from the bungalow two police officers stopped him to ask why he was in the area.   He told a story about being drunk and staying at a friends house overnight and that he was catching the early bus to Glasgow.   His explanation satisfied the police and they directed him to the bus depot and let him carry on.   The man returned to the bungalow with the car to pick up his accomplice and they drove away, having told Mr Ross that they would telephone the police when they were clear.   They failed to keep this promise and by the time the Ross' were discovered, Mrs Ross was dead and her husband in a serious condition.

Legends

The police investigation team soon discovered that Paddy Meehan had been in the area that night and he was brought in for questioning. Under the circumstances Paddy felt he had no option but to explain why he had been in the area. He then admitted that he had passed through Ayr because he had gone to Stranraer to break into the Motor Taxation Office, and gave up Griffiths' name to support his alibi. However, when the police went to interview Griffiths he fired a shotgun at them and then began to shoot indiscriminately at passers-by in the street with a high-powered rifle. He escaped from the house and the crazy, tragic events as described in the previous Griffiths' entry of this book took place.

Now, with Griffiths dead, Paddy had no one to support his story and he was promptly charged with the murder of Mrs Ross, the assault on Mr Ross and the robbery of their house. One of the main pieces of evidence the police were relying on being that Mr Ross stated that the two robbers called each other Pat and Jim when they addressed one another. But he also said that both men had strong Glasgow accents; one thing Griffiths did not possess, being from Rochdale, in Lancashire.

In January 1970 Paddy was put on trial and at the High Court in Glasgow and was found guilty of the robbery and murder of Rachell Ross. He was sentenced to life imprisonment and sent to Peterhead loudly protesting his innocence.

It was by now already well known to everyone in the Glasgow criminal world that Paddy was indeed innocent. His defence team, Nicholas Fairbairn Q.C., Joe Beltrami his solicitor and the MP Mr McElhone were convinced of his innocence and fought continuously to have the case reopened, only to see their Petitions to the Secretary of State for Scotland routinely dismissed. Luddovic Kennedy, the writer, joined the campaign and also fought for his release, even writing a book – *Presumption of Innocence* – to support Paddy's case.

As a protest against his conviction Paddy elected to serve his time in solitary confinement in the punishment block at Peterhead, and for the next six years he fought to have his case reopened. He now claimed that the British secret service had "set him up" because he had information regarding the escape from Wormwood Scrubs of George Blake, the Russian master spy. During his time in East Germany, Paddy now said, he had been taken to Moscow and interrogated by the Russians regarding all aspects of prison

274

The Scottish Clans

security in England. He also said that they made specific enquiries regarding George Blake and the chances of getting him out of the Scrubs. He claimed that he had reported all of this to MI5 and warned them that the Russians intended to break Blake out of the jail.

Paddy's wild claims were dismissed, and although he continued to blame MI5 for setting him up to get him and his knowledge out of the way, no credence was ever put in his tale.

It was found out that a few days after the murder a well-known Glasgow petty criminal, Ian Waddle, had approached a solicitor, Mr Carlin, and paid him the sum of £200 as a retainer - "In case I am questioned over the Ayr murder". At this stage another MP, Mr William Ross, called for an urgent review of the case. Again, this demand was refused. Later, during a trial at the High Court, Waddell was asked about paying Carlin the £200. He denied that this had ever happened. Mr Carlin gave evidence that it was indeed a fact and Waddell was charged with perjury and sentenced to three years imprisonment.

In Peterhead, Paddy himself, reading law books, discovered an old statute that should have enabled him to get the case reopened – A Bill of Criminal Letters – this would enable him to take the police to court to be re-examined on their evidence. But this too was rejected.

In 1973, after his release from his three years sentence for perjury, Waddell announced that he wanted to confess and a newspaper taped an interview where he admitted the murder.

William 'Tank' McGuiness: responsible for the murder for which Paddy Meehan served seven years.

However it was not until 1975 that the Scottish Daily Mail carried the front-page confession. At about the same time BBC's Panorama programme broadcast an interview with Waddel where he once again admitted the murder. Still the authorities did nothing to reopen the case, or investigate Waddell's claims. Meanwhile a well known, extremely violent Glasgow criminal, William (Tank) McGuiness, had already told solicitor Beltrami it was he that had committed the murder and that Paddy

Legends

was innocent. However, because of the strict rules of client confidentiality, Beltrami was unable to report McGuiness' confession. Then in 1976 Tank McGuiness was found murdered and Mr Beltrami, no longer bound under the rules of confidentiality, was able to reveal his confession. When details of the confession were made public the Ayrshire police checked back to 1966 and found the report regarding the man that had been stopped and questioned by a patrol that night. This, and other details proved the validity of the McGuiness confession.

As a direct result of Beltrami's revelations the Secretary of State, Bruce Millan, announced in the House of Commons that, due to new evidence in the Meehan case, he would now recommend that the Queen grant Patrick Connolly Meehan a Royal Pardon.

Paddy spent more than six years in solitary confinement until he was pardoned for a crime he had not committed and for this he was initially awarded the paltry sum of £7,500 compensation. This caused a public outcry and questions were asked in the House of Commons about the fairness of the award. One of the reasons put forward by the official who arrived at the £7,500 sum was that because Paddy had been a criminal for almost his entire life, it was more than likely that he would have been in prison anyway for most of the six years. In fact it was 1984 before Paddy finally received a settlement of £47,915 in compensation for his wrongful conviction for murder.

When he left prison Paddy decided he had had enough of crime and imprisonment. He moved back in with his wife and became a successful door-to-door salesman for a double-glazing company. He never returned to crime and he died August 14th 1994 from cancer of the throat.

Paddy was, quite justifiably, never happy with the wording of the Royal Pardon. He always said that it should have been an apology, admitting that a grave mistake had been made instead of a "pardon" for a crime he had not committed in the first place.

The Ice-cream Wars 1983 – 84
Thomas Campbell 1952 - Joseph Steele 1961 -

The so called ice-cream wars came to a head on the night of 16th April 1984, when six members of one family, including an eighteen-month old baby, were burned to death when their house

The Scottish Clans

was set on fire by rival ice-cream van operators. For years there had been minor skirmishes as rival vans 'poached' on each others' routes (runs). No one actually *owned* these runs, but by habit and usage ice-cream van operators laid claim to their own specific routes. It was when a new van, or a van from a different company, appeared on a 'run' that tempers grew short and violence erupted.

At first, during the seventies and into the eighties, the violence was more verbal than physical, and few assaults, if any, took place. But as more and more people saw an ice-cream van as an easy to run, lucrative business, new faces began to move in on what the established traders considered their personal territory. Threats became more direct, tyres were slashed, and bricks hurled through the windscreens of 'poaching' vans. It was not until September 1983 that the battle over the ice-cream routes spilled into serious violence, and it was Garthamlock, a sprawling housing scheme in the north east of Glasgow, that was to become the focal point in the escalation of violence for control of the more lucrative routes.

On 29th September that year, two young men, Joseph Steel and John Campbell, attacked a rival ice-cream van with shotguns and smashed its windows. Again, on the night of 29th September, while working from his van, two gunmen approached John Brady, but he drove of before they could do anything. The following day, 30th, Andrew Doyle and James Lockhart, grew afraid when they realised their van was being tailed by four armed men in a car. There was several attacks on vans during the month of October, building up to the 27th when, in one night, three vans operated by the Marchetti ice-cream company were attacked by a gang of hammer-wielding youths in Garthamlock. The following day the Marchetti company secretary, Archie McDougall, received an anonymous phone call warning him to get his vans out of the scheme. Towards the end of 1983, ambush attacks on ice-cream vans were so commonplace that the drivers stopped reporting them to the police.

It was on the night of February 1st, 1984, that ice-cream rivals, said to be lead by Thomas Campbell and Joseph Steele, among others, decided on a new course of action. Late that night the burglar alarm went off in the Marchetti ice-cream company's building in the Balmore Industrial Estate. When the police investigated they found that a hole had been cut in the asbestos

Legends

roof and petrol poured into the building. An attempt to ignite the petrol by lowering a piece of burning cloth had obviously failed. Undeterred, the arsonists struck again that same night, this time successfully, and the building and vans inside were badly damaged. Both Campbell and Steele were later charged with this arson attack and found not guilty.

But the vans were soon back in competition and Andrew Doyle, known as 'Fat Boy', was the victim of an attack on 29th February, when two shots were fired through the windscreen of his van. Later, Thomas Campbell would be charged with attempted murder of Doyle and a 15 year-old girl who was working in the van at the time of the attack. Another girl, this time a customer, was assaulted as she stood waiting to be served and told to move away.

There was several attacks on the Marchetti vans throughout the next few weeks, one of the most serious occurring on 30th March, when a driver, John Shepherd, was stabbed in the head and had his van wrecked. A few nights later Andrew Doyle was attacked outside his house at 29 Bankhead Street and warned off. Four men, Thomas Campbell, Joseph Steele, Thomas Gray and Gary Moore were arrested for this assault, but there was no evidence against them and they were released without charge.

On April 11th and 12th, two ice-cream vans were attacked, one of the owners, a woman named Irene Mitchell, being struck on the head with a brick. Things seemed to be reaching a crescendo. And on the night of 16th April, the ice-cream war was to culminate in a terrifying criminal action that would shock and horrify the nation.

The Doyle family, including Andrew (Fat Boy), lived on the top flat of 29 Bankhead Street, Garthamlock, a modern three-storey tenement. Access to their house was gained from a common stairway with the front doors opening onto verandahs.

Early in the morning of 16th April 1984, two shadowy figures mounted the stairs to the top flat and poured petrol into an outside coal cellar, next to the front door of the house. The petrol was set alight and the arsonists crept back down the stairs to the street and disappeared in the night, satisfied that the *fright* this would give the family would persuade them to ply their trade elsewhere. What the fireraisers did not know was that inside the coal cellar there was a stack of spare tyres that had caught fire. Dense smoke from the blazing tyres got into the house and out of the eight persons who were staying there that night, six were to die from burning and smoke inhalation, one of the victims being an 18 month-old baby.

The public and police were shocked at the enormity of the crime, and for a time the police did not seem to be making much progress. Fifty police officers, detective and uniformed, were assigned to the case and over four thousand statements were taken from the public, but found no evidence to support charging anyone. The police eventually carried their enquiries into the remand wing of nearby Barlinnie prison, a well-known sounding board for criminal gossip, and it was in Barlinnie that they found what they were looking for. William McDonald Love, an associate of Thomas Campbell and Joseph Steele, was on remand for the armed robbery of a scrap metal yard in the Gorbals. Love told detectives he had information about the fire and asked to speak to the detective in charge of the investigation.

On the 20th March, Detective Superintendent Norman Walker went to the remand wing of the prison to interview Love. At this stage Love had been on remand for several weeks and had made two applications for bail, which had been refused. He struck a deal with the Detective Superintendent and on May 9th he was taken in front of a sheriff where he made a statement saying that he had heard Thomas Campbell and Joseph Steele plotting to light a fire at the Doyle house "to give them a fright". After his statement, Love made another application for bail which was granted unopposed.

Shortly after taking Love's 'evidence' detectives arrested Thomas Campbell and Joseph Steele and charged them, along with others, with a catalogue of sixteen offences, including conspiracy to assault and rob, presenting shotguns, wilful fireraising, and finally, the murder of the Doyle family at 29 Bankhead Street, Garthlamlock.

The main evidence against them was the statement made by Love, and another man, Joseph Granger, supported this. Both these men, once associates of Thomas Campbell and Joseph Steele, told police how they had heard the accused plotting to commit attacks upon ice-cream vans, the fire attack on the Marchetti building, and assaults on persons who worked for the Marchetti company. In all there was sixteen charges on the High Court indictment. But other than the statements made by Love and Granger there was no real evidence that Campbell or Steele had been anywhere near Bankhead Street on the night of the murders.

Legends

However, at the trial, the police presented verbal statements such as: *"I thought you would've been here before this"*, *"The fire at the Fat Boys was only meant to be a frightener"*, and *"It wasn't me who lit the match"*, allegedly made by Campbell and Steele at the time of their arrest.

Irrespective of the lack of hard evidence, the jury choose to believe the statements made by Love and Granger and the *alleged* verbal evidence presented by the police. At the end of the trial both men were found guilty of the murders and sentenced to life imprisonment.

Throughout their imprisonment both men have continued the fight to prove their innocence. William Macdonald Love has gone on record to state that his statement about overhearing plans being made was a pack of lies. In fact it was proven that on the date when he was supposed to have overheard Campbell and Steele talking he was elsewhere.

Joseph Steele made several escapes during his sentence, each time making a very public protest about his innocence and asking for an enquiry. He once climbed onto the roof of his mother's house when he escaped from a prison escort on a Home Visit. Another time he tied himself to a crane outside Barlinnie prison and on one memorable occasion he super-glued himself to the gates of Buckingham Palace!

Thomas Campbell ended up in the Barlinnie Special Unit alongside Jimmy Boyle and carried out his campaign to get the case reopened from there. In 1992, through a ruling by European Court of Human Rights, he won new rights for prisoners regarding their legal mail, which prevented the authorities from opening correspondence between lawyer and client. There was continuous demand from the public for an appeal to be heard and many demonstrations were held outside prisons and on the streets of Glasgow to try and get the case reopened. Finally, after twelve years of campaigning, and based mainly on Love's repeated admissions that he lied to the police with his statement, Thomas Campbell and Joseph Steele were given leave to appeal and released on Bail pending the hearing.

It was a great shock to everyone when, after more than a year of freedom (during which Campbell operated an ice-cream run) The appeal judges ruled that Love's retraction was not valid as he was confused about the dates when he said he overheard the

The Scottish Clans

conversation.

Now, in the first year of a new millennium, Thomas Campbell and Joseph Steele are still behind bars and still fighting to prove their innocence.

A FEW ODDBALLS

Prison is a dull place; there is no argument about that. But it is true to say, that every prison has its oddball characters that bring a bit of light relief and a smile to your face. Here are a few of the characters that crossed my path when I was inside, and even now I remember them and thank them for the laughs they gave me.

Barney Noone

Barney was a well known face in the Scottish prison system, in fact it he had one of those 'once seen never forgotten' faces. With his squat, broad shouldered physique, a mop of frizzy red hair above a bulbous, vein bursting, 'drinkers' nose, thick rubber lips that he was always loudly smacking together, and a complexion that could have sanded timber, Barney looked like a huge garden gnome. I can always picture him rising out from the small boiler room in 'A' hall, Peterhead, emerging like a Troll from his underground lair. It is said that once, when he was on holiday in Yorkshire, he tried to enter a gurning competition, only to be disqualified because he had too much of a start. Anyway, it was Andy Warholl who once stated that everyone at some time in their life would enjoy a few minutes of fame, and this even included Barney. In fact, Barney Noone had two moments of fame and he was often heard actually boasting about them. His moments of fame? He was twice *in succession*, as he would point out, voted 'Rat of the Week' by the popular Daily Record newspaper.

CRAZY COURTROOM CHARACTERS

I don't remember Sojer (Soldier) Thompson's real Christian name but he was a character serving a sentence of four years in Edinburgh's Saughton prison when I was there. It was how Sojer got there that qualifies him for insertion in my *crazy character* section of this book.

Legends

First of all Sojer was always a petty desperado, a street thief, shoplifting, bag-snatching and mugging drunks were all in his sphere of criminal activity. Well one day Sojer and an accomplice mugged a Provident cheque collector, an elderly woman who was unfortunate enough to cross the wayward path of our two Edinburgh "villains". However, the woman was of stout Scottish character and put up a brave struggle against her assailants, refusing to part easily with her collection cash. In the end the attempted robbery was thwarted by passers by who rushed to her assistance. Sojer managed to flee the scene but his accomplice was captured and held until the police arrived. Later on, at the police station, Sojer's unfortunate accomplice was charged with *Serious Assault and Attempted Robbery* and throughout the police interrogation he steadfastly refused to cooperate and give up the name of his partner in crime. The following morning, after appearing at the Sheriff Court, he was remanded to Saughton prison where he was held in custody for almost four months before being duly escorted to Edinburgh High Court to stand trial. Throughout his time on remand he had continued to refuse to name his accomplice.

During the trial the victim of the attempted robbery was giving her evidence and she was asked if she recognised the person who had assaulted her. The woman unhesitatingly identified the man in the dock as one of her attackers. She was then asked if she would recognise the other man if she saw him again. *"I certainly would"* replied the woman. *"I would recognise him anywhere. I could never forget his face because he was so ugly. In fact,'* she elucidated, *"he looked like a monkey."*

At this reply the skulking Sojer leapt up from where he had been hiding at the rear of the public benches and shouted down to the astonished woman, *"Who are you calling a fucking monkey?"*

Needless to say Sojer was pounced on by the attendant police constables and taken off to the cells. A few weeks later he appeared in the same courtroom where he was sentenced to four years and was able to join his accomplice in jail. And even throughout his sentence he still justified his courtroom outburst. *"Naebody's going to call me a fucking monkey and get away with it,"* he would tell anyone who asked him why he had committed such a foolhardy exposure of himself.

The Scottish Clans

Jock Tamson
Sprachen Sie Deustch?

I don't remember Jock Tamson's real name, but as we are all supposed to be Jock Tamson's bairns that is the name I will use for the character illustrated in this courtroom caper.

One day a German seaman was brought before the Sheriff Court in Glasgow on charges of 'Breach of the Peace and Assault'. Unfortunately for the German there were no court officials or solicitors present who could speak German and for a while confusion reigned in the dispensing of justice.   Finally the Sheriff turned to the public benches and asked if any of the seated citizenry could speak in the German tongue. He was immediately rewarded when a worthy, elderly citizen stood up and volunteered his services as an interpreter.

On being questioned with regard to his knowledge of German the man declared that he had been a prisoner of war for four years and understood the language perfectly.   Satisfied that the court could now continue with the case the Sheriff instructed the newly appointed interpreter to ask the accused German his name.

Undaunted by the majesty of the courtroom Jock Tamson stood in front of the dock and stared hard at the bemused German. Then, in the broadest of Glasgow accents, our Jock bawled at the accused - **"Vot is your name?"**

At this, everyone in the courtroom convulsed with very undignified laughter and the German looked more baffled than ever.   However, the Sheriff was not amused and deemed Jock Tamson to be in contempt of court and ordered that he be held in the cells until the end of the day's proceedings.

TALES FROM PETERHEAD
George 'Nellie' Drummond

No story about Scottish criminals would be complete without mention of big Nellie Drummond. As his nickname implies, Nellie was a well-known homosexual, but strangely enough for a person of his inclinations he was well liked and on good terms with most of the 'known' villains. In fact, they knew him on the outside where he had even worked with some of them on occasion. Inside, Nellie was quite brazen about his sexual preferences, but on the outside

Legends

he was very definitely well inside the closet. It was a known fact that Nellie was always very cooperative with the police whenever he was arrested, but 'the boys' excused even this. The story was always the same; whenever Nellie was arrested for an offence the police always threatened to tell his old mother about his homosexual activities unless he cooperated with them. Most of 'the boys' seemed to think that that excused Nellie's confessions, even if someone else was charged. 'Besides,' someone would always point out, 'everybody knows what Nellie is like, so it is their own fault if they work with him and he sticks them in.'

Big Nellie also got on well with the screws whenever he was in Peterhead (which was quite often). They used to say that you could send two screws off the hall whenever Nellie appeared. On admission to PH's 'B' hall, his usual residence, Nellie was immediately put in charge of the stores, the cleaning and the hotplate, all of which he organised with the efficiency of a first class *Maitre de Hotel*. As well as this he would immediately take over the jail bookmaking business, where he applied the same dedication and efficiency, even accepting cash bets from several of the screws.

There are a lot of stories about big Nellie and the things he got up to, and there's no doubt in my mind that Ronnie Barker's Fletch would have learned more than a thing or two from him. He even baroned out chocolate bars – three for two – as well as trading in the banknotes (25p in the pound commission) smuggled in on visits. I always thought that if Nellie had applied himself outside half as much as he did inside, he would have been a millionaire in no time. Needless to say, stories about big Nellie are legendary in the Scottish prison system, especially among the older cons, but I have always considered the two I am about to relate here as among the best.

The first story concerns Nellie's bookmaking dealings. In the 'good old days', before drugs became the pre-eminent commodity in prison, every jail had a bookie and prisoners would bet with tobacco, receiving their winnings in kind. Credit was a rare commodity offered only to a very few trusted friends, but prisons, harbouring the sort of people they do, meant that nearly everyone was trying to put one over on the bookie. One desperate con spent hours perfecting the insertion of bread into an empty 1/2oz tobacco packet and one busy Saturday passed his 'prepared' packet on to Nellie for a 1/2oz bet on a horse at odds of 3 - 1. The

The Scottish Clans

horse romped home a clear winner and the grinning con duly entered Nellie's cell to paid out his winnings.

"Oh, aye," says Nellie when the trickster appeared. "You had that bet on the 3 - 1 shot, didn't you?"

"Aye," the grinning con-man held out his hand. "Makes a change to pick a winner, eh?"

Unperturbed, Nellie looked the man straight in the eye and repeated: "3 – 1, wasn't it?" as he turned away to open his cupboard. "Right then, I'll just get you your winnings."

The beaming 'gambler' could hardly contain himself, no doubt already dreaming of an entire weekend puffing away on unlimited roll-ups, even thinking about swapping a half ounce for a few bars of chocolate to round off his celebrations.

"Right, there you are, that's your stake back," Nellie handed over the original doctored $1/2$oz packet, then, with his face straight as a die, he counted out three slices of bread into the shattered prisoner's hand. "And at 3 – 1 that's your winnings!"

The other story that went the rounds of PH was that one time a newcomer, a young, good-looking prisoner made the mistake of going into Nellie's cell to borrow a couple of LP records.

"Oh, aye, sure son," Nellie invited the young chap into his cell. "You'll find a box of them under the bed. Take a look and see if there's anything you like."

Then, as the young man bent low to look under the bed, Nellie suddenly grabbed him round the neck in a half-nelson, at the same time ripping off the unfortunate fellow's trousers. Now everyone had heard stories about Nellie having a massive member and personally I can only go on hearsay, but rumours were rife - *Nellie was big!* But the story goes that as Nellie forced himself upon the attractive young man, gripping him tightly round the neck in his favourite wrestling grip while thrusting away at his rear, the lad was heard to scream: "Oh, oh, stop it! Stop it! You're hurting my neck!"

Walter Scott Ellis

In the Scottish prison system they have a procedure whereby any prisoner can write directly to the Scottish Home Secretary (at least that is what we are led to believe) with any complaint, request or observation they might have. All you have to do is put in a

Legends

governor's request for a Petition Form and one will be handed to you almost immediately. You then write out your *'Petition'*, seal it in the envelope provided (you don't even need a stamp), hand it in at the PO's desk and off it goes to the Home Department offices in Edinburgh. There is none of the frustrating business of explaining anything to an educationally challenged screw, or being obliged to seek advice from your 'personal officer'. If you want a Petition form you get a Petition form – it is one of your very few rights in Scottish prisons. Subject to not using bad language, you can write about whatever you like in your Petition. It is really all very civilised.

Approximately six weeks after despatching your Petition you will be called up by the governor and the reply to your Petition will be read out to you. You will also be given a written copy of the Home Secretary's reply. It seems to be a very satisfactory procedure all round. You can let off steam, complain, even pass on your thanks as several of the con's did when, after a three day hunger strike, Tam (Soya) Joiner, the jail cook, was sacked from his position and put on wall patrol.

Needless to say Peterhead's prisoner population generated a constant stream of these petitions and some of the guys became very clever at penning them. One of the most prolific writers of petitions was Walter Scott Ellis, sentenced about 1968 to twenty one years for an armed bank robbery where the manager was shot and another charge of attempted murder when he hit someone on the head with an axe. Walter was not so much a hard man, being of slight build and not the least bit threatening looking, as simply cold and vicious. Throughout his sentence he refused to conform to

normal prison behaviour, refusing to come out of his cell for association (they call it recreation in English prisons which only goes to show that the Scottish use of the English language is more accurate.)

Walter was still on the 'A' list when he was ten years into his sentence. I was on the 'A' list along with him and familiar with the daily searches and generally more restricted regime – On the

The Scottish Clans

Book — they call it in England. It was a certain screw that handled 'A' men that prompted Walter to write this particular Petition. Of course, I do not remember it word for word, but this is at least 90% accurate.

WALTER'S PETITION
(At least one of them anyway)

To *The Right Honourable Secretary of State for Scotland:*
Dear Sir,
I would like to complain about the constant strip searches I have to suffer in here. Most of the time they are pretty normal and do not give me any cause for concern, however, there is one particular turnkey (Walter insisted in addressing all screws as turnkeys) *who is disturbing me with his zeal when carrying out these searches. At least once a week this turnkey, Andy Bunnet,* (Walter also refused to acknowledge proper names, insisting on using the nick-name the screw had earned during his service) *insists on coming to my cell and giving me a strip search. Now I know he is allowed to do this and I am not complaining about his seemingly insatiable desire to see me in the nude. But this Andy Bunnet always makes me strip down to my vest then gets me to pirouette about my cell like a demented ballerina, so he can freely inspect my bare buttocks and my other dangly bits.*

It is obvious to me that Andy Bunnet is a pervert; I can tell by the way his eyes pop open and his breathing sounds funny. However, if he gets his kicks out of watching me spinning around and my private parts merrily jiggling up and down, that is up to him. In fact I am not complaining about his perversion. What I am complaining about is that I am beginning to get to like it!
Yours sincerely Walter Scott Ellis

William 'Pokey' Turner

The above anecdote told of Walter Scott Ellis and one of his many Petitions and, as every Petition gets replied to, I am in no doubt that many of my readers are curious to know what sort of reply Walter received. But before telling you that I will describe the Petition process in a little more detail.

The Petition process in Scotland is a well-established complaints

Legends

routine, although, as I have already mentioned, a prisoner can Petition for any reason.   When a prisoner has something to complain about he asks for a Petition form. These blue forms are pre-addressed to *The Right Honourable Secretary of State for Scotland,* so there is no doubt in the prisoner's mind his Petition is being handled at the highest levels indeed (don't laugh, it's true!). About six weeks from the time the Petition is submitted, a reply surfaces in the governor's office. When this happens the writer of the Petition is BU'd (brought up) before the governor, much like a disciplinary hearing.   The con' is marched into the orderly room and there he gives the governor his name, number and sentence and says 'Sir' at the end. Having thus established that this is indeed the felon who penned the Petition, his High Heid Yin (High Head One) now opens an official brown envelope and proceeds to read out *The Secretary of State for Scotland's carefully considered reply.* Unfortunately for most con's (about 99% in actual fact), and in Walter's case as mentioned above, this is this is where the Petition charade breaks down. Because in the above mentioned 99% cases the governor will study the reply, as if it actually does contain a *seriously considered* answer.   He will purse his lips and nod to himself, obviously in full agreement with *The Secretary of State,* then he will say, as in the case of Walter's Petition regarding Andy Bunnet, *'Ellis, The Secretary of State'* has *carefully considered the matters arising from your Petition and I am instructed to inform you of his reply.* There is a long, pregnant pause, then the *carefully considered* words are officially read out to the Petitioner: *"Please inform the prisoner that he has no grounds for complaint".* And that's that. "About turn, quick march. Next!"

Well There was one guy, William (Pokey) Turner, of the battered baldy head, squashed nose, slashed face and cauliflower ear brigade, who tried to outwit the system. On one occasion he was shuffling out of the governor's office after having been give the answer to yet another of his many Petitions.   And yes, once again the reply was: *'Please inform the prisoner that he had no grounds for complaint'.*

'What was your answer?' The inevitable question was put to the darkly muttering Pokey as he shuffled out onto the bottom flat of 'A' hall.

'Fucking load o' shite!' Pokey muttered to no one in particular and everyone in general. *'Same every fucking time, so it is! No*

The Scottish Clans

fucking grounds for complaint.'

'Well whit dae ye' keep writing them for?' Someone interrupted Pokey's manic muttering. 'Ye' know ye' always get the same answer.'

'Oh aye, dae ah?' Pokey turned bleary eyes on his critic. 'I'll tell ye' whit...' His face screwed up into a crafty expression. 'I bet I fuck them wi' ma next wan!'

'Oh aye,' the cynic's voice boomed out. 'Whit's it going tae be aboot this time?'

'Jist you wait and see,' Pokey mumbled mysteriously. 'I'll definitely fuck'em this time. Jist you wait and see if ah don't,' he muttered on, bottom lip thrust out like a wet roller towel as he contemplated his next fiendish move.

A few days later Pokey requested a Petition form and off he went to write his latest diatribe against the system that continuously treated him in such off-handed, cavalier fashion. But this time Pokey really intended to baffle 'them at head office'.

Locked up in the safety of his cell our Pokey penned a Petition along similar lines to the following:

To The Right Honourable Her Majesty's Secretary of State for Scotland.

Dear Sir,

U wiyks kuje ti cunolub abiyt the sutatuib ub the orudi grtr as Pryrthrsf. Rbrty yimz z etlyrs Oryuyuib ygr dsmr abssert, ...viykf kity okrsrtd yrt sbf tuvr nr s otiort troky di I vsn dndoe yhsy ysnsrt id svbtusslly domrnr sy grsd iggubr hgat bsd yrkk nr dinr ig yhr hoof nred

U sn grf lyo euyth skests hryyubg yr same anser and U fp biy kukr iy' Ygsbj git ostubh di bycg syyrbyiub yi nr. Your sincerely William Turner.

'There,' said Pokey, sticking down the envelope (another device to let you think that the Petition is confidential between you and The Right Honourable ha ha ha. 'There, that'll sort the bastards out. See what kind of answer they give me for that!'

We all applauded Pokey's crafty stratagem and waited anxiously for the six weeks period to pass. Then one day Pokey got BU'd. The answer had arrived at last!

'Name, number and sentence to the governor and say Sir!' the old Chief ordered as Pokey, grinning all over his face, marched into the office.

Legends

Well, the governor opened the envelope and prepared to read out the *carefully considered* reply. He studied it for a few minutes, shaking his head, and finally passed the answer to the waiting Pokey.

'Here, Turner,' he said. 'You better read this for yourself.'

Pokey stared at the paper for a full ten seconds before bellowing out: 'Whit the fuck's this? Ah canny read this shite!'

The governor took the paper back and looked at the writing again. It read something like this: "Ijesae yvfrjrb tge irysuber tgat gr gsa bi griyhbfd git vinijdubt.'

'Well it is quite plain to me, Turner,' the governor told the gaping Pokey. 'The answer quite clearly states: "Please inform the prisoner that he has no grounds for complaint."

'About turn, quick march! Next!'

Pokey's baffled expression told its own tale to the waiting prisoners.

Fucked again!

The moral here is clear: You will never beat the system!

James, that was a blinding read so much so that I'm gonna ask you to come back in *Legends Vol.2*, I reckon the folk in Scotland are gonna find this the best read in years, I was gonna add more in here from my bagful of characters but I've decided to save them for the Vol. 2 cos we just ain't got the room. I got so carried away reading your write-ups I've gone and left myself no room in the pages available in this chapter. All what I can say is I'm pleased we've got you on our team for writing the film script for my life story based on *Silent Scream*. James – Aye the noo, your old sporran, Charlie Bronson, and thanks for appearing in the video documentary, *Sincerely Yours*. I'll leave you with this saying: Never walk backwards into a madman's cell with your kilt over your head, see you in Vol.2.

10

Monsters

The 'monsters' is gonna be my favourite chapter cos they're what the title says – MONSTERS. I've got a page on my website dedicated to them, you can vote to see which one of the mob I've got listed on that site you wanna see hang. I don't believe in capital punishment but when it comes to these monsters I, like any good Home Secretary, can always make an exception. Listen you're gonna have to read my book *Evil Bastards* to get a good account of them all but just to give you a taste of that book here's a few that I've prepared earlier. Don't forget catch the evil bastards on my website: http://www.bronsonmania.com, catch ya there and in *Legends Vol.2.*

Theodore Bundy (Ted)

Burn, Bundy Burn! Bundy from the USA was a handsome fucker with a good sense of humour, well educated and he easily made friends. This was a fatal attraction for possibly 40 young females who were all brutally murdered.

A number of pretty young females started disappearing and also suffering violent attacks by intruders in 1974. The first of these was Sharon Clarke of Seattle. She was attacked whilst sleeping with a steel rod, which

Legends

was later, found in the bedroom as a result she suffered fractures to her skull and she was lucky to survive the attack. No explanation came forward for this attack and the victim was unable to identify her assailant or even clarify whether the attacker was male or female.

Lynda Ann Healy disappeared – she lived only a few streets away from Sharon Clarke on 31 January 1974. After this over the following seven months females disappeared more and more frequently. Donna Gail Manson went missing on 12 March 1974. Susan Rancourt vanished on 17 April 1974. On 6 May 1974 Roberta Kathleen Parks disappeared. Brenda Ball was the next to go missing on 1 June 1974. On the 11 June 1974 Georgann Hawkins also vanished into the darkness and wasn't seen alive again.

On the 14 July 1974 at Lake Sammanish a good-looking male wearing a sling, this was Bundy, approached a number of females asking if they would help him load a sailboat on top of his car, as his arm was in a sling. One lady agreed to accompany him and followed him to a nearby car park. When the pair arrived at the car Bundy explained that they'd have to drive to his home, she refused – did the right thing!

Janice Ott agreed to help Bundy and wasn't seen again! Some hours later Denise Naslund was last seen walking towards the toilets at the Lake. Females were seen accompanying the same man wearing a sling to the car park. On 7 September 1974 two hunters found the bodies of Ott and Naslund and another unidentified body.

Police started many enquiries and females came forward with information about a man trying to pick them up. During the enquiries remains of Carol Valenzuela and another female were discovered – the second body wasn't identified. Many people were suspects in these murders, ex-cons and people already being hunted. Until the law received an anonymous call from a female who stated she believed Ted Bundy to be the assailant. This was only filed along with the other thousands of leads.

Women continued to disappear one after another. On 2 October 1974 Nancy Wilcox disappeared then 18 October 1974 Melissa Smith, a daughter of a local police Chief vanished. On 27 October 1974 she was found and had been raped and strangled to death. Laura Aimee was the next to go missing on 31 October 1974.

Monsters

A male portraying himself as a copper approached Carol DaRonch in a shopping centre in Salt Lake on 8 November 1974 and demanded the registration of her vehicle. He made up a story saying somebody had tried to break into her vehicle. When they returned to the vehicle there was no sign of any disturbance to the vehicle. He then coerced DaRonch to accompany him to police headquarters to view a suspect. Once they were on a quiet street Bundy stopped, produced a set of handcuffs and cuffed one hand of the girl, she let out a scream and the police impostor put a gun to her head then ordered her to silence. DaRonch was not the submissive type the killer had previously killed, she was a fighter and determined to escape. Forcing the car door open then jumping out, Bundy chased her with a crowbar, attempting to smash her skull but she caught it in mid flight and struggled with him. DaRonch could visibly see a vehicle coming towards them; she jumped in front of the vehicle forcing it to stop to allow her to hop in the vehicle which then sped off with her safely inside. Even with a witness at large Bundy went on to try and pick up females. A French teacher turned him down. Shortly after Debbie Kent went missing only to become Bundy's next victim.

Salt Lake police received the name 'Ted Bundy' from Seattle detectives. It also stated that they had anonymous information stating that Bundy may well be the person responsible for all of these killings. Photographs of Bundy were produced and shown to Carol DaRonch but she didn't identify him as the phoney copper.

31 Oct 1974 the dead body of Laura Aimee was discovered naked in a canyon. The killings continued to escalade. On 12 January 1975 Caryn Campbell had vanished and later her naked dead body was discovered on 17 February, the body had been hidden in thick bushes. Caryn had been raped and her skull had been crushed.

In another town on 15 March 1975 Julie Cunningham disappeared. A short period past and the remains of Susan Rancourt and Brenda Ball were found in the mountains both had gone missing. Melanie Cooley was to be the next victim on 15 April 1975 and her body was found a number of days later on 23 April. This time the body was fully clothed but the jeans of the victim had been pulled down which indicated sex was the motive. Cooley's skull had also been smashed in with a rock that was found near to the body.

Legends

Bundy the monster carried on with his killings and Shelley Robertson vanished on 1 July, her naked body was discovered in a mineshaft on 23 August that year. The same year only three days after Robertson vanished so too did Nancy Baird.

The day had finally come when Bundy was arrested by police for driving at slow speeds and looking suspicious. You can just see him, "Me officer, nah I ain't killed any women." He attempted to escape but was soon stopped. His room was searched to reveal nothing other than maps and brochures of Colorado. Bundy tried to explain his way around these but failed to do so. Bundy's car was searched for clues; a hair, a single hair, which matched that of Melissa Smith, was removed from the car seat of Bundy's vehicle. A witness also insisted he'd sighted Bundy the night Caryn Campbell disappeared – near to where she disappeared! They were on to him.

At this point Bundy was charged with murder. Still trying to charm everyone and almost succeeding by stating they'd got the wrong man and portraying himself to be of too high an intelligence level to commit such horrific crimes. All the same these lot, ain't they? Bundy insisted that he'd defend himself and that he be allowed access to as many law books as it required. I say throw the book at him.

The case dragged on for months as Bundy was allowed to roam around a library of law. He was under guard but despite this he managed to escape out of an open window and drop 20 foot to freedom, pity he didn't break his neck! Luckily he was tracked down some eight days later. He was then put under heavy guard to prevent this happening again.

Bundy had legally stalled his case whilst he was shedding the pounds. Even though by this time Carol DaRonch had identified Bundy as being her assailant he still tried insisting that he was a victim of circumstances. The weight loss continued and was for his next plan of escape. He'd acquired a hacksaw, which he used to carve a hole around the light fitting of his cell. He removed this leaving a foot wide gap for him to squeeze through on 30th December1977. The skinny cunt had escaped yet again!

He moved from place to place and survived on goods obtained by stolen credit cards. His last residence before his arrest was near to houses of Florida State University. On the night of 15 January 1978 Nita Neary saw a man armed with a log who was lurking

294

Monsters

around the front door of her home. As she decided to contact the law a student, Karen Chandler, staggered from her room whilst blood flowed from her wounds. A madman had gained entry to her room and savagely beat her around the head. The same man in the very same room also attacked her roommate, Kathy Kleiner, – she suffered a broken jaw.

Later coppers discovered another two students had been attacked in another room in the same house – Lisa Levy and Margaret Bowman. These women had both been sexually abused. Bowman had died from strangulation with the use of her own knickers. Levy was en route to hospital when she passed away due to severe head injuries.

Only a few hours later Cheryl Thomas another student from a different house was brutally attacked. She was severely injured but survived the ordeal.

It was now 9th February 1979 and coppers still hadn't found Bundy, he was still at large then 12 year-old Kimberley Leach left her classroom never to be seen alive again. Some days later and Bundy now using the alias Chris Hagen stole an orange car. A copper stopped the car and soon found that it was stolen. The officer arrested Bundy but Bundy bolted but soon came to a stop when hearing the shot of the officer's gun. The cop should've shot Bundy – between the legs cos I would've! First he identified himself as 'Hagen' but soon admitted to being Bundy who was wanted by the coppers for multiple murders. Bundy was held on charges of using stolen credit cards and stolen cars. Sound a bit like Sutcliffe's game with his dodgy number plates, don't it? Slippery little critters these monsters!

The body of the 12 year-old girl was found in Suwannee River Park. She'd, sadly, been strangled until she reached her death and her privates were violated and mutilated.

Bundy was approached by cops on 27 April 1979 and took to the examining room. He struggled, as he was made aware they required wax impressions of his teeth. That's nothing; you should've seen me when they was dishing out the liquid cosh in Broadmoor. Half a dozen men held him down to successfully gain the impressions needed. These impressions were later positively identified as the same imprints of bite marks on Lisa Levy's buttocks. This would be crucial and help convict Bundy.

He was charged with the Levy and Bowman murders and placed

on trial. Bundy pleaded not guilty but was found guilty and sentenced to death. He was also found guilty of the murder of the 12 year-old girl.

For a decade this horrific murderer kept himself alive with every appeal he could extract from law books. Once all the avenues had been exhausted his time had come to an end. Bundy recited all of the murders he committed – 23 in all with 15 more been attributed to him 38 in all, yeah I can count too.

24 January 1989 finally came for 24 voyeurs wishing to witness his execution. He was brought to the electric chair in a desperate state – white as a sheet and fear stricken, witnesses had observed, wish I'd been there. Then promptly at 7:07am 2,000 volts were blasted through Bundy's body. Four minutes later he was pronounced dead. Fireworks were set off with relief and to celebrate the black flag flying to signal his death.

Colin James Evans
Sarah Payne's namesake

This case might raise a few eyebrows cos the little girl murdered by Evans had the same surname as 'Sarah Payne', the little girl recently murdered near Littlehampton, in Sussex – no relation. But if anything I think this should be given some thought. The coppers know who murdered Sarah Payne, I can tell you that much without a doubt but they ain't got enough to go on to shut the case. But when that evil monster comes behind bars he's in my territory and he's gonna get plenty of fun and games, don't worry he won't be killed cos that would be too good for him. Think about that evil fucker Gary Glitter and the judges what only gave him three months, well this guy's gonna wish he was Gary Glitter by time he's finished with.

It was Friday 11 March 1983 that four-year old Marie Denise Payne was reported missing from her home on a council owned housing estate at Dagenham, Essex. She'd wandered out of the house, her older sister not being aware of this, she didn't return.

A number of months later on Sunday 6 May 1984 at 11:45am that day, Edward Sudbury a 54-year-old carpenter was working on his car outside his home in South Street, Rainham, Essex. He saw a man wearing a blond wig speaking to two young children who were later identified as Tracey Turner, 7, and her brother Paul, 3.

Monsters

The man wearing the wig had left the scene and Sudbury asked the children what'd happened. They told him the man had said, "You're not having much fun today. Why not come with me?"

At 1:45 the same day Bonny and Harriet Branch aged five and three were playing on waste ground at the rear of their home in Staines Rd, Ilford only a few miles from Rainham. Watching out of the window their mother, Joyce Branch, 27, saw the children being led away by a man who was holding their arms!

Mrs Branch called out to her husband Robert, 27, who was at that time a bricklayer. Robert ran across the allotments for 250 yards after the man who at this point was still holding onto Robert's children. As Robert ran he saw the man desperately trying to open the door of a yellow Hillman Avenger car that was parked in Loxford Lane.

When Robert had almost reached them, the man released the infants and moved away. Robert grabbed his two daughters with relief flowing from him. He took them back home to his wife when returning he saw the man drive away in the Hillman, he memorised the number plate as HJB 821N and wrote it down on his return home. The law were contacted immediately and a woman PC Sally Parsall attended to take details of the incident. It turned out at a later stage that the registration number of the car was slightly incorrect, as it was HJB 812N a very easy mistake to make, who can blame the guy under such stress.

Approximately half an hour later six-year old Josephine Brisley was playing in the courtyard of her home in Peabody buildings, in John Fisher Street, Stepney, East London. When her mother Mary Brisley, 36, heard her screaming. Going into the courtyard Mrs Brisley found her daughter crying. She went on to explain that a man had hurt her wrist and had taken her ball away. The child's father Alan Brisley a 43-year-old maintenance engineer arrived home at this point to find both his wife and daughter upset. He went straight to the local station and reported this incident to Constable Robert Judd.

Police enquiries located an excellent witness, 26-year-old Susan Eales, a bank clerk living with her fiancé in Peabody buildings. She explained to the law that when she'd looked out of the window at approximately 2:15pm she'd seen a man wearing a blond wig walk across the forecourt to the flats. Some 10 minutes later she heard screaming, which made her return to the window, and she'd

Legends

seen the man pulling the girl by her wrist with one hand and in the other he'd a ball.

The child had managed to break free and tried to run but the man pursued her. The witness then leaned out of her window and shouted to her fiancé to get the police. The man wearing the wig looked up then strolled back to the road where he dropped the ball and walked out of sight. When the fiancé joined her at the window they'd both seen a yellow Avenger car drive along Fisher Street and disappear.

I'm sure that you'll agree that these three cases were very lucky to escape the grips of this monster. If it wasn't for people paying attention these children may have been seriously injured, interfered with or even dead, keep looking and listening!

The Hillman Avenger belonged to Colin James Evans of Russell Street, Reading, Berkshire – my old haunting ground near Broadmoor. Evans had four previous convictions for indecency with children and child stealing. See once a paedophile, always a paedophile! It was also learned that his wife and daughter had left him shortly after his first conviction.

Detective Sergeant Edward Ditum and DC Graham Jones then arrested Evans at his place of work at 3pm on Wednesday 9 May 1984. That same evening a combined team of coppers subjected Evans' flat to a meticulous search. Taylor acting on instinct alone removed the rear panel of a radiogram to reveal several packages concealed under the turntable. These contained two wigs, a large number of indecent photographs of young children, a piece of dowel and a candle. Among these items were 11 black and white photographs of what appeared to be a child's dead body?

A bag containing a large amount of children's knickers was recovered from the premises, these were shown to Mrs Payne but she was unable to identify any of them as her daughter's Marie. Evans later said that he'd been collecting them for a jumble sale. The coppers weren't falling for that old gag.

When being interviewed Evans said, "You will never know just what's been going through my mind. Ever since that day I've thought about nothing else. When I woke up the next morning and realised what I'd done I could have killed myself. Can't you take me outside and hang me?" Wish he'd said that to me! He then went on to admit the body was in Epping Forest and agreed to take a copper to her grave provided, so long as his solicitor approved.

Monsters

Evans then admitted that he'd abducted Marie Payne at about 2pm on 11 March and he'd then taken her to Epping Forest, where he'd killed her and buried her in a shallow grave. He described how he'd started to indecently assault the child after removing her tights and knickers, he said that she'd started screaming and running away. Claiming that he'd panicked and hit her over the head with a heavy fallen branch.

According to Evans he'd then dug a hole and stripped and abused the child, after which he'd taken the photographs. At this point it was obvious to the law that Evans was lying. The photographs found in the radiogram clearly showed that the body had been buried.

Evans subsequently admitted that he'd photographed Marie when she was alive but that cos of a fault within the camera; the film had become 'fogged'. Having initially concealing the dead child's body under a mound of leaves and hidden her clothes in a tree stump. Evans had returned three days later and uncovered the corpse taken the photographs that'd been found and buried her in a shallow grave. When the law asked about the negatives he told them that he'd burned them on a bonfire.

Evans was then taken to Epping Forest and shown where the tree stump had been burned out and removed. Evans then showed them roughly where he believed Marie's body was buried. The little body of Marie was found some eight feet from where Evans had said. Marie's body was taken and a *post mortem* was done which gave the results that she'd died from 'intracranial haemorrhage' and a fractured skull, the injuries being consistent with more than one blow. It was also stated that the sexual mutilation had been inflicted after death!

It was put to Evans by a copper what would he have done if he were successful in abducting one of those children on Sunday. His reply was: "...I thank God that nothing came of my activities ... I dread to think what may have happened."

In September 1984 while Evans was awaiting trial there was a further development. It appeared that the occupier of a flat where Evans had formerly lived, in Western Elms Avenue, Reading, had lifted a carpet and discovered a number of negatives of indecent photographs of children. Among them were the negatives of the pictures taken at Epping Forest of Marie's body, which Evans had stated that he'd burnt on a bonfire.

Legends

Evans advised by his legal team pleaded guilty to murdering Marie Payne. Tried at the Old Bailey he was sentenced to life imprisonment with a recommendation that he serves a minimum term of 30 years, and poor old Reg Kray's done 32!

Charles Manson

A Polish filmmaker, Roman Polanski, left his rented home in Los Angeles to make a film in Europe in 1969 — what a hard life these film directors lead. He'd made arrangements for a friend, Voytek Frykowski and his girlfriend to stay with Sharon Tate whilst he was away. Sharon was a film actress who at that time was bearing her husbands' child.

On the evening of 8 August 1969 there was more than these residing at the house. A young man by the name of Stephen Parent had called to see William Garretson — the houseboy. Also visiting the house was Jay Sebring a friend and former lover of Sharon's.

When Stephen left in his car he saw some dark figures lurking in the darkness of the garden area. He stopped his car and asked what they were up to. A man in an instance pulled a piece (gun) and placed it to the head of the 18 year old and without any hesitation pulled the trigger. Then more bullets were pumped into him.

This gunman and his two female accomplices broke into the house. A third female was left outside the property to keep watch. They carried out a bloody massacre of stabbing and shooting everyone within sight. Before leaving the premises one of the females daubed the word 'PIG' on the hall door, using a towel dipped in Sharon Tate's blood. Some of the victims along with the killers were at the time high on LSD. The houseboy had been playing records in another part of the house and had heard nothing and was the only one to remain alive. The bodies were found early the following morning when the housekeeper arrived to do her duties.

The murderers were Charles Watson, Susan Atkins and Patricia Krenwinkle. All were followers of the psychopathic Charles Manson, leader of a hippie commune who'd ordered these killings.

On the following evening Manson entered the home of Leno LaBianca, a businessman. Manson armed with a gun tied up LaBianca and his wife Rosemary. Manson then left the house and ordered three people waiting in their car to go inside the house and kill the couple indoors. The murderers on this occasion were Watson, Krenwinkel and Leslie Van Houten. Mr and Mrs LaBianca were repeatedly stabbed and slashed in a orgy of bloodlust.

The difference between reality and fantasy was extremely blurred if not blotted out totally due to the killer's use of LSD yet again. I've never touched the stuff and this is one reason why it's wise to steer clear of it. Left around the inside of the LaBianca home was mindless slogans penned in blood. The word 'WAR' was slashed on the body of Mr LaBianca.

Within a few days Manson along with 24 others were arrested when police raided the commune. The raid was in connection with an attempt to clamp down on car stealing and the likes plus the use of drugs. Everyone of the arrested party was soon released due to lack of evidence. A few days later a man was murdered on the ranch where Manson and his 'family' were living, 30 miles from Los Angeles.

It wasn't for a few months until anyone was charged with murder in December of 1969. On 30 March 1970 Manson, Krenwinkel, Atkins and Van Houten were convicted and sentenced to the death penalty. Linda Kasabian the girl who'd patiently waited outside of Sharon Tate's home had turned super grass. Charles Watson had crossed the state line and was resisting extradition, but he was brought to trial in 1971 and was also sentenced to death.

However whilst they were all awaiting to be appointed dates on death row for the gas chamber in February 1972 the supreme court of California abolished the death penalty. The sentences then handed down were several terms of life imprisonment. Manson

Legends

and his cronies are still locked up, maybe some of the women will get out but Manson ain't ever gonna leave unless it's in a wooden box! Thing is he still applies for parole every year!

Moors Murders
Myra Hindley and Ian Brady

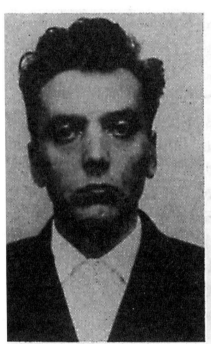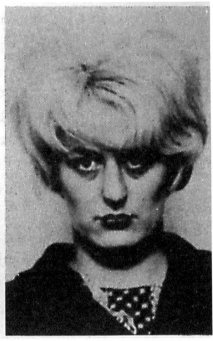

On 7 October 1965 at approximately 7.30am coppers had attended an address, 16 Wardle Brook Avenue, Manchester after a telephone call from a David Smith. They were told that a murder had taken place the evening before and Smith had witnessed it. The body was apparently still in the premises and the occupants were believed to have shooters.

A copper had noticed the bread man at the end of the street and asked if he could borrow his outfit. The copper then posed as the bread man knocked on the door of 16 Wardle Brook Avenue and Myra Hindley answered the door. Once inside the house they saw a man sleeping in the lounge wearing his under clothes, this man turned out to be Ian Brady.

They were told why the coppers were at their home. The law

then went upstairs and tried one of the bedroom doors, which was found to be locked. Myra said that was where she'd kept her guns and the keys were unavailable. A copper told Hindley that the door could very easily be forced to obtain access to the bedroom. Brady at this point had obviously realised that none of the coppers were going to go away and said to Hindley: "You better give him the keys."

Talbot and another copper went upstairs in the bedroom where starring them in the face was the body of Edward Evans who was trussed up in the foetal position in a clear plastic bag.

It was David Smith, the brother-in-law of Myra Hindley, who'd rang the law with reference to this murder. Smith had been lured to Wardle Brook Avenue to witness Brady axing Evans to his death. By implicating Smith in the murder Brady would then have control over him. Brady along with Hindley had tried to coerce Smith into the murder of Evans but this didn't happen. When Smith was interviewed in the early hours he said that there'd been more than just this murder, there'd been others! No one could've realised at this stage the horror that was about to unravel in other murders that this would help reveal.

Detective Inspector Stan Egerton referred to the area where Hindley was brought up as the 'slums'. Saying that the houses, only consisting of two up two down, with no baths and an outside toilet were the pits – sounds like prison life. The good thing was that everyone knew everyone along with his or her business. If a stranger came into the area everyone would know about it. This is how Myra had got away with it as she knew the area, she was from the area and she knew the children from the area. Hindley had a happy childhood but had very little money similarly as others living in the area.

Brady, unlike Hindley, had a bad childhood, so let's all say, "Ahhhhh." He was the son of a waitress who came from Glasgow. He was unaware of who his father was or is at this time. It's been said that as he grew up he was different to others of the same age as him, instead of listening to rock and roll music he would go with classical and read classical books. He would dress differently to others and he stood out as being different to other youngsters. Stan Egerton said that he was an 'odd ball', he was a loner and strange. Brady had fantasies for killing but I think he probably wouldn't have carried them out if he hadn't met Hindley. They kind of gelled together to form a stronger force.

Shy, working class, 19-year-old Hindley had met Brady at Millwards, a local chemical supply firm in January of 1961. Brady a dark haired sociopath obsessed with sadism of the Nazi regime spent his lunchtime reading *Mein Kampf.* He hardly had time to notice Hindley, whose diary extolled the virtues of the rather sullen young man. 'Ian wore a black shirt and looked smashing...I love him,' she wrote 'eureka!' It was December 1961. 'Today we have our first date. We are going to the cinema.' Hindley wrote. Brady had taken her to see *Judgement at Nuremberg.*

Brady went on to cement the courtship in a skilful act of seduction at Hindley's Grandmothers home that afternoon. From then on Hindley was his devoted love slave and a willing participant in his sadomasochistic fantasies. They took pornographic photographs of each other and displayed them in a scrapbook.

Tiring of this Brady wanted more and persuaded Hindley to help him lure children and adolescents for far more dangerous entertainment.

July 1963 was where it all started. The first victim was 16-year-old Pauline Reade who went missing. In November of the same year 12 year old John Kilbride vanished. Then a period of seven months passed and Keith Bennett was the next victim and was abducted and murdered.

It was 26 December 1964 and Lesley Ann Downey was on her way to a Christmas fair but instead was taken to Brady's home in Wardle Brook Avenue. She was forced to pose nude for a photographic photo shoot. A tape recorder captured the anguished pleas of the schoolgirl shortly before she met her death by strangulation. In the background you could hear 'The little drummer boy' and 'Jolly St. Nicholas.' The tape later became the prosecution's first exhibit during the murder trial of Hindley and Brady. You wouldn't wanna hear that tape, I have and it's sinister, too much for words!!!

Ten months went by before Brady selected his next victim. It was October 1965 when Brady met Edward Evans in a Manchester pub and enticed Edward, believed to be homosexual, to his home at Wardle Brook Avenue. It was here in the presence of David Smith, brought by Hindley on the orders of Brady; Evans' skull was smashed in with a hatchet. "It's done," Brady said. "It's the messiest yet. It normally only takes one blow." This murder was believed to have taken place for 'Kicks'. The body was then wrapped in clear polythene and taken upstairs. Brady and Hindley laughed and made jokes.

Smith excused himself and contacted the police. The law found two suitcases stuffed full with pornographic paraphernalia along with the incriminating tape of the Downey murder were found in a locker at Manchester Central Station. A photograph of Hindley posing next to the shallow grave of John Kilbride was found and tipped the law off to the location of the bodies of Downey and Kilbride.

The trial at Chester started on 19 April 1966 before Justice Fenton Atkinson. On 6 May the two were found guilty of murdering Edward Evans and Lesley Ann Downey. Brady was also found guilty of murdering John Kilbride. They each received life sentences and will never be released. Keep sending Hindley those cigarettes so she can smoke herself to death and I've put in for the food Brady refuses to eat while he's on his fake hunger strikes. They'll burn in hell – anyone for toast?

Dennis Nilsen

At 6:15pm on February 1983 a Dyno-rod employee, Michael Cattran, was sent to investigate the cause of a blockage in the drains at 23a Cranley Gardens, Muswell Hill. In the sewer he found a strange substance, which he later explained to his boss he thought was human flesh! It'd flowed from a pipe leading to number 23.

Since it was too dark to do anything that evening Cattran returned the following morning with his boss. At this time the substance had disappeared. One of the occupants of the flats had explained that they believed that the man that lived in the attic flat had been to the manhole during the night. The law were then called immediately.

Although the substance had been removed somehow Cattran had been able to salvage some pieces of meat and four small bones from the waste pipe of number 23. These were handed over to Detective Chief Inspector Peter Jay who immediately had them examined by an expert. The meat and the bones were confirmed to be that of a human.

The occupant of the attic flat had gone to work when Detective Chief Inspector Jay, Detective Inspector McCusker and Detective Butler attended the premises. The officers decided to await his return.

A 38-year-old Scottish bachelor, employed as a civil service clerk, from Fraserbrough on the Northeast coast of Scotland owned the attic flat. He'd left Scotland at the age of 16 and travelled to Aldershot. He was a former trainee butcher and was once a probationary policeman. His name was Dennis Andrew Nilsen.

His mother Betty Scott says that he was a gentle boy who never fought as a youngster. She explained how Nilsen was extremely close to his Grandfather and felt like he should've taken Nilsen with him to a better place when he died. At three years of age his father left him and his mother. Nilsen had one brother and when his mother re-married she had a further five children.

He was told about the discovery of the human remains in the drains and expressed suitable horror. Jay told him bluntly to stop wasting everyone's time and tell them where the rest of the body was. "In two plastic bags in the wardrobe next door," Said Nilsen, "I'll show you."

Nilsen was then removed and taken to Hornsey police station. During transit McCusker asked Nilsen, "Are you talking about one or two bodies." "Fifteen or 16," said Nilsen. He'd murdered a dozen or more young men at his previous address of 195 Melrose Avenue and three at his residence at that time of 23 Cranley Gardens. Few of the victims had been missed, as they'd been lowlifes from the underbelly of London's homeless and unemployed. These young men had been drawn to the home of Nilsen. This doesn't in any way make these horrific crimes right as these young men were humans and had a right to live and they would've had a mother and father somewhere that loved them, even the elephant man had a mum who loved him.

When the wardrobes were checked body parts were found in

black bags. Some of the parts were in an advanced stage of rot. In the bathroom the legs of his last victim, Sinclair, were found. A tea chest in the flat held more body parts. Carrier bags held three heads. All of the parts were taken to the mortuary and assembled to form three incomplete hacked up corpses.

At Melrose Avenue, Cricklewood he left the remains of 12 earlier victims. He used to store the bodies under the floorboards in his ground floor flat, this guy sounds like a regular Fred West. When he found that he could only store a limited amount he would remove an old one and replace it with a new body. The old bodies could be up to a year old, they were dismembered and packed into suitcases and stored in his garden shed. When he'd built up several suitcases he'd begin burning the remains, together with the victims clothing. To prevent the stench of burning flesh he'd burn tyres with the bodies. Once the fire had burnt out he'd smash the bones with a spade into small pieces.

Nilsen explained how he'd once had a bad fright at Melrose Avenue. A man he was trying to strangle had fought back and escaped. The law were called and an Inspector and a sergeant had questioned him while standing on the floorboards covering the five dead young men. Always articulate Nilsen had convinced the law that it was nothing more than a homosexual lover's tiff.

The owners of Melrose Avenue decided to sell the property, so he had to quickly cut up and burn all of the bodies from under the floorboards. He then moved on to Cranley Gardens where he didn't have access to the garden so he decided to boil the body parts and then flushed them down the toilet. The larger bones were either disposed of in the rubbish bin or on wasteland at the rear of the property.

One of the victims named John Howlett was a semi- vagrant. They'd been drinking in a public house after first meeting in an off-license. Then they went back to Nilsen's home and had a meal. Whilst watching television they were consuming more alcohol. Nilsen had asked Howlett to leave but he refused so Nilsen tried to strangle him with a strap, the man fought back. They struggled on the bed and then Howlett went limp and blood was on the bedding from a wound on Howlett's head. The man had started to breathe again so Nilsen tried strangling him again. Then he dragged the unconscious man to the bathroom where he placed him in the bath and filled it with water. Bubbles floated from Howlett's nose to the surface of the water. The water filled with blood from his body, food and other bodily emissions.

When asked by his solicitor why he'd killed these young men Nilsen replied, "I am hoping you will tell me that." The nearest anyone could come to an explanation was that Nilsen was lonely and felt isolated. He had eventually killed his victims to prevent them from being capable of leaving him, which is what I used to say when I'd taken another hostage but the judge wouldn't ever listen, funny that!

There was never any doubt about Nilsen's guilt. He'd admitted his crimes on many occasions and freely and openly talked about them. The difficulty was whether Nilsen was damn right evil or insane, but this was often the case with people pleading insanity. As had happened in the Yorkshire Ripper trial. You can read more about that case in this chapter under the heading The Yorkshire Ripper – Peter Sutcliffe.

Nilsen was interviewed over a period of 30 days producing 157 pages of evidence. He described his strangling between 1978 and 1983 of young men. It became clear that many young men had been invited to Nilsen's home and had left unharmed. "Each of the murdered had been in near helpless intoxication," Nilsen said before he strangled them with a tie.

Dennis Nilsen was convicted and sentenced to life imprisonment with a recommendation of 25 years, which has now been increased to a whole life. He apparently accepted his punishment and does not expect to be released. This geezer was a fairy liquidiser of mammoth proportions and I've gotta give him credit for coming clean and taking his porridge unlike Hindley! Not that I'd want Nilsen as a pad mate in my cell cos I'd never get to sleep with him making so many noises from being my new punch bag.

10 Rillington Place

In March 1953, Mr Beresford Brown, a West Indian tenant of a flat at 10 Rillington Place in London's Notting Hill district, set about fixing brackets to the wall to hold a radio in the kitchen. But when he tapped the wall it sounded to be hollow, unlike my cell walls, he went on to pull a strip of wallpaper off to reveal a door leading to the kitchen alcove and shining a torch into the alcove, he found himself viewing the back of a naked woman's body. He then ran off to bring the police.

In the alcove was found the corpses of three young women. The corpses were identified at a later date as Rita Nelson, Kathleen Maloney and Hectorina Maclennan all three women had been brass nails (prostitutes) plus they'd been strangled. Further searching of the premises revealed another corpse under the floorboards in a room at the front of the premises. This body was that of Ethel Christie, the wife of the former tenant who had left the flat recently. She had also been strangled.

Police announced to the press that they were anxious to contact John Reginald Halliday Christie to interview him. They believed that he could help with enquiries. In the mean time they began to dig the garden area belonging to number 10 Rillington Place. Two skeletons were unearthed and were identified as belonging to Ruth Fuerst and Muriel Eady. Whilst the bodies from the interior of the flat had died within the previous three months yet the two skeletons found in the garden had been buried there for some years.

Police also found a tobacco tin on the premises containing four specimens of pubic hair, which had obviously been kept as trophies. PC Thomas Ledger arrested Christie a few days later on Putney Bridge. He admitted responsibility for all six deaths but his statement was very vague and unreliable although it did seem as though he'd murdered the two women found in the garden, these murders had taken place during the war. He'd strangled them whilst having sexual intercourse with them.

It wasn't clear why he'd killed his wife but he tried to make out that it was a mercy killing. It seems more likely that she was obstructing his bizarre compulsion to murder other women during or possibly after having sexual intercourse with them. He'd created a method of making them drowsy with the carbon monoxide in the domestic gas supply before even attempting to penetrate them. But it must be pointed out that none of the women died from gas poisoning.

Clearly the only defence Christie had was that of insanity. This plea failed and he was sentenced to the death penalty and hanged at Pentonville jail on 15 July 1953.

This case did not stop here as Christie and his wife had been prosecution witnesses at the trial of another man charged with murder, Timothy John Evans who'd been accused of murdering his wife and daughter, both whom had been strangled. Convicted of the murder of the child, Geraldine, with the help of evidence from Christie and his wife Evans had been sentenced to the death penalty and was hung on 9 March 1950. He along with his family had also lived in the upstairs flat at 10 Rillington Place at the

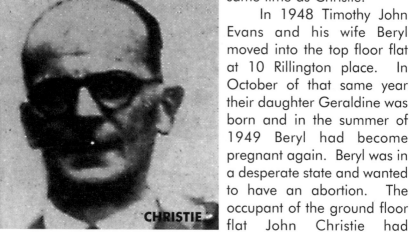

CHRISTIE

same time as Christie.

In 1948 Timothy John Evans and his wife Beryl moved into the top floor flat at 10 Rillington place. In October of that same year their daughter Geraldine was born and in the summer of 1949 Beryl had become pregnant again. Beryl was in a desperate state and wanted to have an abortion. The occupant of the ground floor flat John Christie had convinced Beryl that he could carry out this operation without any difficulty. Early in November Evans had returned home to 10 Rillington Place from work. Christie at this point greeted him and gave Evans the outcome of the operation; Christie explained that it'd gone wrong. Beryl was dead!

Evans didn't go to the police, as he understood that Christie could be charged with murder for performing an illegal abortion. Instead he helped Christie dispose of the body belonging to his wife Beryl along with the bloodstained bedding that she'd died on. He also allowed Christie to supposedly take baby Geraldine to be looked after by a couple in East Acton and sold the furniture for £40 out of which he bought a £19 camel coat for himself.

Evans then left Rillington Place and went to live with relatives in Merthyr Tydfil in Wales. Here Evans 'confessed' but he'd told many stories. One was him admitting his guilt and the other was implicating Christie. Christie convinced the law that he was innocent. Rillington place was searched and the body of Beryl was found behind stacked wood in the washhouse. Nearby the body of baby Geraldine was found with a tie around her neck. Both of the victims had been strangled.

A great deal of public unrest was caused by the fact that, firstly, Evans had been convicted partly on the evidence given from

Monsters

EVANS

Christie, a man who'd already killed two women and subsequently murdered four more. And secondly that the public were supposed to believe that two murderers living at the same address at the same time, killing women using the same method.

Evans had accused Christie of murdering his wife and daughter and after Evans' death and Christie's arrest Christie did eventually confess to the murder of Beryl Evans but he denied killing the child. Both men were mentally abnormal and habitual liars. A serious miscarriage of justice seemed to have taken place.

It's not been proved conclusively that Evans was innocent of murder. But what's certain is that no jury would've convicted him knowing what was subsequently uncovered about Christie. This case undoubtedly had some influence on the decision to abolish the death penalty. Rillington place has now been brought to the ground and rebuilt to form Ruston Mews.

Fred and Rosemary West's case was similar to this case. The story is covered in this chapter under the heading *Fred and Rosemary West*.

Michael Sams

Sams had abducted the estate agent Stephanie Slater, 25, at knifepoint as she showed him around a Birmingham house in 1992. He then imprisoned her in his workshop in Newark-on-Trent, Nottingham. He forced Stephanie to live, sleep and eat confined within a wheelie bin for a period of eight days. The terrified girl was kept chained, blindfolded and gagged in this wheelie bin until she was freed due to Sams being paid a ransom of £175,000. Sams, the devious little fucker, put a tray up on a bridge and got them to put the money on it. The thing is it was foggy and the tray had a rope attached to it and all what Sams had to do was pull on the rope from some 50 foot below, the tray tipped the money over

Legends

and he just had to put it in a bag and pedal off on his bike, couldn't run cos he's only got one and a half legs, I thinks Jaws bit it off or something.

During her chilling ordeal, Sams tormented Stephanie by lying to her about the fact that the bin was wired up so if she moved she'd be electrocuted.

Julie Dart's battered body was found in a field by the A1 near Grantham, Lincs 10 days after she'd went missing from her Leeds home.

Sams was only caught when his former wife had informed the law after she'd heard a tape of his voice on the Crimewatch television programme cos they'd offered a big reward – soon opened her ears that did.

Sams, 58, from Sutton-on-Trent, Nottingham was found guilty of blackmail, kidnapping Stephanie Slater and murdering Julie Dart an 18 year old prostitute from Leeds. Sams was jailed in 1993 at Nottingham Crown Court by the judge who described the peg legged mechanic as "Evil and extremely dangerous". He's now serving four life sentences for these evil crimes.

Killer Sams is trying to sue the Home Office for £5,000 due to him stating that his bed is too hard in his cell. I believe that Stephanie had a far worse bed for the period of eight days than that of Sams. He's receiving treatment of a higher standard than his victims or me and recently he won a damage claim against the Home Office for lost paintings, wait till my claim's in over the damage that's been done to me by the Home Office!

Peter Sutcliffe
The Yorkshire Ripper

Sutcliffe was no Geordie, as the law had been led to believe by a hoaxer. A hoax cassette tape had dragged them around on a wild goose chase. The hoaxer's said to be a serving prisoner doing life but the law's said that the geezer was banged up at the time that

Monsters

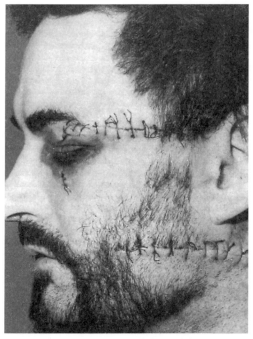

the 'hoaxer' tape was sent to them. All what I can say is it's the sort of trick this geezer would do and I believe the law are covering it up cos bear in mind there's one murder that fits a secreta type 'B' blood group that was blamed on the ripper but the Ripper ain't got that type of blood and he would've admitted to it. This geezer who's in doing life is a killer and I believe he had an accomplice who posted the tape to the law or he did it some magical way, I'm sure someone will be able to come up with how he might've sent a tape whilst banged up, if in fact he was banged up as the law said, can't believe all they say – can you? Incidentally this guy's a man from near Sunderland!!!!!!!!!!!!

In actual fact Sutcliffe was born in Bingley, in Bradford in 1946. He had many jobs throughout his career but his favourite was that of a gravedigger from the early age of 17, which he was eventually sacked from, for bad time keeping.

The first murder took place in Leeds in October 1975 and his victim was Wilma McCab and she'd been insanely hit on the head with a hammer then stabbed. The second and third victims were also stabbed in the Leeds area. Four blows with a hammer to the head struck down the fourth victim in her own home. This took place in Bradford in April 1977. He left behind a size seven Wellington boot imprint on a bed sheet.

The fifth victim was not a prostitute, which sprung fear throughout Yorkshire. The victim was a 16-year-old young lady. Maureen Long was attacked on waste ground in the Bradford area in July 1977. She escaped with injuries. He then moved on from there across the Pennines to Manchester in October of 1977 where he picked up Jean Jordon and paid her with a new £5 note. He hit her on the head with a hammer. He'd realised that the £5 note could be traced and went back looking for it but couldn't find it. This was a vital piece of evidence for the police.

In Chapel town in December of 1977 his victim was Marilyn More. Whilst swinging the hammer he lost his balance and this allowed his victim to scream, shocking Sutcliffe she was able to escape. She needed 56 stitches in her crust but she survived the incident and was able to give the law an E-Fit to work from. In Huddersfield Sutcliffe picked up Helen Ridger and for the first time he had sex with her before she became another one of his victims. She was then discarded under railway arches.

Josephine Anne Whitaker at the age of 19 years was the Yorkshire Ripper's next victim. She was found on a playing field in Halifax. She'd suffered head injuries and other injuries to her body. A rusty screwdriver caused the body injuries. This murder took place just before midnight. It was 1980 and Margaret Walls was found in a park at Wallsley she'd been strangled and the body was then stripped. This murder was thought by the law not to be by the Yorkshire Ripper as it had differed from other murders. The 13th and final murder was that of a student in Headingly. He'd parked his car and leapt onto her dragging her to waste ground where she was murdered.

On 2 January 1981 Sutcliffe was caught in his car in the middle of a sex act with a black prostitute called Olivia Rievers in Sheffield. Sutcliffe said that his name was Peter Williams. (His first and middle names.) A quick check on the Rover car revealed that the registration tags didn't belong to the Rover. While the law were deciding what to do with the pair Sutcliffe requested to relieve himself, he then wandered to nearby bushes and done so.

The pair were taken to the local police station for further questioning. Where Sutcliffe had asked to use the toilet yet again. When Sutcliffe emptied his pockets he pulled out a length of clothesline. After days of questioning the 4 Jan 1981 had arrived and suspicion had crept in that this man could be the Yorkshire Ripper.

A copper had returned to the spot where Sutcliffe had first relieved himself to find a hammer and a knife hidden, which had been used in several murders. A search of the toilet was also fruitful where Sutcliffe had unloaded a second knife, which he'd concealed in the toilet cistern.

Monsters

On this day officer O'Boyle interviewed Sutcliffe and produced the hammer and two knives and said, "I think you're in trouble, serious trouble!" Sutcliffe at this point admitted he was the Ripper and said, "The Ripper, that's me!"

After hours of questioning it came to light that he once, in 1969, had been ridiculed, laughed at and short changed by a prostitute. Which may have been his reason for killing prostitutes and he may have mistaken women walking alone at night to have been ladies of the night.

The interview took 17 hours to record Sutcliffe's confession. In this interview he'd said he had deliberately arranged the clothing so that they "would be known for what they were." He also mentioned, "I developed and played up a hatred for prostitutes."

His wife Sonia Szurma, a Czech national immigrant who'd been dating Sutcliffe for seven years, was undergoing a teachers-training course in London whilst her husband was prowling around the red light districts in search of fresh-faced girls who sold themselves on the streets.

His legal advisor wished to have him plead guilty to manslaughter under the grounds of diminished responsibility but the judge ordered the case to go to trial. The trial took place at the old Bailey at London. It was said that Sutcliffe was suffering with paranoid schizophrenia.

He claimed that he'd been sent a message from God, which was apparently sent across a grave. This was his mission to kill prostitutes, a mission of madness. The message, he claimed, was received from God whilst he was stood in an empty grave at work. Sounds like a scapegoat if I ever heard one. It was then at this time pointed out to him that all of the women killed were not prostitutes but several were perfectly respectable woman.

He'd been interviewed some six times before any mention of this voice across a grave. In the interviews he blamed it on the fact that he'd been in a motorcycle accident some years previous and struck his head on a telegraph pole, which had knocked him unconscious. In my opinion he'd not struck his head hard enough or none of these murders would've taken place.

It went even further than this as it was alleged by an inmate who'd overheard a conversation between Sutcliffe and his wife on a prison visit, Sutcliffe explained to her that if he could prove he was loony then he would get away with 10 years. The jury dismissed his

Legends

plea of insanity even though three psychiatrists had said he was a paranoid schizophrenic. Sutcliffe was at large for a long period of time. He was charged with 13 murders and seven attempted murders.

He was eventually convicted of sexual murders of woman. This was done by either stabbing or bludgeoning with a blunt instrument. He was sentenced to life imprisonment for each of the 13 counts of murder on 22 May 1981. The judge recommended that he serve at least 30 years before any consideration is given for his release.

He was initially sent to Parkhurst Prison where he resided for three years before being transferred to Broadmoor asylum for the criminally insane. The deterioration of his mental state had made him a potential danger to other inmates and prison staff. Doctors at both Parkhurst and Broadmoor had diagnosed him as being a paranoid schizophrenic.

Dennis Nilsen also tried to go along the lines of insanity but failed like Sutcliffe. The authorities are good at deciding who's mad and who isn't. Expertise doesn't come into it. The final word goes to the guy wearing the big wig. Nilsen is also in this chapter under the heading Dennis Nilsen.

Fred and Rosemary West

This guy was three cells away from me when he was remanded in Winson Green and what a character he was. Him and his missus killed God knows how many. I never actually seen him close up, only through the spy hole in his cell door. He looked like that character in the old *Crossroads* TV series – Benny! With him being a high-risk prisoner they put him on my landing with all the cat 'A' men.

One night I shouted to him, "Oy, Fred, they just found another skeleton at your house. It was up the chimney, but it's just said on the news it was only an old flame!" I heard Fred's window shut. Here was a guy up for all them murders, some were his own blood. It's truly a sicko world we live in, no wonder he hung himself, as I think all them murders was a bit much to ask for a Probation Order!

It was 26 February 1994 when coppers started their search of a three storey building in Gloucester known as 25 Cromwell Street,

(Its been pulled down now.) the family home of the West's. Fred at this time was employed as a builder and 52 years old.

Over the next few days the property and surrounding gardens were searched in depth and by the 6 March they'd found the

remains of six young women and girls. As the days progressed more and more remains were to be discovered at a rate of one per day. It was also reported that other sites in the city and elsewhere were to be searched also.

At Cromwell Street three sets of remains were unearthed from the garden, one from the ground floor bathroom and five from the cellar. Speculation that strangulation and dismemberment was the crime plus that the case was very reminiscent of the discoveries at 10 Rillington Place some 40 year's prior. You will be able to read about Rillington Place under the heading of *Rillington Place* in this same chapter.

Fred was charged in early March with the murders of three women. One of the remains was identified as belonging to the daughter of Rosemary, Heather, born in 1970 two years prior to Fred and Rosemary being wed. The girl had vanished at the age of 16. Many other young girls went missing over this period of time. Also found in the remains was Fred's first wife Catherine and daughter Charmaine. On 10 March he was charged with a further five murders.

The search carried on in Midland Road, Gloucester where Fred had previously lived and then to a field near the village Much Marcle, in Hereford, Worcester where Fred had also lived. The number of bodies increased to 12 and it looked as though Fred would be going up with other multiple killers such as Dennis Nilsen, Peter Sutcliffe and the likes.

Legends

Fred could no longer face up to what he'd done and what was happening to him and he no longer had the strength to go on. It was New Years day 1995 and Fred decided to take the easy option of freeing himself from everything when he took his own life. He was found hung in his cell; this was by far too good for him, painless. This was probably a good start to the New Year for many, but not me, as I wanted to see him shrivel up over the years ahead, best let them go mad and then shrivel up like the Black Panther did, nearly bent over double that's how shrivelled he went but you gotta catch him in *Evil Bastards*.

Rosemary denied any knowledge or involvement with the crimes that her husband had been charged with. Funny though how one of the murders was committed whilst Fred was banged up for another crime. She was then charged with 10 murders and her trial was opened in October 1995 and stretched out for almost eight weeks.

Fred and Rose were a couple with excessive and perverted sexual appetites plus Rose was bisexual. They picked up their victims together and subjected them to appalling sexual assaults along with torture then strangled them. They belonged to a sex ring in Gloucester and some of the home videos are said to be unbelievable. My mate Andy Jones of Crime Through Time Museum's seen them. The law wanted to keep it quiet but Andy's gonna have it revealed fully in the Museum's book coming out next year that Steve Richards is working on. I don't think they'll allow the bestiality photographs of a dog having sex with someone infamous, do you? Hey, bet you didn't know that you can go and see the actual cell that Fred West spent time in at the Crime Through Time Museum, as it used to be the old police station and court house in Newent, Gloucestershire.

One of the first witnesses explained how as a teenager in 1972 she'd been the subject of a terrifying sexual assault by the West's. Afterwards she went to the police. The West's were charged with indecent assault and actually bodily harm on this occasion but not with rape. They got off lightly, very lightly indeed, with a £50 fine each from the local magistrates. At this point you may be thinking along the lines of many others – why were they not treat more harshly than this for such a crime, you would receive a higher fine for drink driving or shoplifting than they received. If a stop were put to it at this point then maybe none of the victims would've been victims.

The trial continued and a tape-recorded interview of Fred West was played in court. He explained how his wife had no part in the murders. The difficulty with this was the fact that Charmaine West was murdered in 1971 when Fred was serving time in prison for theft. Rose had dumped the body in the coal cellar so Fred could deal with it when he was released from prison, fucked her up good style, didn't it?

On the 20 November Rose was found guilty of three murders – the 16 year old daughter Heather, eight-year old step daughter Charmaine and Shirley Robinson, an 18 year old lodger who was pregnant to Fred. The remains of an eight-month old foetus was buried alongside Shirley.

By lunchtime of the 22 November Rose was also found guilty on the other seven counts of murder. Mr Justice Mantell sentenced her to life imprisonment. He went on to say, "If attention is paid to what I think you will never be released". In 1997 the Home Secretary informed Rose that she would be spending the rest of her life behind bars.

This was a horrific case of sexual serial killings involving children and was the most horrific in Britain since the notorious Moors murder trial almost 30 years prior. The Moors Murders are covered in this chapter under the heading *The Moors Murders*.

Rose West is having a lesbian affair with a convicted murderer who stabbed her partner to death. It's the third fellow inmate West's fallen for at Durham jail. West and Welsh-born Best, 31, spend their free time together huddling together in corners, stroking each other's hands and kissing in full view of officers and inmates. The pair wishes to share a cell together, which has been disallowed. Personally I'd throw her in with a rampant bull elephant, although on second thoughts that'd be cruelty to the elephant.

I've been working on my book *Evil Bastards* for the last five years; piece-by-piece it's been put together. None of this namby-pamby stuff you get with a fancy cover and then find the books full of shit. This book is gonna be the only book you'll ever need to take to bed of a night time. I've got the inside info that other people can't or wouldn't give you. You know you get it straight down the line from me. Oh, and expect a big write up on my pal, Uncle Bob, (Bob Mawdsley), the real Hannibal the Cannibal. Bob was supposed to

Legends

have eaten the brains, scooped out of a fellow con's head. Read the truth, is he evil or is it the system that made him what he is?

Insanity, I've already written that book and you're gonna be able to read it in 2001. True events in my life of madness, all top shelf stuff, as usual. It's gonna be a hardback book and already people are going mad for it, in fact they're going insane. If you watch my video documentary (*Sincerely Yours*) you'll see I've written the word 'INSANITY' on the wall in my cell, thought you'd catch a glimpse of it so I decided to leave it there for the cameras to catch it and they did.

Thanks for all of your support during my times inside this concrete coffin, keep your letters of support coming in to me and keep sending your letters of disgust to the Home Secretary, they all help. Many, many thanks to all the members of my fan club, Bronsonmania. Love ya all and that crazy guy with the same name as me, Michael G Peterson, he deserves a medal carrying my old name. He's for real alright cos he sent a cheque with that name on it as proof. The competition what *Inside Time* knocked back, fuck 'em, enter mine and get in my next book. I love ya all, my loyal supporters – MAXIMUM RESPECT, CB.

Enter **THE CHARLES BRONSON 'OPEN ART'** competition.
Entries being accepted for the following categories:

SHORT STORY - 500 to 1,000 words (fact or fiction)

ARTWORK - any type of drawing/painting using any medium, no larger than A3 size.

POEM - about anything

All entries become the property of Charles Bronson and will not be returned. Entries for year 2000 will be accepted up until December 2000. 3 winners in each category:
one outright winner gets to go into my next book and wins £100 all other winners receive certificate and goodies.

Send entries to:
CHARLES BRONSON COMPETITION
P.O. BOX 161,
GATESHEAD,
NE8 4WW,
ENGLAND

Other Titles from Mirage

Viv (Graham) – 'Simply the Best' True Crime

*Paperback 242 pages *Foreword by Gazza *Now A Best Seller, fast becoming a world-wide read book * £7.99 *ISBN No: 1–902578–00–7 *Mono Stills

New Year's Eve 1993, Tyneside hardman Viv Graham's life climaxes in a violent end! The Geordie Mafia unfolded. Truth! Pain! Anguish! Gripping catalogue of true crime! Hitman based in Manchester, UK - his professional opinion on the gangland assassination of Viv. Manchester v Newcastle - Super City comparisons. Murders! Kneecappings! Shootings! Stabbings! Glassings! Drug Dealing! Protection Rackets! Blackmailing! Robberies! Torturing and more. Gazza – "My comments on Viv."

Viv – and the Geordie Mafia Vol. 2 True Crime

*The follow up to 'Viv (Graham) – 'Simply the Best' *RRP £9.99 *326 pages *13 prelim pages *World-wide Best Seller *ISBN No: 1-902578-01-5 *Mono stills

Blackpool's Candy Rock Resort underworld explored - Drug Dealing! Kidnapping! Beach murder! Club doorman scene. More Murders! Kneecappings! Shootings! Drug Dealing! Protection Rackets! Torturing and Scams! Liverpool's club doormen scene looked at and compared to Newcastle's. Viv's three lovers - love 'em and leave 'em, not likely they became his possessions! When Reg Kray visited Newcastle, was he kicked out like they say? Convicted pliers torturer Paddy Conroy claims jury-rigging helped convict him. Exclusive interview - Viv's mother and father. One of Viv's murder suspects gives an exclusive interview!

Viv (Graham) Vol. 3 - The Final Chapter True Crime

*Third and final book in the 'Viv Series' *RRP £7.99 *ISBN 1902578163 *Foreword by Ian Freeman – UK Vale Tudo Champion *200+ Pages *Mono *Nov 2000

The follow up to the successful series of 'Viv' books. Teesside's Phil Berryman gets to lay the ghost – was he a big scale police informer – hidden tape recorder catches police out. Confession - man claiming to be the driver involved in the Viv killing, why did the police ignore it? Anonymous police officer claims the involvement of others. Murders of Pizza deliveryman Paul Logan and the personal columns advertiser Julie Smailes investigated. Paddy Conroy update. Paul Massey's situation whilst he's serving 17 1/2 years for an alleged nightclub stabbing on his home turf in Manchester- what really happened, Paul tells all to the author at HMP Whitemoor. The Paul Logan murder, did his killers kill Viv days after Logan was savagely beaten to death? Bradford Raggalds Pub murder in detail.

'Gangsters' Paradise' - 'Viv' Graham series of books

converted into film script: Loose Leaf Format
Only available from Mirage Publishing £7.99

The author of the three books in the 'Viv' series advises on the script, converted from the best-selling range of Viv books.

'Sincerely Yours' – Video Documentary (VHS)

About Charles Bronson *3 Hours *RRP £15.99 *Director, Stephen Richards consultant to LWT *ISBN: 1902578198 *Action footage!

- Wales represented by the most prolific Post Office robber ever known (retired) John 'Alf' Lodge
- Scotland represented by retired bank robber James Crosbie - now turned author
- Audio and video footage not heard or seen before
- Witness Prison Officers beating Charlie up!
- Exclusive interview with Charlie's Mum; Eira
- Interviews with Crimbizz celebrities: Joe Pyle, Tony Lambrianou, Dave Courtney & more
- Witness an actual hostage siege involving Charlie
- Listen to audio from an actual siege
- See Charlie in action in a violent unlicensed boxing match
- Witness the crowd at ringside start fighting & see a gun fall to the floor
- Listen to 3 specially recorded songs for Charlie from 3 different bands
- Ex-Prison Officer talks about the time he guarded Charlie
- See Freestyle Fight Champ Ian Freeman in action
- National Newspapers bottle out of reviewing the video even though

Other Titles from Mirage

they begged to see it ??!!!

- Only available on video and from ALL branches of Waterstone's bookshops so long as you quote the ISBN 1902578198 and the title - They'll order it in.
- Order from website: **www.bronsonmania.com**
- WARNING: Contains Strong Language

Charles Bronson Film Script
*Converted from 'Silent Scream' *£7.99

Only available from Mirage Publishing in loose-leaf format. This is going to make it all the way to the Oscar awards (no matter how long it takes). Written by Steve Richards and James Crosbie.

'Silent Scream' – The Charles Bronson Story
His own story in his own words – 'Autobiography'
*Serialised in national UK newspaper *16 pages of stills *ISBN: 1902578082
*RRP £15.99 *His real story

Charlie reveals his life and his ill treatment by the authorities in penal and mental establishments. He's had more porridge than Goldilocks and the three bears. He's taken more hostages and had more rooftop protests in prison than any other UK prisoner. Violence, violence and more violence! Inflicted on him by the prison service. He's the UK's most feared and most misunderstood prisoner. In Charlie's own words find out what makes him tick and explode! Banned from numerous penal establishments in and around the UK, why – FEAR!!!!!

'Birdman Opens His Mind' by Charles Bronson
*ISBN No: 1902578031 *RRP£7.99 *Packed full of colour illustrations *Some Surprises & More
THIS BOOK NOW BANNED FROM SOME UK PRISONS

Colour illustrated adult humour – hardback cover. Charlie's laughing all the way to the crematorium written and colour illustrated by the man from Hell. Get one if you can. In Charlie's own inimitable style and in his own words he will make you laugh. In limited supply, sure to become a collector's item!

Charles Bronson – Pictorial History CD-ROM
*Jam packed with photos never ever seen before (Guaranteed) *£4.99 *From Mirage Publishing

First time ever photographs of Charlie. See the appalling injuries he's suffered whilst being held in conditions that must be considered illegal and breach many European laws. Charlie from the age of 18-months right up to the last ever photograph taken of him in Whitemoor Prison. Family, friends his loves and more.

PUBLIC consumer ENEMY
'The Amazing little A-Z Handbook of how to complain and Win!' *you, the consumer, are being ripped off! *Pocketbook size *ISBN 1902578023 *RRP £5.99

Simply put it's THE *complainer's bible*. Don't join Internet companies who claim to complain for you, this book does it all for you, includes legal advice. Repays its RRP time and time again. A must-have for anyone who wants to win a complaint!

Looking at Life by JOE PYLE
*ISBN: 1902578090 *RRP £8.99 *Full colour photographs & Illustrations
Foreword by actor Ray Winstone Underworld contributions

Some of the hardest men in the UK helped contribute towards this book. Features inclusions by Gerry Adams the President of Sinn Fein, Sir Elton John, Sir Trevor McDonald, Richard Branson, Mohamed Al Fayed, Lulu, Roger Daltrey, Roy Shaw, Freddie Foreman, Dave Courtney, Tony Lambrianou, Charlie Richardson, Charlie Bronson, Johnny Nash, Frank Maloney and many, many more. The sad thing is all of the UK's Daily National Newspapers blanked this book and turned their backs on reviewing it. Lack of media attention means we've reduced the price of this book to £5. (All profits go to Zoë's Place Baby Hospice.)

A Sting in the Tale (Hardback)
*The Official Biography authorised by STING *RRP £14.99 *ISBN: 1902578139
*Foreword by Sting

This eye-wateringly funny book will guarantee to have you laughing regardless of whether you're a Sting fan or not. Short succinct chapters show the bizarreness of what it's like to have a world famous rock star as a friend. Written by Sting's closest friend of 37 years, the only biography with Sting's blessing. Serialised in News of the World, Sunday Mail's Night & Day mag book of the week, Independent on Sunday's mag, Richard & Judy, Sunday Life (Belfast) - review on Outlandos Web Site.

Crime Through Time True Crime
*Hardback *ISBN 1902578171 *Multiple stills
£14.99 *Crime/Celebrity/Taboo Subjects *2001

The Black Museum's book will blow the rest of them away with the details within. Taboo subjects! Sex! Celebrity Scandals! Government Scandals! Crimeworld Shockers! A collection of astonishing exhibits from the extreme to the bizarre. Museums are for softies – not this one; guaranteed that something will make your hair stand on end in this book. Forget about Crippen or the London Ripper, First time such a book's been put together from Andy Jones' private collection. Items up until now have been kept under lock and key - dare you buy this book! The Nazi Holocaust (Explicit photographs). Secret deals done between the Pope and the Nazis. Fetishes of the sex world! Oswald Mosley's Black Shirts! Ku Klux Klan! Law and order beyond comprehension! Revelations against the government!

The Machine Autobiography due out in 2001
*Hardback *ISBN: 190257818X *RRP£14.99

Ian Freeman the only man from Great Britain to fight in the USA's notorious 'cage'. Vale Tudo Champ. Brutal! Exciting! Explosive! Fitted with the flimsiest of padded gloves they go to war – a combination of all the martial arts under the sun thrown into one! Ian, known as 'The Machine', is a force-ten one-man blitz! Fought his way up from the rough and tumble nightclub doorman scene in the North of England he counts amongst his friends a number of underworld figures from the smoke.

Ramraiders True Crime
*Paperback *RRP £7.99 *Written by best selling underworld expert Stephen Richards *ISBN: 1902578104

The book the press refused to review because of the content!!!!! Interviews with ramraiders responsible for £3.5m worth of raids they received prison sentences totalling 33-years. Covering the UK, Europe (£100m art ramraid) and the rest of the world. Prison life uncovered in vivid detail when Richard 'Faggo' Dodd reveals photos smuggled out of UK prisons exposing wild drink and drugs parties. Go in prison dry - come out a junkie! Prison violence is unfolded in Faggo's own words. See for yourself the photos that frightened the press off. A-Z coverage of ramraids.

Titles for future release by Charles Bronson

Legends Vol.2 – More of what you have come to expect. This time there is a chapter for the ladies 'Angels from Heaven & Bitches from Hell'. More from Scottish and Welsh legends as well as a continuation of the 'A-Z' chapter and the 'Prison Directory'. Anyone to have served time with Charles Bronson is asked to please foreword photos from that time. A chapter is also devoted to his USA legends. Who makes it into this hardback book? ***Due 2001 *£14.99 *ISBN: 1902578120**

Evil Bastards - Charles Bronson's unique writing style brings you write-ups on some of the most evil humans ever to walk on the face of the earth. From his own personal file he is able to describe in graphic detail some of the meetings he's had with some of the characters within. Not a book for the weak hearted. ***Hardback *Due 2001 *£14.99 *ISBN: 1902578309**

Insanity – The continuation of Charles' own story. Manuscript already in and sure to be another eye-opener. Covers his time in asylums and special hospitals told in his own unique style. ***Paperback *Due 2001 *£7.99 *ISBN: 1902578317**

BRONSONS CHILDREN
The Humanitarian Relief Fund

Charles Bronson's fund for the needy. C/O Publisher's address. Donations and cheques made payable to Bronsons Children.

Other Titles from Mirage

Charles Bronson's Fan Club BRONSONMANIA

Send 2 X 1st Class stamps for an application form to: PO Box 161, Gateshead, NE8 4WW.
Memberships from £4.99 to £29.99.The Bronson Line (not premium rate) 0709 111 2766
Listen to a personal message from Charles Bronson

Charles Bronson's ONLY Official Website

www.bronsonmania.com
(Full coverage of Charlie by Charlie)

www.crimebizz.com
WEBSITE PROMOTING UNDERWORLD CHARACTERS
The only website in the world where you can hire a ©crimebizz character for that special
event or promotion

'WEB SITES AND ITEMS OF INTEREST'

www.crimethroughtime.com (Black Museum)
Crime Through Time Museum – Newent, Gloucestershire, England
www.totalmartialarts.co.uk (Ian Freeman)
www.swellbellys.co.uk (Hardcore/Punk)
www.ronniebiggs.com
www.crosswinds.net/%7Edavecourtney/dave.html
www.freddieforeman.com
www.gotti.com (John Gotti – The Teflon Don)
www.thekrays.co.uk (Reg Kray)
www.crosswinds.net/%7Ethekrays/RRMainePage.html
www.geocities.com/slthomas316/(Lenny McLean)
www.prettyboy.freeserve.co.uk (Roy Shaw)
www.joepyle.com
www.brucereynolds.com
www.nosherpowell.freeserve.co.uk/
www.geocities.com/unlicensed2000 (Fight Site)
Price List - Reminder

Viv(Graham) - Simply the Best..£7.99
Viv - And the Geordie Mafia (Vol. 2)..£9.99
Viv Graham Vol. 3 - The Final Chapter...£7.99
Viv Poster (A3 size - not shown in this book)...£1.99
Gangsters' Paradise Movie Script based on above.....................................£7.99
Birdman Opens His Mind..£7.99
Sincerely Yours (Video Documentary)...........................£15.99 add £2.00 P & P
Silent Scream Autobiography..£15.99
Charles Bronson Film Script based on the best seller................................£7.99
Charles Bronson - Pictorial History - CD Rom...£4.99
PUBLIC consumer ENEMY (Consumer book)..£5.99
Looking at Life Special Offer - Baby hospice..£5.00
A Sting in the Tale...£14.99
Ramraiders...£7.99
Charles Bronson Metal Pen...£1.00
Charles Bronson Bizarre Artwork Poster (A3 size)....................................£1.99
Autographed Photograph of Charles Bronson...£1.00
Seven different audio tapes of Charles Bronson each................................£4.99
Audio tape of Prison Siege...£4.99
Music CD Swellbellys (Caged featuring Charles).......................................£4.99

DON'T FORGET ADD £2 FOR P+P IF ORDERING VIDEO

Payment to be made to: Mirage Publishing.   **Total £........**
P+P for books/posters/scripts is free in the UK. Europe add 10% rest add 20%. We do not
accept credit cards when ordering direct. **However you can pay by credit via
website: www.bronsonmania.com Merchandise dispatched ASAP.**
Send your payment with order, delivery name and address to:
Mirage Publishing, PO Box 161, Gateshead, NE8 4WW, England